COUNTING WHAT COUNTS

Turning Corporate Accountability to Competitive Advantage

MARC J. EPSTEIN
BILL BIRCHARD

PERSEUS BOOKS
Cambridge, Massachusetts

Many of the designations used by manufacturers and sellers to distinguish their products are claimed as trademarks. Where those designations appear in this book and Perseus Books was aware of a trademark claim, the designations have been printed in initial capital letters.

A CIP record for this book is available from the Library of Congress.

ISBN 0-7382-0313-0

Copyright © 2000 by Marc J. Epstein and Bill Birchard

Text design by Ruth Kolbert
Set in 11-point Caledonia by Carlisle Communications

Perseus Books is a member of the Perseus Books Group.

1 2 3 4 5 6 7 8 9 10——03 02 01 00
First paperback printing, February 2000

Perseus Books are available at special discounts for bulk purchases in the U.S. by corporations, institutions, and other organizations. For more information, please contact the Special Markets Department at HarperCollins Publishers, 10 East 53rd Street, New York, NY 10022, or call 1-212-207-7528.

Find us on the World Wide Web at http://www.perseusbooks.com

For more information on the issues explored in this book, please visit http://www.countingwhatcounts.com

COUNTING
WHAT
COUNTS

Other Titles by Marc J. Epstein

THE ACCOUNTANT'S GUIDE TO LEGAL LIABILITY AND ETHICS

MEASURING CORPORATE ENVIRONMENTAL PERFORMANCE

THE SHAREHOLDER'S USE OF CORPORATE ANNUAL REPORTS

INTRODUCTION TO SOCIAL ACCOUNTING

CONTENTS

Preface   *vii*

P A R T   I
THE PROMISE OF ACCOUNTABILITY

Chapter 1   The Accountability Advantage   3

P A R T   I I
THE SEARCH FOR WISDOM

Chapter 2   Facing the Crisis   25
Chapter 3   Calling for Governance   50
Chapter 4   Inventing New Measures   73
Chapter 5   Managing the System   99
Chapter 6   Lifting the Veil   115

P A R T   I I I
THE NEW ORDER OF ACCOUNTABILITY

Chapter 7   The Accountability Cycle   143
Chapter 8   Financials Revisited   168
Chapter 9   Beyond Financials   190
Chapter 10   A Social Accounting   216

P A R T   I V
OPPORTUNITY BEYOND CRISIS

Chapter 11   The Accountable Manager   245

Notes   *255*

Selected Bibliography   *281*

Index   *299*

PREFACE

On many a shelf, in many a home, there sits an old music box. A box filled with memories and probably a few cracked pins. The box may malfunction, but from time to time many of us take it down, wind it up, watch the drum go round and round. We probably nod with approval as a melodious tune floats through the air. We wince as the bad pins plink and buzz.

The state of accountability in corporations today reminds us of such a music box. A lot goes well inside companies, but the internal workings of many organizations have a pattern of weak spots when it comes to accountability. These weaknesses prevent companies from consistently delivering the sweet sounds of value, whether measured in the plink of cash or the hum of satisfied customers.

Many people who work for companies, who buy from them, and who supply investment capital often feel they're dealing with defective music boxes. They are aware of the dead spots in performance, and they periodically want to throw up their hands at annual reporting time and banish the corporate boxes to the attic.

But the glitches in accountability have a fix. We have assembled in this book the makings for that fix.

- We explore the reasons for the lapses in accountability.
- We present a new model that clarifies the concept of accountability (Chapter 7).

- We tell the stories of executives who champion the principles and practices of accountable management.
- We offer an action plan—four best practices—for using accountability as a lever to deliver unparalleled performance.

We offer a richly detailed book that is part research document, part how-to book, and part business manifesto. We blend the most thought-provoking elements of the latest academic research, company cases, and firsthand executive experience to document the state of the art in accountable management. We integrate our findings into a prescription for turning accountability into competitive advantage. We issue a call to action for top executives, general managers, financial executives, and accounting professionals to look for the next edge in business in the venerable concept of accountability.

The ideas we present in this book came to us not in a bold stroke. More than twenty-five years ago, Marc Epstein began researching, writing, and consulting in financial accounting, managerial accounting, and social accounting. He produced thirteen books and nearly one hundred academic and professional papers. His work covered everything from the use by shareholders of corporate annual reports to the use by managers of nonfinancial measurement in decision making to the preparation by accountants of reports on environmental performance. The research seemed to follow a zigzagging course of investigation. On the one hand, it included research into the role of accountants and auditors in society. On the other, it included a twenty-year comparison (since 1975) of how shareholders from all fifty U.S. states use company accounts and make investment decisions. This was a diverse stream of research, but it always flowed from a single source of inspiration: the notion that the financial, operational, and social aspects of business must be tied together as integral aspects of the accountable organization. This book is the concrete outcome of that insight.

Beginning more than ten years ago, Bill Birchard began writing about a broad array of business topics, as editor of *Enterprise* magazine, as contributing editor to *CFO* magazine, and as contributor to *Tomorrow* magazine. In the last five years, he specialized in topics related to performance measurement, governance, environmental management, and accountability. He reported, in his articles on environmental management, a startling development: Seemingly overnight, starting in the early 1990s, managers in company after company were reversing their guarded approach to reporting their successes and failures. They had become answerable for their performance, which was measured quantitatively. They answered to their bosses. They answered to their boards. And they answered to the public. This turned out to be a tip-off: Corporations had begun to use accountability like never before—and not just to improve environmental performance. This book stems from that initial realization.

In our partnership as authors, in which we merged two independently conceived book proposals into a new, stronger one, we bring together the best of two worlds—a book that combines the research, inspiration, and insights of an academic with the reporting, writing, and conclusions of a journalist. Although we bring our book to life with story after story of chief executive officers, chief financial officers, and other senior executives who are leading accountable organizations, readers can rest assured that our message stands on a broad and deep base of academic research and expertise.

In writing the book, we started out looking for companies that we would consider paragons of accountable management. We found none that were perfect in all respects. We found that many were doing a terrific job in one way or another, improving their operations through at least one piece of accountable management. By telling the stories of these many companies, we provide in one volume a composite view of the accountable firm of the future.

Executives in many corporations—in finance, operations, research and development, marketing, and human resources—have begun to use accountability to tremendous advantage. We show that by adopting a new model of corporate accountability—comprising improved internal and external performance measures, reporting, management systems, and corporate governance—they are delivering untold benefits. They have given the dead spots in the corporate music box a bright new sound of life.

Of course, our book draws on conversations with many unnamed executives, consultants, and university faculty and students, many of whose own work appears in the bibliography. To them, we are deeply indebted. Special thanks go to valued and trusted colleagues, mainly at Harvard, Stanford, and INSEAD (European Institute of Business Administration), including Robert Kaplan, Krishna Palepu, Robert Simons, William Bruns, Jr., Srikant Datar, Kirk Hanson, Jean-François Manzoni, and Moses Pava for their guidance and friendship over the years. Special thanks also go to Carolyn Brancato, Robert Monks, Baruch Lev, Steve Hronec, David Norton, Bennett Stewart, Dan Keegan, Robert Howell, Alan Brache, Shelley Taylor, Thomas Stewart, and others who have devoted their careers to issues of corporate accountability.

We also thank the executives who took time to tell us their experiences for this book, and who took the time once again, just before publication, to review passages in the book for accuracy and currency. In particular, we thank Jerry Choate, Tom Wilson, and Loren Hall at Allstate; Dana Mead, Bob Blakely, Barry Schuman, and Richard Wambold at Tenneco; Bill McGuire at United HealthCare; Gerry Isom and Tom Valerio at CIGNA Property & Casualty; Dennis Kozlowski and Philip Hampton at Tyco International; Earnie Deavenport, Virgil Stephens, and Jimmy Tackett at Eastman Chemical; John Roth, Megan Barry, and Mark Brownlie at Nortel Networks; John Shiely at Briggs & Stratton; Bob Hoffman, Steve Stetz, and Tom Hartley at Monsanto; Leif Edvinsson, Gordon Boronow, and Jan Hoffmeister at Skandia Group; Ralph Hake at Whirlpool; Bob Wells at Bank of Montreal; Fran Corby at Harnischfeger; Terry McClain at Valmont Industries; Gordon Petrash at PricewaterhouseCoopers (formerly with Dow Chemical); Ron Loeppke, Marlene Giesecke, and Jerry Howell at PhyCor; Bill Blackburn at Baxter International; Don Mullane at Bank of America; Mark Green at Pitney Bowes; Geoffrey Bush at Diageo; Mark Lee at Business for Social Responsibility (formerly with VanCity Savings); Robert Stasey at Analog Devices; Fred Larcombe at Cambrex Corporation; Bob Banks at Sun Company; Don Macleod at National Semiconductor; Phil Hillman at Polaroid; Tom Hellman at Bristol-Myers Squibb; Ed Lewis at Mobil; Chris Tuppen at British Telecommunications; and scores of other people in companies that helped in big and small ways to supply the information for this book.

We especially thank four anonymous reviewers who read the entire manuscript and gave many helpful comments.

We also thank our agent, Helen Rees, and our editor, Nick Philipson, for their support and encouragement.

Finally, we thank our wives, Joanne Epstein and Sue Birchard, and our children and their families, Simcha, Debbie, Emily, Scott, Judy, Amanda, Jake, and Kye. We owe them all at least one well-run music box to make up for their indulgence in putting up with the demands of the research and writing life.

PART ONE

THE
PROMISE
OF ACCOUNTABILITY

1

The Accountability Advantage

In the spring of 1989, Ed Woolard, then chairman of DuPont, gave two speeches that would help him make his mark as a maverick. The then-freshly minted DuPont chief executive declared that, among other goals, DuPont would cut toxic air emissions by 60 percent, carcinogens by 90 percent, and hazardous waste by 35 percent.

Woolard stood at the podium and made gargantuan commitments without knowing exactly how the company, the biggest U.S. polluter, could comply. "My people told me I couldn't do that!" he later recalled. "I said, 'Well, I've done it, done it publicly. Now you guys have to do it—it's your job!'"[1]

At the time of the incident, many people inside DuPont would maintain that Ed Woolard had lost his management sense. With the benefit of hindsight, however, they would unanimously say the reverse: He had brought new sense to management.

Woolard was choosing public accountability—naming targets and promising to report on progress publicly—in a stunning drive to boost company performance. It worked wonders. By the time he retired as chairman eight years later, in 1997, DuPont had cut toxic air emissions by 60 percent, carcinogens by 75 percent, and hazardous waste by 46 percent—all documented quantitatively in an annual environmental report.[2]

In the annals of management, the most remarkable move by Woolard was not that he set a new course on the environment— although that was noteworthy—but *how* he set it. "The first thing we did," he explains, was to declare that "we're going to measure everything, and we're going to make public commitments."[3]

Woolard followed up, too. He called upon DuPont's thirty-three highest-level managers to sign "The DuPont Commitment." The document obliged every executive to drive his or her operations toward zero waste generation, zero emissions, and zero accidents. The single page ended with the pledge: "We will measure and regularly report to the public our global progress in meeting this commitment."[4]

Few managers fully understand the notion of accountability. They can't define the concept clearly. Nor can they readily apply it to gain day-to-day or long-term advantage. However, developing full accountability can give an organization a powerful competitive edge in implementing strategy and in helping individuals, teams, and business units deliver unparalleled performance.

Unfortunately, most people interpret accountability as a code word for organizational policing. The concept evokes the image of a higher authority, stern-faced, banging the table for an explanation— while the culpable party, lips pursed, gets squeezed uncomfortably to come clean. When people embrace the notion of accountability, they often do so for the wrong reason—for the satisfaction of making the *other* guy accountable.

However, this menacing, autocratic form of accountability contrasts with an appealing, empowering variety. Rather than act as a stick to keep people in line, the principles of accountability can act as a carrot to keep them climbing to higher levels of performance. The greatest beneficiary of accountability need not be some higher authority, an outsider, or a special-interest group. It can be the organization itself, propelled by goals set by leaders like DuPont's Woolard.

It is time to revise the meaning and use of the concept of accountability. To realize its potential, managers must turn its reputation around. They must throw out the bad cop and bring in the good one. They must use accountability as would an inspiring, if demanding, teacher, to rally people to fulfill lofty ambitions.

Because the word accountability appears in many contexts—business, law, morality, government, politics—few people agree on its meaning. However, the true test of an accountable organization is specific: whether it measures performance quantitatively—with financial and nonfinancial numbers—and reports it publicly to audiences inside and outside the organization. Anything less than hard numbers, broadly disclosed, reveals an organization hesitant to commit to full accountability. The act of one party answering to another in qualitative terms alone is not enough. Accountability requires data. As Charles Handy says, "Counting makes it visible, and counting makes it count."[5]

Indeed, the late Coca-Cola Chief Executive Roberto Goizueta repeatedly declared shareholder value his objective, so he measured and reported the closest quantitative proxy he knew for showing his company was accountable for building that value—economic profit.

Tenneco Chief Executive Dana Mead has repeatedly declared cost and quality his objective, so he has measured and annually reports the single most pertinent figure that shows the company is succeeding: reductions in failure costs (the sum of scrap, rework, warranty, litigation, and other costs).

Skandia Chief Executive Lars-Eric Petersson declares developing customer relationships a prime objective, so Skandia's multiple insurance units report satisfied customer indexes, insurance-policy surrender ratios, and other hard-edged numbers.

Former Allstate Chief Executive Jerry Choate declared equal employment opportunity a prime objective, so Allstate publishes race and gender data, by job category, as reported to the Equal Employment Opportunity Commission.

Executives like these recognize that traditional practices for measuring, managing, and accounting for performance are no longer enough. They find accounting according to generally accepted accounting principles (GAAP) awkward and outmoded, hardly up to helping managers compete effectively in global capital, labor, and product markets. They recognize what leading thinkers like Michael Porter have maintained for years. Individual companies cannot operate at peak performance, nor can the economy as a whole effectively allocate capital, without an overhaul of accounting.

In a landmark report in late 1995, Porter and Robert Denham urged the Securities and Exchange Commission (SEC) and the Financial Accounting Standards Board "to undertake a project to develop generally accepted principles for measuring salient categories of nonfinancial information." They cited such categories as customer satisfaction, process quality, and work-force training.[6] To achieve record-breaking performance, companies must retool their management and accounting systems.

What managers will find is that new forms of measurement have tremendous power to enlighten and empower decision making internally. That's where the magic of accountability starts. These measurements also give the accountable company an entirely new advantage: the ability to enlighten decision making with the insights of outside stakeholders. That's where the concept of accountability explodes with new possibilities—in enabling the company to win advantage by inspiring loyalty in all stakeholders vital to corporate interests. This one-two punch—first, measuring, managing, and reporting performance internally; and, second, presenting the numbers externally—promises corporations a new competitive advantage.

This book explores how companies can gain this advantage. First, it offers an inside look into how leading managers have embraced the practices of accountable management. Second, it shows how companies have used accountable management as a springboard to better performance. Drawing on the best practices of these companies, we portray a composite view of the accountable organization— along with a model of that organization, an approach to building it, and the tools for realizing its potential.

THE ACCOUNTABLE PERFORMANCE

The job of building the accountable organization, in spite of the focus on data, is not first or foremost a task of accounting—even if accounting numbers are the *lingua franca* of accountability. It is a task of management. In the same way that a critically acclaimed theatrical production calls for a well-wrought script, a cast of skillful characters, and plenty of direction and support backstage, the accountable organization calls for a set of rigorous practices; strong leadership; and robust management, accounting, and information systems to support them. The final show—the accounting of performance—represents untold discipline behind the scenes, starting with the dedication of general managers, financial executives, and top operations managers to adopting the full complement of practices that typify the accountable organization.

Most companies today have only begun to fit together all the pieces of a critically acclaimed show of accountability. However, across industry, companies have created a remarkable buzz of activity. In the first half of this book, we chronicle that buzz. To be sure, we find that no single company today operates with every element of accountability. Still, many companies are crafting masterful one-act dramas that fit into the larger accountability play. In the second half of the book, we show how all companies can bring together the pieces—the best practices—in a single model to create a production of an accountability masterpiece.

Our research, based on hundreds of interviews with company managers, our own extensive studies and surveys over twenty-five years, and a review of the vast academic and managerial literature, shows that, as managers create the buzz of activity, they plunge deeply into four different approaches to accountability: governance, measurement, management systems, and performance reporting. Managers create active, independent governance; balanced financial and nonfinancial systems of measurement; integrated, closed-loop planning, budgeting, and feedback systems; and thorough, regular public reporting procedures. A combination of these four approaches defines what we call the accountable organization. (See Figure 1-1.)

This combination of efforts is daunting, but our research shows that managers, collectively, have begun to define accountability in just this way. They are looking at the notion much more broadly than in the past. They have jumped beyond accountability as a splinter issue, like paying for performance. They have fashioned inventive solutions to using accountability as a tool for delivering on the promise of the wealth and well-being that can flow from the free-enterprise system. This creates a rich story of accountability never before told. We bring it to life by weaving together the four elements of accountability.

Figure 1-1
The Elements of Accountability

Governance

Who could have missed the most prominent effort today by top managers to address a vacuum of accountability: revamping governance by the board of directors? Managers now roundly concede that traditional governance mechanisms have fallen short of their target of institutionalizing firm, independent oversight that holds management's feet to the performance fire. Recent innovations to improve board governance, although not fully assuaging investors' concerns, are perhaps the most polished act today in the new play for full accountability.

General Motors (GM), for example, rewrote the role of the board of directors after its stumbling performance in the early 1990s. The company so thoroughly recast its governance principles that a commission led by governance expert Ira Millstein cited GM as a model.[7] Among other things, GM requires that the board contain a majority of independent directors, that directors themselves nominate new directors, that a committee annually assess the performance of the board, and that outside directors select a lead director to chair regularly scheduled meetings of outside directors.[8]

Measurement

Managers have struggled for decades with financial and managerial accounting that fails to measure all the variables that drive long-term value. Without taking into account quality, turnaround time, customer satisfaction, and other leading indicators of company wealth creation, managers at all levels have simply made bad decisions. Leading managers have attacked the issue of accountability by inventing many new ways to measure financial, operational, and social performance.

What Peter Drucker said in his classic editorial in 1993 is as true today as ever: "Financial accounting, balance sheets, profit-and-loss statements, allocating of costs, etc., are an x-ray of the enterprise's skeleton. But much as the diseases we most commonly die from—heart disease, cancer, Parkinson's—do not show up in a skeletal x-ray, a loss of market standing or a failure to innovate do not register in the accountant's figures until the damage is done."[9]

Companies are rapidly devising ways to go beyond the x-ray and create much more insightful leading indicators for making decisions and creating value. Arthur Andersen developed a number of key measures for gauging its performance worldwide. Along with financial indicators, the firm measures such factors as customer satisfaction, flexibility, resilience, market share, and employee satisfaction.[10]

Managers have realized that, paradoxically, the best way to stimulate peak financial performance is often not to spotlight the financials at all. A menu of nonfinancials, to complement the financials, can make just about everyone better able to contribute to the ultimate financial health of the company. Clamping managers in the irons of financial targets may actually dull peak performance.[11]

New balanced measurement systems like the ones at Arthur Andersen and Sweden's largest bank, Swedbank, show the future. Swedbank's branches deliver a report card of performance that shows measures of "customer value added" (for example, depth of relationships, loyalty), "people value added" (perception of leadership, perception of competence), and "economic value added" (profit before credit losses, bad debt ratio).[12]

Management Systems

Try as they might, managers have always had trouble linking the systems for corporate strategic planning, business-unit planning, annual budgeting, performance review, and compensation. The systems often have worked at odds with each other. Managers today are trying to make them work as one. The objective is to make the measures defining strategy at the top lead to actual implementation of that strategy at the bottom.

Robert Kaplan and David Norton, in a 1996 study with *CFO* magazine, found 57 percent of respondents reporting only "little" or "some" linkage between the priorities of the long-range strategy and the annual budget. More than two-thirds (69 percent) said that strategic planning had only "some," "little," or "no" influence on the company's overall success.[13]

Senior managers are starting to forge links between isolated pieces of their management systems. They are breaking down top-level measures into subordinate measures for division and team performance. They are asking managers to determine the indicators of success—the *drivers* of long-term value. The measures, then devised by the people accountable for them, gain buy-in. People take ownership for them and the measures keep people focused on the strategies, objectives, tactics, and targets for which they are accountable.

As Kaplan says of frontline workers, armed with measures they understand: "You transform them into people who really deliver the strategy day to day."[14]

Top managers are finding that measures also offer a way to evaluate the strategy itself. Are customers satisfied, say, with the new-product strategy? A proxy for that level of satisfaction is whether they are clogging phone lines with help calls. Are shareholders satisfied with their financial returns? A simple measure is the percentage by which stock-price gains exceed those of the firm's peer group. Are employees going to remain satisfied? One measure is whether, according to surveys, the brain trust of key people in research and development say they are happy—and not inclined to walk. A mix of new and traditional measures gives hard, cold, diagnostic data for evidence. Managers no longer need rely only on end-of-quarter financial numbers, which yield a flow of insight that runs only ankle deep.

Reporting

Finally, managers have begun to push the envelope where chief financial officers often cringe, in reporting data more broadly, both within the company and outside. In an age when most workers inside the company depend on information to innovate, many managers have come to believe the company holds information too tightly for rapid decision making. Hence comes the popularity of "open-book management," in which managers share detailed cost figures with every employee.[15]

However, managers are not stopping with broader reporting inside the company. At a time when company outsiders have more choices than ever to invest their capital, serve an employer, conduct a partnership, and buy products and services, many managers are offering more information to sway decisions in the firm's favor. Managers are concluding that they have no compelling reason to operate with so much performance data hidden backstage. Executives in every function are taking a fresh look at what information they need to run the company. They are providing insights to accountants to help them provide that information, and are drafting plans to disseminate a distillation of that information to people inside and outside the company.

In short, executives have begun to develop corporate communications strategies based on increased transparency. Along with a narrative that tells the story of their corporate strategy, executives are giving more hard data, and hard-hitting descriptive information, to woo shareholders, (prospective) employees, business partners, and customers. What is the payoff? Engaging the collective efforts of all stakeholders—who have a new window on corporate performance—in a never-ending effort to generate ideas and spark innovations to better the business.

The notion of broadly reporting performance numbers publicly is not new. Philosopher Jeremy Bentham, John Stewart Mill's teacher, recognized 200 years ago the power of public accountability. He wrote about the "open-management principle," "all-aboveboard principle," and "transparent-management principle." Publicity, Bentham maintained, commits companies to their duties. "The more strictly we are watched, the better we behave," he wrote.[16]

Bentham, the founder of Utilitarianism, foresaw as far back as the eighteenth century the power that managers like Ed Woolard exercise today: using a public commitment and accounting spurs unparalleled betterment *inside* the company. The combination of indisputable quantitative figures, along with public disclosure, keeps people focused on their goals.

Of course, managers aren't going public with secrets that hurt competitiveness, but a growing number are realizing that the line separating confidential and public information has shifted sharply. Although on-time shipping performance may have fallen squarely within the domain of proprietary data a decade ago, today it may fall into the domain of numbers that, reported publicly, give the company an advantage.

In any case, the flow of information within society and among business has exploded to such a degree that it calls into question any strategy based on knee-jerk confidentiality. In years past, companies (and managers) could reliably gain an advantage by withholding information or selectively releasing it. They could err on the side of stamping every memo "company confidential." That advantage has turned into a disadvantage, however, as managers on top of the pyramid can no longer easily control the information, like product quality, that reaches the marketplace.

Those managers striving to apply accountability as a tool for high performance are working on all four fronts—governance, measurement, management systems, and reporting—as described in Chapters 3, 4, 5, and 6. However, the company that puts all four of these elements together into a single, broader concept of accountability, as described in Chapters 7, 8, 9, and 10, will stage an unbeatable accountable performance. Top managers at some companies are starting to put this model together. They are winning an audience of investors, customers, employees, business partners, suppliers, and even the public. They are positioning themselves to use accountability's power to spark glittering performances by individuals, teams, business units, and their entire companies.

THE JOYS OF PERFORMING

The power of accountability remains underappreciated. Many managers haven't thought much about it. Most, faced with the idea of hanging out their report card, good or bad, recoil at the thought.

The concept of full accountability is a bit much, if not altogether foreign.

This attitude prevails above all, despite the fact that the accountability as we describe it is a synthesis of practices that managers around the world have already embraced. Nearly all managers have woven at least a few strands of accountability into their managerial fabrics. After all, they comply with SEC regulations to file financial statements and other information. They compile and share defect data for the sake of total quality management efforts. They survey and report customer and employee satisfaction indexes. They rely heavily on these and much other data to make decisions, review performance, and pay bonuses.

Still, many firms are likely to kick and scream on their way to the high altar of accountability that we describe. They will view accountability only as a means for third parties to obtain information from them. They will act as if the idea were invented by overzealous regulators, rather than by innovative managers. They will see a regulatory bad cop with a truncheon for punishing the errant, rather than a management good cop with white gloves pointing the way to the land of high performance. They will belittle calls for more publicly disclosed measurement information as a heap of useless red tape and as unwarranted prying by outsiders.

Admittedly, their point of view responds to a long tradition of lawmaking. When Congress passed the Securities Act of 1933, it prescribed mandatory disclosure to clean up rampant abuse of investors by managers and financial manipulators. That legislation started a process that has seemed to gain momentum ever since. Congress has repeatedly mandated public reporting as a curative, passing disclosure laws on everything from occupational safety and environmental management to equal employment and community reinvestment. In 1997, Representative Paul Gillmor (R-Ohio) even sponsored a bill to mandate disclosure of charitable giving, saying shareholders have "a right to know."[17]

Indeed, the use of public disclosure to force companies to paint a vivid picture of their performance has a long history. In an oft-quoted comment, Justice Louis D. Brandeis observed in 1914: "Publicity is justly commended as a remedy for social and industrial diseases. Sunlight is said to be the best of disinfectants; electric light the most efficient policeman . . . [the] potent force [of

publicity] must . . . be utilized in many ways as a continuous remedial measure."[18]

However, the measure of an astutely run business is not participation in a remedial accountability program. Seventy years after the
1929 stock market crash, managers can reap huge rewards by
snatching the lead from regulators and peer companies. Even if
they stop short of practicing full accountability—even if they just
engineer new measures and internal reporting—accountable managers stand to markedly strengthen their companies.

The rewards from building the accountable organization are a lot
like those from building the quality organization—the more committed the managers and workers, and the more integrated the concept with company line operations, the more benefit. As a first step,
managers must build the accountable systems and practices within
the company. They then can build bridges to the outside. As they
move toward full accountability—well governed, measured, managed, and publicly responsive—they will position themselves to
reap many benefits.

- **Improving decision making.** The accountable
  organization generates a wealth of information on
  performance, which informs decision making with facts, not
  intuition. People both inside the company and outside can
  make more effective decisions to further company strategy
  and goals.
- **Accelerating learning.** The accountable organization
  installs the feedback systems that yield a rapid-fire means of
  learning from people both across the company and outside
  the company. The company with the most feedback loops—
  internal and external—wins.
- **Executing strategy.** The accountable organization
  communicates each strategy and tactic with specific
  measures that align direction in a way written objectives
  cannot. The hard measures then give managers a month-to-
  month reading on whether the strategy is working.
- **Empowering the troops.** The accountable organization
  thins the ranks of middle managers that distill and convey
  information, and it apportions new decision-making
  authority to the frontlines. As management articulates *what*

it wants with the unvarnished concreteness of quantitative measures, workers have unmistakable guidance as they figure out *how* to deliver it.

- **Communicating the story.** The accountable organization delivers its story of value with credible financial and nonfinancial numbers. As senior managers report more numbers externally, exposing performance transparently, shareholders and analysts will have less reason to undervalue their stock.

- **Inspiring loyalty.** The accountable organization markets its value based on reliable performance measures. The no-smoke-and-mirrors approach spurs cooperation and inspires the loyalty of investors, customers, suppliers, employees, business partners, and even communities.

Reaping these benefits requires plenty of stamina and courage—stamina to implement systems internally, courage to submit to the rigor of a fuller public accounting. In a world where every company is looking for ways to elbow aside competitors, however, managers may have no choice but to exercise that courage and summon that stamina. If not, competitors will. When Coca-Cola snaps up capital by selling its superior accountability to shareholders, millions of investment dollars become unavailable for everyone else—in its industry or in any other.

Top managers will understandably worry about potential liability from all the measurement and reporting that characterizes the accountable company. They may suffer from litigation. They may fear losing proprietary secrets. Many believe reporting costs will skyrocket. Even if these risks were real, and we argue they are specious, they would pale compared to the alternative of not acting.

If a company fails to stage an accountable performance, it cedes the advantage to others. Its competitors can run with more precise information, with leaner workforces, and with better-informed workers. Its competitors can reap more lessons from accelerated learning and from empowered decision making at each level. Its competitors can execute strategy with more diverse feedback. Its competitors can deliver their messages of progress with greater credibility to a more trusting shareholder, employee, or customer. Its competitors can gain an edge by inspiring increased loyalty in people who supply capital, labor, and purchase orders. Over time, competitors can commandeer the basis on which the company must compete in the future.

Managers can instead seek to gain first-mover advantage—first before politicians, first before regulators, first before competitors. By moving first, they can free themselves from the treadmill of remedial accountability. They can run at the head of the pack—with financial performance like that of Coca-Cola, environmental performance like that of DuPont, quality performance like that of Tenneco, and diversity performance like that of Allstate.

ALL THE WORLD IS A STAGE

As managers embark on building the accountable organization, they can easily become embroiled in an age-old argument: To whom is the firm accountable? The battle lines are typically drawn between two parties, those who answer shareholders and those who answer one or several other stakeholders, typically customers, employees, and community. The argument can stir strident philosophical debate.

As the interests of society and business increasingly overlap, the stakeholder question stirs far fewer debates in practice. Neither the company nor its multiple stakeholders can ignore the benefits offered by the other, and neither can bite the hand that delivers benefits. On the contrary, company managers must work cooperatively with investors, customers, employees, suppliers, and communities to create value together.

Tom Copeland, formerly a partner at McKinsey & Company and now with Monitor Company, has long argued that managers are accountable first to shareholders for creating shareholder value (measured by discounting cash flows). Still, he maintains that in practice, managers have to take the interest of other stakeholders into account, since shareholders are residual claimants on corporate cash flow. Indeed, empirical research supports the notion that increasing shareholder value does not conflict with creating value for all stakeholders. "A winning firm wins in all directions." Copeland says.[19]

Research by John Kotter and James Heskett relating the value that top management places on various stakeholders to long-term performance, yields similar conclusions. Winning companies, like Hewlett-Packard, don't necessarily balance stakeholder demands. Nor do they necessarily give priority to one or the other. Instead, they put all of them on a pedestal. "You're accountable to more than one constituency," Kotter says. "Once you accept this, the job gets tougher, not easier. If you can't handle that tougher job, you can't handle the tougher economic environment we're facing right now."[20]

Without the governance, measurement, management systems, and internal and external reporting that is at the heart of the accountable organization, managers simply won't make optimal decisions. They will suboptimize, and their short-sighted decisions will come back to bite them.

If business enjoys the best of what society produces—trained software engineers, uncongested roadways for quick deliveries, attractive tax abatements—the members of society expect benefits in return. Even shareholders seem to think such an approach makes sense. In a national survey in which we asked shareholders to rank their preferences of where to allocate more corporate funds, most ranked pollution control and product safety higher than increased dividends.[21]

So the accountable company measures the winnings and impacts on both sides, makes decisions based on the data, demonstrates the value provided through candid reporting, and parcels out the spoils to keep the relationships healthy. The company that operates to give its stakeholders a fair exchange of value will win favor for the future. It can also expect enduring, trusting relationships that lower transaction costs for years to come.

You might expect executives who ardently declare fealty to shareholder value to think differently. Not so. Francis Corby is CFO at Harnischfeger Industries, the $3 billion manufacturer of paper-making and mining machinery, which in 1993 declared economic value added as its primary measure of performance. "I just don't think being responsible to stakeholders is in conflict with shareholder value," he says. Stakeholders "can prosper just as well as your shareholders can."[22]

To be sure, not every stakeholder wins an equal share in every corporate decision. Managers are often faced with tradeoffs that pit the interests of shareholders against those of society or those of customers against those of employees. This book provides guidance on making such tough choices. Our research, revealed throughout this book, has uncovered a lot more examples of win-win decisions than many managers might believe. Often, such decisions simply revolve around an analysis of short- versus long-term corporate interests. In many cases, viewed in the long term, the same course of action pays off handsomely for both the company and its stakeholders. A company *can* increase the bottom line while also benefiting employees, customers, and society.[23]

Of course, many in business today believe that stakeholders, and often society as a whole, place more demands on the corporation than they are due. They also believe that stakeholders' demands, like support for education, extend beyond what the company is able to fulfill. Whatever the answer philosophically, experience since the late 1980s has shown that many institutions of society—religious, political, social, and educational—are floundering while the corporation thrives. In attempting to cure society's ills, people from all walks of life are looking to the corporation to serve as more than a machine to generate shareholder value—if only because corporations have the money to do so. Witness how the failure of many schools to graduate literate teenagers creates pressure on companies to provide basic education.

As executives try to unravel what makes sense for their businesses, they have to deal as much with perception as with reality. More than half of Americans think a corporation's top obligation is to its employees.[24] It may well not matter, with activist unions, employee groups, and a sympathetic media, if managers disagree. They have to meet societal expectations.

Many people believe the public gives business a "license to operate," that business operates at the pleasure of the public. For good reason or not, small groups of stakeholders can threaten to pull that license. They can pull it, if not in the court of law, in the court of public opinion. So managers will find it in their interest to remain sensitive to outside demands. A prime way of remaining sensitive is to determine if outsiders are happy, to measure the impacts the company has on various stakeholders, to factor a knowledge of those impacts into daily decision making, and to demonstrate with numbers how the company is paying its due.

In many instances, companies will recognize that decision-making power is shifting away from corporate managers to communities, reg-

ulators, and the public. If companies do not proactively give an accounting to society, these constituencies, to remain loyal, will demand it. Often, through the political or regulatory process, these
demands will lead inexorably to more reporting. So in the same way
that a company can adopt full accountability to remain competitive,
it may find that taking action to gauge and report its social performance will help ensure its continued free operation as a valued institution in society.

In the end, the difference between working in the shareholders'
interest and working in the stakeholders' interest is small. Of
course, sometimes it doesn't look that way, as when a bloated firm
runs into trouble and turnaround managers have to cut and wrestle
their way back to levels of profitability that pay shareholders a fair
return. Moreover, in the short term, it sometimes isn't that way, as
executives push win-lose transactions for short-term gain that cost
stakeholders far more than they benefit. In the long run, however,
what's good for business is often good for society. Managers must
take a broad look at performance, measure its many aspects, and report fully on their effect on all constituencies.

As the late Roberto Goizueta, long-time chairman of Coca-Cola,
said, "We cannot for the long term exist as a healthy company in a
sick society."[25]

THE MISSING ACTORS

Into the hands of top executives falls the main responsibility for
making the organization accountable. They must set a new cultural
tone, stressing fair appraisals, open disclosure, and continuous
learning. They must mandate measurement systems that shift people from a pure financial focus to a balanced focus on building financial, operational, and social value. They must dedicate the
people and money to build the information systems that support
quantitative measurement and fast, reliable, consistent reporting
worldwide. They must courageously set targets and report on
progress publicly to show how they have performed for shareholders and other stakeholders.

Although senior managers will provide critical leadership, their
efforts will remain insufficient to transform the organization completely. The directors of the corporate board must oversee and

legitimize the managers' work. An active, independent board will ensure trust and rigor in the systems of accountability. Meanwhile, managers throughout the organization, taking their cue from their bosses, must similarly imbue their units with a philosophy of accountability, adopt quantitative measures of performance, and embrace forthright target-setting and transparent internal reporting.

Accountants play a special role in fulfilling the potential of the accountable organization. They have to complete the revolution started in the late 1980s by Thomas Johnson and Robert Kaplan in their landmark book, *Relevance Lost.*[26] Johnson and Kaplan showed that companies had developed management accounting over the course of decades to mainly serve financial reporting. Management accounting had evolved to yield good data on, say, average costs of inventory, but precious little on, say, the real cost to make one product versus another. It provided much data on lagging indicators based on historical costs according to GAAP, but it reported little data on such leading indicators of performance as time to market. The result was that management accounting failed to give managers the information they needed to make daily decisions on how to adjust strategy or run their operations. While pointing out these flaws, Johnson and Kaplan called for delinking the management and financial reporting systems; otherwise, managers would simply make lousy decisions.

Subsequently, Kaplan, Robin Cooper, and others spread the gospel of developing financial numbers for management accounts based on activity-based costing, and of supplementing financial data with a variety of nonfinancial measures.[27] More than a decade has passed since then, and their recommendations have caught fire. The job of managers and accountants is to finish the return of relevance to management accounting. With that return, they not only lay the groundwork for the accountable organization, but they will enable companies to relink management and financial reporting. The numbers provided by management accounting can once again come first. These numbers and other important managerial information can feed financial reporting, in particular the broader set of information that accountable companies will want to disclose. Accountants and senior managers can then mount a corporate communications strategy to ensure that all stakeholders receive the information they need. This information includes a broadened universe of both facts and data to help outsiders, first, to evaluate past corporate performance and, second, to make projections about future performance.

Top financial officers play a special role. They must set aside the money and dedicate the people to complete this revolution in accounting, returning relevance to financial reporting. As they do, they will have to expand their role beyond stewards of the financial figures. They will become stewards of performance measures that allow line managers to factor financial, operational, and even social impacts into decision making. They must insist that the organization draw on the richness of a newfound universe of measures to voluntarily report performance to stakeholders.

Now is not the time for managers to suffer stage fright. They must take steps to begin building accountable organizations. With new corporate culture, governance, measurement, management systems, and reporting, they will become more productive, profitable, and innovative while boosting the standard of living and social well-being of the people with whom they do business. As a first step, they must assess the level of accountability in their own organization. As they do, they will probably find, as we show in the next chapter, that the level simply fails to come up to par.

PART TWO

THE
SEARCH
FOR WISDOM

2

Facing the Crisis

Nobody runs a contest to grade companies on accountability. If someone did, the judges would find only a handful of firms vying for a blue ribbon. Most companies fall short of the ideal. Some don't even come close. The result? Both the company and its stakeholders suffer.

Just ask Dana Mead, an executive who knows firsthand both the rewards of accountability and the punishment from a lack of it. Mead joined Tenneco at the invitation of chief executive Michael Walsh in 1992. It was a time when Walsh, new himself, had a mandate for drastic action to turn the ailing conglomerate around. One of Walsh's earliest moves was to bring in his own team, including Mead, to run the corporation and put it back on the road to financial health.

Mead agreed with Walsh that the company had gotten complacent. Although business-unit heads committed themselves to financial budgets, corporate executives above them routinely tolerated missed targets if there was a good excuse. Corporate finance executives even allowed business-unit finance chiefs to lower targets during the middle of the year—without alerting the chief executive. The compensation system supported this blasé attitude, doling out stock "as long as you were warm, all present, and hadn't done anything egregious," says Mead.[1]

Tenneco's very existence was at risk. The "scissors curve," a graph of rising costs slicing upwards against falling prices, told the story of a company well on the way to bleeding to death. As the scissors closed, Tenneco lost $748 million from operations in 1991. Debt soared to a high of 69 percent of total capital by the end of September, just as the newly arrived Walsh was putting in motion a successful financial rescue of the company.

Accountability was, in a word, nonexistent. Neither Walsh nor Mead (who was named chief executive at Walsh's tragic death) could find measures that detailed the health of operations. They didn't have any control systems except for financial accounting. They didn't find forthright internal reporting that might have delivered insights for improvement or oblige commitment to change. "When you asked for information," says Mead, "it just wasn't there."

Tenneco's case is unusual. In 1992, it was a conglomerate of six different businesses, from automotive parts to shipbuilding. However, its crisis in accountability is not unusual at all. Many companies today run without the governance practices, performance measures, management control systems, and internal and external reporting that define the accountable organization.

In particular, a huge number of companies fail on two counts: managing performance with a broad selection of financial and nonfinancial measures; and delivering a detailed accounting of results to people inside and outside the organization. We closely scrutinize these two aspects of accountability throughout this book.

The failure in measurement stems from managers too often running their operations with measures devised decades ago, largely unadjusted for advances like quality management, just-in-time manufacturing, lean management, environmental management, and reengineering. Those traditional measures don't work in the new, more complex field of business today. Perhaps that's why 64 percent of companies, according to the Institute of Management Accountants, are experimenting with new performance measures.[2]

The failure in reporting stems from managers still keeping information too much under wraps—so much so that people across the company don't know what's going on or what's going wrong. Most managers refuse to reveal their performance numbers anywhere but behind closed doors, whether the data show they deserve a blue ribbon or the booby prize. Although some managers are opening the doors on their performance data to a broader audience, most are still holding the opening to a crack.

THE POVERTY OF MEASUREMENT

Managers have brought the crisis in accountability down upon themselves. For six decades, they have increasingly confused the goals of management accounting and financial accounting. The two are simply not the same, even when they do overlap. Financial accounting is a machine tuned since the 1930s to satisfy the requirements of the SEC. It cannot serve as the wellspring of corporate performance measurement nor as the performance gauge. Accounts derived solely from generally accepted accounting principles, or GAAP, give a blinkered—financial-only—view of performance.[3]

Managers that look at financial ledgers alone are likely to manage like cartoonish, armchair general contractors. They will track construction of their new buildings by peering through a financial peephole in the fence. They will see the percentage completion of the work, the resources going in and out, and the quantity of steel piled up for raising new floors. However, they won't be able to gauge progress inside. When the lights go out, they won't know if their people forgot the wiring, tripped over a switch, or need more training in configuring lighting systems. Managers simply don't have the detailed financial and nonfinancial information to tell them what's going on, what their priorities should be, or how to do better next time. They don't have the data of accountability.

Financial Accounting

The source of weakness in financial accounting is also the source of its strength. Accountants have developed a system over the last 500 years to report financial numbers to people outside the company, not to managers on the inside. The system errs heavily on the side of compiling data that is *reliable*, like the amount paid for an asset. It thus often leaves out a lot of information that may be *relevant*, like the current value of real estate, intellectual property, and brands. It's a system perfected for a companywide counting of beans, a trustworthy record for outsiders peering in.

In fact, the system works pretty well to show investors how well managers are stewarding their capital; that is, not stealing it. It also works well to help tax collectors compute their share of profit for the state. However, the system has become a limited tool for giving shareholders and financial analysts the information they need for their judgments—the likely future performance of the company and its stock price. Some assets are valued at historical costs. Many are not valued at all. Information that might prove useful as leading indicators of performance goes unreported altogether.

Financial accounting also has limited value as a management tool. It actually hampers decision making because it turns people's attention toward historical figures. Thus, facing backward, people learn about the botched or beautiful work of the past, but they get a foggy or faulty reading of the future. The system essentially yields old weather records, unfit for dealing with the storm of business challenges ahead.

If managers could reliably extrapolate the future from the past, they might find the financial accounts more helpful, but even then they would find that the records aren't even available when they need them. Despite the speed at which accountants close the books these days, useful reports arrive on managers' desks weeks or months after the fact—too late to make mid-course corrections.[4] At Tenneco, nobody even knew week to week the performance of each division—shipbuilding, farm and construction equipment, automotive parts, packaging, natural gas, transportation, and chemicals.

Looking through the financial lens alone to make decisions has come to the point of being silly. Managers need to know if their strategy is working, and financial numbers rarely tell them. At Tenneco, Walsh and Mead initially had to look backwards through a single financial peephole called IBIT, or income before interest and taxes, to understand the problem. IBIT was the company's main measure of success.[5] What they needed instead was a way to gauge the success of their new strategy: to regain leadership in their markets through low costs and improving quality. They wanted to drive decision making, as Walsh liked to say, by looking through the windshield, not through the rear-view mirror.

IBIT just wouldn't do. To be sure, it did show how bad things were. In 1991, Tenneco's Case unit reported an IBIT of negative $1.1 billion, including more than $400 million in restructuring charges, on $4.4 billion in sales. As Case was losing another $260 million from operations the following year, Mead even attempted to sell the division for $1, along with Case's $4 billion in debt. He found no takers. What Tenneco needed instead was a way to stimulate and gauge progress in executing a new strategy. It adopted a broad set of measures of everything from cash flow to environmental infractions.

Just one of Tenneco's new measures was the "cost of quality." In every business unit, to this day, managers work tirelessly to reduce these costs, which Tenneco calculates separately, as failure costs (scrap, rework, warranties, lawsuits) plus prevention and appraisal costs (inspection, testing, training, planning). The measurement was a key vital sign demonstrating the return of the company's health. In 1992, it cut $215 million in quality costs; in 1993, $246 million more. In 1996, the company was still at it, cutting $230 million, followed by another $236 million in 1997.

Just one mark of the value created was that in 1994 Tenneco sold 56 percent of the revived Case. The public offering raised $750 million. The cost of quality, along with the long menu of non-financial measures, had guided Tenneco away from the bite of the scissors curve. Since then, says Executive Vice President Robert Blakely, CFO since 1982, "We've taken a company driven on financial accounting systems to one driven on performance systems and forecasting."

Getting to full accountability through the financial accounting system fails for another reason. The accounting is based on scores of assumptions that may not reflect economic reality. Even the near-sacred earnings and returns figures may mask this reality. When the company carries real estate at 1950s prices, it overstates return on capital. When it recognizes revenue after shipping product to a distributor, as opposed to when the distributor ships to a customer, many people believe it overstates revenue. When a software firm capitalizes R&D, many people believe it misstates earnings.

Accountants may argue the details, but they agree that financial statements can offer alternative views of the truth. Take the hypothetical case of two essentially identical companies. One capitalizes most R&D. The other expenses all R&D. The balance sheets of the two will show wildly different values. One might have a book value of 10:1; the other, 5:1. In the firm that writes off the R&D, managers no longer have to answer tough questions about the return on the investment in product development because that investment is not on the balance sheet; its expensing deflects many, possibly embarrassing, inquiries.

Of course, the bodies that set accounting standards provide a lot of choice in financial reporting in part because they want to allow companies to portray results in a way that best fits their businesses. The discretion allowed also increases the quantity of information companies supply because standards don't block inclusion of relevant data by specifying regulatory pigeonholes.

Still, for purposes of accountability, the ledger entries portray a variable truth, and that truth may change year to year, too. Plenty of accounting changes lie very much within generally accepted accounting principles. From one year to the next, companies can increase earnings by switching from accelerated to straight-line depreciation, by lengthening depreciable lives, by increasing assumed returns on pension assets, or even by reversing earlier write-offs.

The flexibility in accounting begs the question: Who is to say which numbers give managers firm footing to stand on when building the accountable organization?

The trouble raised by accounting assumptions is exacerbated by managers who give in to the temptation to manipulate financial results. Under intense pressure to deliver on year-, quarter-, or month-end budgets, they can delay spending to another quarter to help earnings in the current one. Who hasn't been asked to put off travel plans to help shine the upcoming numbers? Who hasn't pulled sales into a current quarter by offering customers irresistible deals? Who hasn't gotten caught in year-end sales-closing antics, not always closing deals at an acceptable profit?

Managers should not lull themselves into thinking that the practice of managing earnings goes unnoticed. In a harsh rebuke to managers and accountants, SEC Chairman Arthur Levitt took to the podium at New York University in September 1998 to scold companies for "accounting hocus-pocus." He assailed companies in particular for engaging in five kinds of "trickery," including inflating revenues and padding gargantuan write-offs for restructuring and acquisitions. He then promised new rules from the SEC to tighten accounting practices gone astray. "Too many corporate managers, auditors, and analysts are participants in a game of nods and winks," he said.[6]

Levitt's crackdown stems in part from an undisciplined attitude by many business people toward holding the line on good accounting practices.

In a study of a regional group of accountants, respondents said they had few qualms about massaging the bottom line through operating-decision manipulation. They rated the practice of deferring expenditures by a month as a 3.38 on a scale of 4 (ethical) to 0 (unethical). They rated deferring expenditures into the next year as a 3.12. They even tolerated, to a lesser degree, practices that violate generally accepted accounting principles. They rated the deferral of the recording of supplies received to future accounting periods as a 1.71 on the same scale.[7] Referring to this kind of erosion in earnings quality, Levitt said, "Managing may be giving way to manipulation; integrity may be losing out to illusion."

Surveys suggest that Levitt is right even when it comes to the executive ranks. In answer to a 1998 *CFO* magazine conference questionnaire, 45 percent of respondents said they had been asked to misrepresent results. An astonishing 38 percent said they did so.[8] Apparently, neither accountants nor managers nor executives reject out of hand the finagling of numbers to improve the earnings report.

Management Accounting

Many companies have turned to their management accounting systems to bypass the limitations of financial accounting. Some of them have developed best practices that give them a firm foundation for true accountability. We discuss them in Chapter 4 and in the second half of this book.

However, many companies have not gotten beyond the crisis in management accounting that crept into place early in the century. That is, they use management accounting as not much more than a data-gathering device for determining product costs and compiling external financial accounts. As Thomas Johnson and Robert Kaplan argued in 1987, management accounts are driven by the cycle and procedures of financial accounting.[9] The information is most useful for tasks like valuing inventory and aggregating costs across the company. It is an incomplete basis for measuring performance.

Any company that has not radically changed its management accounting risks finding it produces problems similar to those created by financial accounting. The two most critical problems are prodding managers into, first, an incessant financial focus and, second, a near total reliance on historical, or lagging, indicators for decision making. The product and service costs that managers receive, the meat and potatoes of managerial accounting, often reveal little about the nonfinancial factors of performance that create costs, like complex product designs or defective customer service. The cost data help managers keep the financial score but not necessarily how to improve their long-term batting average.

Unfortunately, the data from traditional cost systems are often just plain wrong—not a little wrong but wildly so. A classic example is the case of Tektronix's circuit board division in Forest Grove, Oregon.[10] In the late 1980s, the cost accounting system nearly ran the division out of business. Sales of the unit rose briskly, breaking $50 million, but profits tumbled. Managers from sales, marketing, engineering, manufacturing, and finance could not agree on the root cause.

The circuit board division had already adopted just-in-time techniques, statistical quality control, and total quality management. Inventories were shrinking, quality rising, and delivery improving. The cost system, calculating standard costs, even said margins were just fine. Yet, as the plant manager at the time, Gene Hendrickson, later lamented, "the more we sold, the more money we lost."

Exasperated, Hendrickson adopted activity-based costing (ABC), which guided the plant to profits four times the industry average. Using ABC, accountants assigned overhead according to its actual usage by product, not, as in standard costing, by averaging costs across the plant. The retabulation revealed that one printed circuit board the division sold for $1.00 cost $4.30 just to manufacture. Including overhead, it cost a staggering $20.30. Yet, the standard cost accounting system's numbers were a fraction of that—just $0.67. The division was losing nearly $20 on each such unit sold.

Why such a wild difference in accounting? The board was made in lots of one or two, which consumed, in some cases, the same amount of overhead time as lots of thousands. The per-unit overhead cost of small lots was actually huge. Most debilitating was that more than half the division's product line sold in small (undercosted) lots. So faulty product costing was helping drive the division toward extinction. Tektronix was caught in a death spiral, so long as it profited only on large (overcosted) lots. By using ABC, the unit could calculate not just product costs accurately but customer costs as well, leading Tektronix to sell only profitable products to profitable customers.[11]

Even when cost systems do provide accurate measurement data, they can still distort decision making, eroding the basis for full accountability. A classic example of this problem is that of Analog Devices, which recognized long before other companies the pitfalls of a dominating focus on financial accounts. Now a $1.3 billion Norwood, Massachusetts, integrated circuit board maker, Analog had grown by an annual 25 percent into the mid-1980s when suddenly growth slowed to less than 10 percent. Analog pinpointed one problem: too low a yield, or too many scrapped chips. So, like Tektronix, it adopted total quality management.

Analog found right away, though, that the signals from the accounting ledger, right or wrong, encouraged behavior that clashed with quality efforts. Standard cost accounting, for example, would goad people into building too much work-in-process inventory. That slowed down manufacturing cycle times and lengthened lead times. It also angered customers. The cause? A desire by managers to reduce the cost of goods sold (with the help of the averaging of standard cost accounting) and thus increase margins and profits at quarterly reporting time.[12]

Another tough problem is that traditional financial measures would encourage people to ship high-value orders early, even if that meant shipping low-value ones late. Art Schneiderman, then vice president of quality, polled twenty of his peers in 1986, asking those who regularly dealt with customers what they heard when angry customers called. The answer, chastening, was predictable: "Where's my order!?"[13]

Time and again, Analog found, financial figures are too late to act on, too distorted, too encouraging of the wrong behavior, too lacking as leading indicators. In short, as many companies have found, financial figures alone aren't an adequate foundation on which to build an accountable organization, especially when linked to pay. Executives who rely on traditional financial figures risk making decisions they will kick themselves for later, like dropping the wrong product lines and cutting staff rather than cutting costs from poor quality.

The lesson is that companies that depend on financial accounting and traditional management accounting systems are in crisis because they are missing the first element for making the accountable organization: relevant and comprehensive measures of performance. Without systems that extend beyond the financials to nonfinancials and that accurately tally product costs, few managers or executives can deliver a maximum of value to shareholders, customers, or anyone else.

Managers widely recognize the problem today. In a study by Deloitte & Touche, 45 percent of companies said their performance measurement system had a neutral to negative impact on long-term management. What's more, respondents who reported the least satisfaction with their performance measurement systems used financials more intensely and used fewer nonfinancials than did respondents who reported more satisfaction. Little surprise that 65 percent said most of their measures came from the current-year financial results.[14]

Analog chief executive Jerry Fishman began wrestling with the inadequacy of the financial accounting systems back in the late 1980s when he was executive vice president. Once the distortions in the system became clear, he stumbled upon the next managerial problem. Top managers were arguing about priorities in the corporate agenda. They were asking, Which comes first, financial or nonfinancial goals? "Your job," Fishman told Schneiderman, in a phrase that captures the challenge we address in the second half of this book, "is to integrate them."[15]

THE DROUGHT OF REPORTING

When managers work with the right numbers, and even integrate them, many still face a crisis in accountability. The main cause is a culture of confidentiality. Managers worry so much about letting go of information that could benefit competitors—or litigators—that they don't release information that will benefit their own organization. Their attitude is, if in doubt, don't give the information out.

The practices and behaviors that protect legitimate company secrets can run amok. People may believe that hoarding data yields more benefit than sharing it. They may habitually keep their information to themselves, sensing that an ace up the sleeve can trump a political foe. They may use the data to hide troubles, manipulate others, or build power. They serve themselves at the expense of the organization.

This is partly a legacy of command-and-control management. Managers once amassed information only at the top of the hierarchy. They squelched dissemination of critical performance data. Today, however, without ample and credible information, employees can't accelerate continuous and breakthrough improvement. They can't win the trust and loyalty of people outside the company, the customers, shareholders, suppliers, and others they depend on to conduct business.

Reporting on the Inside

In few companies today do managers share their measures of success widely. Some "open-book" companies are the exception, at least in sharing financial data.[16] AES Corporation, the $835 million independent power producer in Arlington, Virginia, goes to an extreme: It has long given employees so much information that all are classified by the SEC as insiders. AES also annually surveys its employees' opinion of company values—of integrity, fairness, social responsibility, and even fun. Until 1994, when AES grew too large to report comparable data across divisions, it even published the survey results in its annual report.[17]

But few large companies circulate financial and nonfinancial data throughout the organization, from team to team, or division to division. Even if they have the systems to do so, they don't. They consider the data too sensitive.

One company that saw the mentality of sealed lips and secrecy drag down performance was CIGNA Property & Casualty. Before Gerry Isom took over as president in 1993, the company operated without any means of broadcasting the critical measures of its success around the company.[18] At the time, the company was suffering a financial crisis. Hit by claims from the Mississippi and Missouri River floods, Los Angeles riots, environmental cleanup, and Hurricanes Hugo and Andrew, the Property & Casualty (P&C) unit lost $1 billion between 1990 and 1993. Its combined ratio in 1992 was 129 percent—it was shelling out $1.29 in claims for every $1 coming in.

The poor circulation of data was hardly the only cause, but Isom noted some of the behavior it prompted: "While everybody's intentions were pure, a strong dynamic had developed between the divisions and corporate. In particular, the mission of P&C's financial staff had evolved into an ambiguous one. On one end, they were tasked with supplying P&C's management with the necessary financial information.... On the other, they'd developed the habit of filtering the information they distributed inside, and leaking selected other information to corporate, unbeknownst to the P&C management team."[19]

The information Isom wanted spread around for better decision making, strategy execution, and organizational learning had become a commodity for squirreling away and parceling out. The filtering of information complicated Isom's goal of providing a strong, consistent message that would align the efforts of everyone in the organization. It also blocked organizational learning, a capability Isom believed was necessary to succeed with a new strategy of specialty insurance. The tight-fisted treatment of information meant that employees didn't even know precisely how their performance was being measured. Nor did they see clearly how to fit their efforts into the strategy.

Poor internal reporting contributes to the crisis in accountability in other ways. One of the most important is in reducing commitment to delivering results. To gain the commitment of people, teams, business units, and functions, managers need peer-reviewable targets, measures, and results, but many organizations keep the goals and results of business groups at all levels behind closed doors. At both CIGNA Property & Casualty and Tenneco, none of the business-unit heads knew the results of their peer-level executives—until the changing of the guard in the early 1990s.

Disclosure on the Outside

Although many companies fall short of full accountability by failing to share performance measures widely within their organizations, even more fall short by failing to share them outside. By operating with poor external disclosure, companies count themselves out of the rich feedback that spurs learning. They complicate informed decision making by financial analysts, shareholders, customers, suppliers, and others with whom they interact. They forgo the opportunity to develop enduring stakeholder loyalty, an increasingly valuable edge in business today.

Most companies try to fill the information gap with public-relations fodder, but PR is a flimsy tool to engage stakeholders in making decisions in the company's favor. Moreover, PR often comes with an implication that the company is stonewalling, hesitant to come clean with all available facts. By relying on PR alone, executives risk losing that most valuable commodity: credibility. Something more than PR is needed to engage the hearts and minds of the people who provide low-cost capital, talented labor, steady business, and reliable alliances. Hard data, fresh from the company's data warehouse, is that something.

Few companies provide a complete report of performance information. Surveys spanning two decades show that even in the publication of annual reports, the key document portraying firm performance, companies don't come close to satisfying investors. Only 21 percent of investors, surveyed randomly, believe the annual report is "very useful." The good news is that figure is up from 14 percent in 1973, but the figure is still appalling. What business in America would consider a key product successful if only one out of five customers liked it?

The survey further shows that even the financial statements don't please the customer. Nearly one out of three investors still has trouble understanding the balance sheet and cash-flow statement—at a time when the cash flow has become one of the most trusted measures in the report. More than a third of the investors surveyed wanted more explanation of the balance sheet and cash-flow statement and more than a quarter wanted more explanation of the income statement and management discussion and analysis.[20] They also wanted more disclosure of forward-looking information that would help them to make better forecasts of future corporate performance.

With the awful ratings, you would think business would declare an emergency—and assign a crack team to engineer a new product. However, many corporate finance chiefs fight new disclosure requirements every step of the way. They have greeted recent Financial Accounting Standards Board (FASB) proposals on derivatives exposure, stock-options costs, and a more complete earnings figure called comprehensive income with disdain. Compromised rulings have forced many critical facts into obscure footnotes. The result is that companies now portray some huge liabilities in their financial statements as having no cost at all. Such a distortion is not worth the divot thus whacked from management credibility.

A pair of reports in 1998 brought to light, for example, the mountainous liabilities companies have accrued as they have doled out employee stock options. The more conservative report, by Bear Stearns, calculated that had DuPont, for example, expensed options costs like other pay, company net earnings in 1997 would have taken a hit of 8 percent.[21] Had Silicon Graphics done the same, net earnings would have evaporated. Factoring in the rising value of unexercised options, Smithers & Co. Ltd. (London) came to even more alarming conclusions. The one hundred largest publicly traded U.S. companies, concluded Smithers, would have reported, as a group, 34 percent lower earnings in 1996 if all options costs had been expensed.[22]

A survey of Wall Street's star analysts revealed enormous dissatisfaction with company disclosure. Thirty-five percent of these respected analysts have trouble understanding footnotes; 18 percent have trouble with the statement of cash flows. Even analysts who say they understand the statements feel poorly informed: 55 percent want more explanation of the footnotes; 34 percent want more on the cash flows.[23]

The reaction of analysts to other parts of the annual report isn't much better. For example, 49 percent would like more explanation in the management discussion and analysis—including data on product-line profitability, budgeted year-ahead income statements, earnings forecasts, and explanation of strategy.[24] The analysts aren't fooled by inconsistent approaches to reporting year to year, either. Half say they believe companies purposely write in obscure language when they aren't doing well. They say they want full disclosure in both good times and bad.[25]

Annual reports leave plenty of room for management to volunteer better information. You might think managers would grab the opportunity to improve a faulty information product. Yet, few do. In interviews with twenty-five of the most influential institutional investors in Europe and the United States, performed by Shelley Taylor & Associates in 1998, seven of ten investors said they consider clearly stated objectives and their comparison with actual achievements very important. Yet, in a concurrent study of annual reports for 100 of the world's largest firms, only 76 percent clearly state objectives, and a mere 24 percent showed results against objectives.

These institutional investors also said they are intensely interested in disclosure of forward-looking information, but in only 37 percent of the annual reports did companies divulge forward-looking information including earnings forecasts, and in only 41 percent did they disclose, in financial-statement footnotes, planned expenditures.[26] What's remarkable is that not even the people most managers feel ultimately responsible to—the owners—are satisfied with the information they receive on their share holdings.

In the light of history, perhaps this gap between what investors want and what they get makes sense. After all, the SEC and FASB have over the years dictated most disclosure practices. Managers have understandably come to view disclosure as an act of compliance, which they associate with a storm of red tape and strong-willed bureaucrats. They have thus begun to develop a compliance mentality. Disclosure gets lumped into the reviled category of business activities, like taxes, managed to meet the letter of the law. It is no surprise that in a 1998 survey of 308 large companies by the American Society of Corporate Secretaries 44 percent reported they divulge no more than what is legally required.[27]

The crisis in accountability becomes particularly acute when it comes to disclosure of nonfinancial information. At a time when many companies crank out reams of quality, customer satisfaction, employee satisfaction, turnaround time, environmental management, equal employment, charitable giving, employee treatment, and other data, they spend too little time examining how they could use the data for gaining an advantage through both internal reporting and public accountability. They should be managing disclosure as a competitive opportunity and should start by making a more transparent communications strategy a critical component of corporate strategy.

Managers may pooh-pooh the value of further nonfinancial disclosure. They may obsess over the costs and risks—of data processing, paperwork, potential litigation, and loss of trade secrets—but they will find they are not meeting the demand for this information any better than the demand for better financials. In 1997, Ernst & Young's Center for Business Innovation, in

Boston, studied investment preferences of 275 portfolio managers. They found that decisions are 35 percent influenced by nonfinancial factors. A company's ability to attract and retain talented employees, for example, ranked fifth in a list of twenty-nine factors investors use to pick stocks.[28]

A raft of such data sought by outsiders, however, remains locked in the vault of corporate confidentiality. Managers should not stop short of achieving full accountability simply for want of fuller disclosure, of either financial or nonfinancial items. The few companies that do release more data, as we will see in later chapters, are breaking new competitive ground.

THE SEASON OF DISCONTENT

Solving the crisis in accountability has become more urgent in recent years. The competitive pressures are only half of it. Pressures from stakeholders are the other half. Not only are these outsiders dissatisfied with corporate accountability, but they are campaigning like never before to improve it. They are striving to part the corporate veil, with whatever tools they can muster, whether managers like it or not.

Most executives misunderstand the gathering forces arrayed against them. They fail to sense the full scope of the discontent. They let marketeers field the gripes of customers. Investor-relations people take the heat from shareholders. Local line managers catch the criticism of communities. Various staff handle the stones hurled by public-interest groups. They allow the many extremities of the corporate body to absorb the multiple pinpricks of pressure. The company consequently treats many demands for greater accountability in isolation and as nuisances.

What senior managers should grasp is that the pinpricks are symptoms of one overarching trend: the growing belief by company outsiders that corporations should provide a far better public accounting of performance—and the growing commitment by those outsiders to use everything from the power of persuasion and peer pressure to hungry journalists and sympathetic lawmakers to press their case. Managers who view these pressures in isolation make a mistake. They should view them, and handle them, as one.

Outsiders today simply believe they have a right to know what is happening inside corporations. No company can escape the rising tide of external activism, whether from shareholders or other constituencies, to examine the inner workings of corporations large and small. A look at some of the activism facing companies today reveals how the inexorable growth of pressure for greater accountability is forcing many managers to change the way they manage.

Regulatory Heat

Regulators remain a prominent force for greater accountability, whether the Occupational Safety and Health Administration, the Environmental Protection Agency, or any other federal, state, or community agency. If not by the force of law, they press their cases through the force of will.

No agency better exemplifies the regulatory posture toward disclosure than the SEC. In opening a speech at the University of Virginia, SEC Chairman Arthur Levitt quoted Samuel Johnson, who said, "Where secrecy or mystery begins, vice or roguery is not far off." Levitt maintains that it was precisely to protect investors from the danger Johnson observed that the SEC was created in the aftermath of the 1929 market crash.

Levitt, fond of reminding people of the SEC's historical mission, quoted Joseph P. Kennedy: "Publicity," said Kennedy in his very first speech as the first chairman of the SEC in 1934, "will be an important element in the new conditions, publicity, not of an occasional nature, but regular and informative. It will not be enough for a new enterprise to be candid in its original prospectus; it will supply its investors, from time to time, with publicity of such a nature that all will be as well informed as any individual could be."[29]

The SEC never considers that mission quite fulfilled. Levitt and other commissioners remain on the lookout to make disclosure ever more informative. Steven Wallman, commissioner until late 1997, even laid out a new, radically expanded approach to disclosure. "The purpose of accounting and financial reporting is to provide information that is useful to investors, creditors, monitors, and others—increasingly including employees and major suppliers and customers—in making investment, credit, monitoring, and other decisions."

He then outlined disclosure that would suit this cast of characters. He suggested data the likes of which few firms would consider
reporting today: off-balance sheet intangibles (for example, the
value of brands), customer satisfaction (as in J.D. Power survey results), and "intellectual capital" (for instance, the value of a trained
workforce).[30] This proposal has not been adopted, but whatever its
merit, it reveals an entrenched principle of regulatory thinking, a
principle not just alive in the SEC but in agencies across the land:
More disclosure is better disclosure.

Accountants on the Move

The accounting profession, represented by the American Institute of Certified Public Accountants (AICPA), contributes to the
pressure for accountability in a different way. Long worried about
the growing irrelevancy of traditional financial statements, AICPA
leaders felt in the early 1990s that they had to make some recommendations for change. After all, the group is the main think tank
and standards counselor for public reporting practices. So in the
early 1990s, the AICPA tapped Edmund Jenkins to lead a committee to figure out what to suggest. Jenkins, now head of the FASB,
came back in 1994 to suggest that companies throw open the door
on disclosure.

The so-called Jenkins report ran 200 pages, reflecting what users
of financial statements wanted. Backing it up was a 1,600-page
database of research, mainly results from a Lou Harris survey of
1,200 investors and creditors, discussion groups with investors, and
analyses of investment documents. Among a deluge of suggestions
in the report, the Jenkins committee prescribed a new model for
business reporting. It called on standards makers to require "high-
level operating data and performance measurements—which help
users understand the linkage between events and their financial impact on the company and the factors that create longer-term
value."[31]

The report ignited a firestorm of criticism. Some observers forecast a short shelf life and quick burial, but the AICPA formed a
committee to follow up on the recommendations. In early 1997, a
sister committee, studying assurance services, chaired by KPMG
partner Robert Elliott, released a report strongly endorsing the
Jenkins reporting model.[32] In 1998, the FASB, headed by Jenkins,

voted 7–0 to take up a project to pursue the recommendations. The Jenkins report, though temporarily a sleeper, hardly died.

Today, work continues behind the scenes to develop new, expanded, high-quality reporting practices. Businesses can safely bet that they will feel unceasing pressure for greater transparency, mandated or voluntary. Accountants will increasingly want to fulfill key recommendations of the Jenkins committee. Among them,

- "Provide more information about plans, opportunities, risks, and uncertainties.
- "Focus more on the factors that create longer-term value, including nonfinancial measures indicating how key business processes are performing.
- "Better align information reported externally with the information reported internally to senior management to manage the business."[33]

Clout of the Customer

The clout of customers may yet overwhelm the pressures from either regulators or accountants. Although customers have not risen to a powerful force in opening the disclosure doors in many industries, managers can hardly afford to ignore them. In a sign of what's to come, consider the health-care industry. In their dealings with everything from small hospitals and physicians' practices to giant managed-care organizations, health-care customers in many regions have already gained so much power that they are, in effect, issuing orders on what, when, and how health-care organizations should disclose performance data.

The irony is hard to miss. An industry maligned for managerial backwardness has taken what appears to be a five-year lead over the rest of industry in measuring and reporting to customers all kinds of data—quality, customer satisfaction, administrative performance, and so on. As far back as 1993, managed-care giant United HealthCare, whose story we tell in Chapter 4, reported such detail as administrative costs per member and appointment wait times.

How has it happened that an industry of managerial laggards jumped to the lead? The answer is equally ironic. Coalitions of business customers, often with poor disclosure records themselves, banded together to wring nonfinancial information from their health-care suppliers. Hospitals, physicians' groups, health-maintenance organizations—they have all been taking a crash course in measuring and reporting performance to comply with the ultimatums of their customers.

Consider northeastern Ohio, around Cleveland, as just one example of the forces at play. In 1989, Cleveland's biggest employers formed the Cleveland Health Quality Choice Program (CHQCP). Every Cleveland hospital that valued these companies' business had to measure and report mortality rates; lengths of stay; patient satisfaction; and outcomes for medical, surgical, obstetrical, and intensive-care patients. The hospitals had no choice. To this day, they prepare a twice-yearly report card, which helps steer patients to the highest quality, most efficient health-care providers.[34] Not only has the CHQCP created accountability, it has increased patient satisfaction and sharply reduced mortality rates.

Managers who don't feel they should get ready to take advantage of (or avoid getting hammered by) such customer power should note how the CHQCP's maneuverings played out. When the first round of data was released in 1993, the numbers proved that hospital quality varied widely. Some hospitals that charged the most even offered the poorest results. Within a year, by the release of the third report in spring 1994, health-care managers could plainly see that the power of publicly disclosed numbers would restructure the industry.

Health-care customers, principally health-maintenance organizations, threw their old vendor arrangements out the window. In 1994, MetLife announced it would pare its hospital network, redirecting its 70,000 Cleveland-area enrollees from twenty-eight hospitals to just eleven.[35] Aetna Health Plans of Ohio created a subnetwork of eleven (of thirty-two) hospitals, telling its 400,000 members that they would get a 25 percent discount for using the smaller, higher-quality network.[36] One local physician network shifted 275,000 patients from one four-hospital group to another.[37]

The story of Cleveland, where some hospitals saw their business plunge overnight, is being repeated around the United States. Doctors, hospitals, and health networks have been offered deals they can't refuse—measure and report or risk losing hundreds or thou-

ments very important. Yet, in a concurrent study of annual reports for 100 of the world's largest firms, only 76 percent clearly state objectives, and a mere 24 percent showed results against objectives.

These institutional investors also said they are intensely interested in disclosure of forward-looking information, but in only 37 percent of the annual reports did companies divulge forward-looking information including earnings forecasts, and in only 41 percent did they disclose, in financial-statement footnotes, planned expenditures.[26] What's remarkable is that not even the people most managers feel ultimately responsible to—the owners—are satisfied with the information they receive on their share holdings.

In the light of history, perhaps this gap between what investors want and what they get makes sense. After all, the SEC and FASB have over the years dictated most disclosure practices. Managers have understandably come to view disclosure as an act of compliance, which they associate with a storm of red tape and strong-willed bureaucrats. They have thus begun to develop a compliance mentality. Disclosure gets lumped into the reviled category of business activities, like taxes, managed to meet the letter of the law. It is no surprise that in a 1998 survey of 308 large companies by the American Society of Corporate Secretaries 44 percent reported they divulge no more than what is legally required.[27]

The crisis in accountability becomes particularly acute when it comes to disclosure of nonfinancial information. At a time when many companies crank out reams of quality, customer satisfaction, employee satisfaction, turnaround time, environmental management, equal employment, charitable giving, employee treatment, and other data, they spend too little time examining how they could use the data for gaining an advantage through both internal reporting and public accountability. They should be managing disclosure as a competitive opportunity and should start by making a more transparent communications strategy a critical component of corporate strategy.

Managers may pooh-pooh the value of further nonfinancial disclosure. They may obsess over the costs and risks—of data processing, paperwork, potential litigation, and loss of trade secrets—but they will find they are not meeting the demand for this information any better than the demand for better financials. In 1997, Ernst & Young's Center for Business Innovation, in

Boston, studied investment preferences of 275 portfolio managers. They found that decisions are 35 percent influenced by nonfinancial factors. A company's ability to attract and retain talented employees, for example, ranked fifth in a list of twenty-nine factors investors use to pick stocks.[28]

A raft of such data sought by outsiders, however, remains locked in the vault of corporate confidentiality. Managers should not stop short of achieving full accountability simply for want of fuller disclosure, of either financial or nonfinancial items. The few companies that do release more data, as we will see in later chapters, are breaking new competitive ground.

THE SEASON OF DISCONTENT

Solving the crisis in accountability has become more urgent in recent years. The competitive pressures are only half of it. Pressures from stakeholders are the other half. Not only are these outsiders dissatisfied with corporate accountability, but they are campaigning like never before to improve it. They are striving to part the corporate veil, with whatever tools they can muster, whether managers like it or not.

Most executives misunderstand the gathering forces arrayed against them. They fail to sense the full scope of the discontent. They let marketeers field the gripes of customers. Investor-relations people take the heat from shareholders. Local line managers catch the criticism of communities. Various staff handle the stones hurled by public-interest groups. They allow the many extremities of the corporate body to absorb the multiple pinpricks of pressure. The company consequently treats many demands for greater accountability in isolation and as nuisances.

What senior managers should grasp is that the pinpricks are symptoms of one overarching trend: the growing belief by company outsiders that corporations should provide a far better public accounting of performance—and the growing commitment by those outsiders to use everything from the power of persuasion and peer pressure to hungry journalists and sympathetic lawmakers to press their case. Managers who view these pressures in isolation make a mistake. They should view them, and handle them, as one.

sands of patients. The stakes are huge. Some buyers' groups represent the Goliath of all customers: the federal government, the administrator of Medicare and Medicaid, known as the Health Care Financing Administration.

Managers in other industries may pass this off as a one-industry event. That would be a mistake. Customer power is growing everywhere. When customers gain a critical mass, they will often demand hard numbers. Their collective muscle can pry the doors off the lockbox of proprietary corporate performance data. As just one other example, note how outraged consumers, with the help of celebrities, are working to publicly expose corporate labor-practice data. Shoppers want assurance they aren't supporting child labor or sweatshops. What does this mean in the future? As an indicator, two-thirds of Americans, according to an Ohio State University survey, favor labels that tell consumers clothing was made by socially responsible manufacturers.[38]

A decade ago, few health-care executives would have dreamed that they would now be baring their operational soul. Now, in a development other industries should heed, full accountability has become so much a part of standard industry practice that the Joint Commission on Accreditation of Healthcare Organizations (JCAHO)—the premier accrediting group for the nation's hospitals—launched a program in 1997 requiring hospitals to report at least two quality measures (of their choice). Starting in spring 1998, the hospitals that don't report at least two can't gain accreditation. The requirement gradually rises to twelve measures by December 2000.

In a sign that the JCAHO plans to push the accountability trend forward, it also gave health-care managers the option of going beyond compliance. Hospitals can step into the limelight by joining the elite ORYX PLUS program (the program's name, not an acronym). ORYX PLUS hospitals will start immediately reporting to JCAHO at least ten measures from a standardized list of thirty-two.[39] They can then release, with the seal of approval of the JCAHO, the broader list of figures to customers. The ORYX PLUS program will give participants a huge advantage over their competitors, especially because the JCAHO will display data that compares individual hospitals with national averages.

As the JCAHO says, those hospitals adopting ORYX PLUS will "quickly become recognized by consumers, employers, payers, and government bodies for their commitment to self-evaluation and accountability through their willingness to share performance information with the public."[40] We can predict that health-care organizations failing to follow the leaders will put themselves at a marked disadvantage. We can also speculate that those industries that go too slow in recognizing the rich returns of investing in accountability may handicap their future competitiveness.[41]

Interest-Group Intensity

Corporate watchdog groups are always ready to raise the alarm of a crisis. Forever loyal to their programs, they nip continuously at the corporate conscience for more accountability. They have such power and sophistication that, today, companies ignore them at significant cost. These organizations include not just the citizen-action groups that like to advance their cause via raising a public ruckus but also the new breed of organizations that sit at the table with business people and *negotiate* for greater accountability.

Consider the California Reinvestment Committee (CRC) in San Francisco. CRC, which monitors banks' reinvestment of deposits in local communities, has signed oversight agreements with six California banks. These letters of understanding, executed by, for example, the chief executives at Bank of America and Wells Fargo, detail reinvestment pledges, like how much multifamily housing they will invest in and in what cities. CRC meets with bank officials twice yearly and requires a performance report and verification of progress. Over the last decade, CRC has gone so far as helping banks meet their goals. At one time, it steered Wells Fargo into using the low-income housing tax credit profitably to create what has become a multimillion-dollar low-income housing loan portfolio.[42]

Consider the Coalition for Environmentally Responsible Economies (CERES), which lobbies hard to get companies to provide an exhaustive, voluntary public report on environmental performance. In its early years, CERES enrolled a contingent of small do-gooder firms. Today it targets and enrolls the biggest names in business, from Sun Company and Polaroid to General Motors and Coca-Cola. The CERES commitment requires companies to answer a tough, 110-part questionnaire that portrays every aspect of their environmental performance, from waste recycling to energy consumption.[43] "We really feel like we're baring our soul in answering those . . . questions," says Philip Hillman, head of environment at Polaroid.[44]

Consider the Interfaith Center for Corporate Responsibility (ICCR), an association of 275 religious groups that together hold $90 billion in assets. The ten staffers at ICCR, while wearing the hat of social activist and exerting the influence of monied shareholder, raise a wide array of issues, from environmental affairs and equal employment opportunity to hiring in Northern Ireland and doing business in Burma. ICCR has convinced 150 companies to release their equal employment opportunity data, triple the number of ten years ago. In one case, that of Schering-Plough, a single meeting prompted executives to hand over the desired document.[45]

When the powers of persuasion hit resistance, ICCR staffers don't hesitate to turn on their shareholder activism. In 1998 alone, ICCR-related shareholders sponsored 158 shareholder resolutions at 114 companies. At Con Agra and Barnes & Noble, for instance, these groups filed resolutions calling for disclosure of the equal employment opportunity numbers, essentially the data supplied to the government in EEO-1 reports, often held secret from the public. ICCR also filed 41 resolutions calling for adoption of the CERES principles.[46]

The pressure exerted by groups like the CRC, CERES, and ICCR on individual companies sends waves of influence toward other companies that shy from taking a seat at a table with a public-interest group. Amoco, for example, prodded repeatedly to adopt the CERES principles, declined, but the influence of CERES still left its mark: Amoco sponsored the Public Environmental Reporting Initiative (PERI) with nine other companies (including DuPont, Dow Chemical, and Polaroid). The industry-led effort created a parallel standard for environmental reporting. From 1992 until its acquisition by British Petroleum, Amoco reported environmental performance against the PERI guidelines, disclosing an unprecedented amount of information.[47] Action by Amoco and similar firms demonstrates that public interest groups have gotten managers' attention, convincing many managers that disclosure counts more than ever.

Pension Power

As in most stories of power and influence, one character stands out as the 800-pound gorilla. In the accountability story, that character is the institutional money manager. These managers together control such vast capital that their wish often carries the weight of command. The most active of these managers today are the public pension-fund managers, whose story we tell in the next chapter. Suffice it to say for now that a few pension gorillas can bring incredible urgency to top managers' efforts to create better accountability.

With the voice of the pension-fund manager added to the mix, corporate managers will find that stakeholder calls for full accountability are calls they cannot ignore. Even if they choose not to build an accountable company for internal reasons, as a way to make their operations more competitive, they may well have to build one for external reasons, as a way to make their operations acceptable to outsiders. That is part of the price they pay for access to labor, capital, and product markets. That is also part of the price for their license to operate in a society that views business as intertwined with other social institutions.

LOSING THE LEAD TO OUTSIDERS

Because few managers comprehend that a crisis of accountability engulfs them, even fewer have acted quickly to turn the crisis into opportunity. Just the opposite. Other organizations have taken the prerogative to specify the terms of the corporate accountability equation. In case after case, independent groups have cropped up to measure and publicly report corporate performance. To the extent that companies could gain advantage by reporting for themselves, especially with audited figures, managers have largely lost the opportunity forever.

Among the independent organizations grabbing the lead is the Families and Work Institute. In the *Corporate Reference Guide*, it rates company performance in three categories to produce a "family-friendly index."[48] *Business Week* similarly grades more than fifty companies on family friendliness.[49] Other organizations taking the lead are Wichita State University and the University of Nebraska–Omaha, which publish annual-airline-quality ratings, based on data the airlines report to the government.[50] University of Michigan's Business School and the American Society for Quality Control rate quality at more than 200 companies on a 1–100 scale.[51] The National Association for the Advancement of Colored People (NAACP) issues report cards on the employment of African Americans at hotel chains, giving only the best an A, expecting the grades to swing traffic to the more diverse hotels.[52] *Fortune* magazine, working with the Council on Economic Priorities, even inaugurated in 1998 a list of the fifty best companies for Asians, African Americans, and Hispanics.[53]

Of course, most stakeholders who are trying to gauge the mettle of a company prefer such independent measurement. Still, the emergence of so many rating groups sends a two-part signal that managers should heed: (1) People want more decision-making information than companies produce today, and (2) companies have been too slow to produce it for either insiders or outsiders. It's a simple message, really. It sums up the root cause of the crisis in accountability.

The challenge for managers is to do something about this crisis. In the next four chapters, we explore what companies *are* doing about it: revamping governance, devising new measures, revitalizing management planning and control, and expanding reporting. In Chapter 3, we start at the top of the power pyramid, looking at efforts to reform the governance of the corporation.

3

Calling
for Governance

The drama of the accountability crisis has not yet reached a climax at many companies, but, like most dramas, it has already put one set of people under the bright lights. These are the people that most outsiders view as the power brokers responsible for the problem, the chief executive and the board of directors.

The notion has emerged that a corporation without an active, independent organ of supervision cannot be fully accountable. That is why companies have begun actively experimenting with the first element of corporate accountability, governance. (See Figure 3-1.) They are concluding that the board must comprise a set of directors who are completely independent, who ensure the accountability of the chief executive. Those directors must run the board with strict, new governance practices, which ensure their accountability to outside constituencies.

At a special meeting of shareholders on July 2, 1997, Dennis Kozlowski, chief executive of Tyco International, showed just how much good board governance counts in improving decision making and strategic execution. Kozlowski knew his audience wouldn't be entirely happy on that day. Many shareholders thought that, in the interest of empire building, he was asking them to vote for a deal from tax hell, namely a proposal to acquire

Figure 3-1
The First Element of Accountability: Governance

burglar-alarm giant ADT, in which they would have to pay capital-gains taxes on their Tyco stock.

Some shareholders recoiled. Long-term shareholders would have to pay big taxes, because the stock had doubled in just the previous two years. The reason for the taxes was that in buying ADT as a white knight, Kozlowski had arranged a complex transaction in which Bermuda-based ADT would legally be acquiring Tyco, the Exeter, New Hampshire–based conglomerate, which makes fire systems, underwater cables, medical supplies, circuit boards, and packaging.

The chief executive of the $18 billion firm (after recent acquisitions of U.S. Surgical and AMP) admits that the board didn't warm up to the deal at first. Even when he flew to New York to win them over in a special meeting, the debate lasted ten hours, about seven hours longer than he expected. He argued the merits of the deal, of course. The combination would make Tyco the largest fire and security business in the world. The company would expand operations to fifty countries. Tyco would acquire 1.8 million ADT customers. He assured directors that the deal, detailed in a 200-page proxy statement, would lift the stock price significantly. Still, recalls Kozlowski, "There wasn't a director who didn't question [the deal] and agonize over it."[1]

This is why, at the July meeting, Kozlowski relied on more than the suggested merits of the deal to convince shareholders. He relied also on his and the board's record of accountability for performance. Long-time Tyco director Philip Hampton was called on to defend the plan. He reminded shareholders that all seven directors owned stock (all but one owning more than 10,000 shares). He said the board would take the tax hit along with everyone else. He further proposed that if anyone in the room could suggest a better way for Tyco to take over ADT, the board would delay the vote.

At many companies around the world, getting the board to take such an active, objective oversight role has taken center stage as a means to create greater accountability. Strict board governance practices, the thinking goes, will reassure company outsiders that the board has the processes in place to ask the right questions and to monitor management effectively. Such practices help convince naysayers that executives and directors will act first to fulfill their obligations to shareholders and other stakeholders, and not to themselves. They reassure outsiders further that when the going gets tough, the company won't suffer from one of the root causes of the accountability crisis: a board that does the chief executive's bidding as opposed to a chief executive who does the board's bidding.

At Tyco, shareholders could look to a history of strong oversight to reassure them. Since 1992, the board has run itself according to principles that stimulate decision making independent of the CEO. Hampton, for instance, was the formally designated lead director. He had run regular board sessions without Kozlowski. He gave the chief executive his annual review. He evaluated each board member's performance.

So the comments by Hampton, a holder of 25,000 Tyco shares, carried a lot of weight at that July meeting. Shareholders came into the meeting with a respect for the legacy of accountability and performance of the CEO and the board. Although nobody can say how much this legacy contributed to the vote, shareholders voted to go ahead with the ADT deal. The deal worked as Kozlowski promised. After its consummation, Tyco stock rose steadily from about $60 to trade in the mid-$80 range within three months.

Of the four ways companies are pursuing full accountability—by means of governance, performance measurement, control systems, and reporting—governance has received the most visibility in recent years. How strongly it figures among the four components of full accountability is arguable. What is certain, however, is that modern governance practices like those at Tyco inject a huge measure of shareholder confidence into the decision making of management—confidence that corporate bosses and their boards can use to their advantage.

THE BANKRUPTING OF GOVERNANCE

Changes in corporate governance like those at Tyco have come in response to a tradition of board management that had gone bankrupt. Ingrained and abused, that tradition had come to fail in exacting accountability from company executives. Up to the late 1980s, many chief executives had come to routinely stuff boards with friends, family, business associates, and company executives. The directors were the people the boss lunched with, sent holiday cards to, hired to do taxes. All this coziness compromised the directors' ability to take a hard look at performance.

The board, in concept, comprises a panel of objective overseers.[2] These overseers counsel corporate managers and monitor performance. However, few directors proved they could adequately fulfill that role until recently. They weren't active counselors, vigilant monitors, or skeptical judges. Most dined on the information fed to them at the boardroom table by chief executives. They digested the data on their plate but never called for more. They certainly never stomped into the kitchen for answers. So they had no means to gain insights for hard-edged dialogue over the direction of the company.

Boards became—and many still are—the sugar daddies of chief executives. This is essentially what Adolph Berle and Gardiner Means said would happen. In their classic 1932 book, *The Modern Corporation and Private Property*, the two economists predicted how power would shift within the company as ownership splintered into thousands of slivers divided among small, powerless shareholders. Top executives would hold all the power. The company bosses would become "princes of industry," and the princes would make decisions in their own interest, not in the shareholders'.[3]

Who could or would stop them? Certainly not the small shareholders. If they didn't like what was going on, they would sell. Certainly not the board members. Handpicked by the chief executive, they remained loyal to the company boss, cowed by pay and pensions. They had little at stake. Many directors didn't even own stock. Remarkably, directors' wallets were free from hurt if they failed at their sole job—acting as fiduciaries to steward and grow shareholder capital.

The board had become impotent. It was not so much a question of people's competence as it was a question of a derelict governance process. Even if stuffed with talent and led by a top-flight chief executive, the board couldn't contribute credibly to assuring accountability. If performance lagged, it couldn't summon the means or power to bring management to account. This breakdown in the rigor of oversight hurt the board, hurt management, and hurt shareholders.

By the end of the 1980s, chief executives who practiced so-called mushroom management—leaving directors in the dark and shoveling them manure for information—were alarmingly common. At some companies, governance became a costly charade. At others, it became worse—an illusion that even the directors believed in.

Today, governance is rapidly improving at the biggest companies, but the improvement has come too slowly in many people's eyes. In a recent survey, nine out of ten of Wall Street's star analysts (87 percent) believe that the board did a good job of representing company *management*. Only one out of ten (8 percent) felt it did a decent job of representing shareholders.[4]

THE RESTRUCTURING OF GOVERNANCE

The spotty corporate record in upgrading a doddering governance institution has spurred change. Chief executives like Kozlowski have fashioned a model that brings out the full potential of the board. This is the model that all corporations should heed, a model that uses accountability, of executives to the board, to boost performance. None of the particulars of the model are uncommon, but they take courage and conviction to implement at the top of the corporate hierarchy.

An Emerging Model

No chief executive has contributed more to the model of governance than David W. Johnson, who took the reins of Campbell Soup in 1990. Johnson grasped right away that in hidebound board governance he had found a buried competitive opportunity. He insisted on revamping governance practices to such a degree that Campbell became a paragon of board practices trumpeted far and wide. Governance reform quickly became the fashion and a powerful means to improve performance.

In a precocious move, the Campbell board published its twenty governance standards in 1992. In the spirit of a search for excellence, it tinkers with the standards continuously. It then republishes them every year in the proxy statement. The board actually scores its own performance on a scale of 1 to 5 in sixteen categories, summarizing the results in the proxy. In 1997, it dinged itself for less-than-perfect handling of performance evaluation, succession planning, and capital spending.[5]

Among other things, Campbell requires a majority of outside directors, bans insiders on the nominating committee, requires stock ownership of 6,000 shares within three years, rejects a poison-pill provision, and requires yearly elections of all directors. In 1997, the board even created a new process to evaluate each director, rating people on independence, accountability, participation, preparation, and even stature. In 1998, it further committed to creating a process for evaluating the performance of each board committee.[6]

Research shows that Johnson recognized earlier than almost anyone else how governance can contribute to performance. A study in 1997 by Paul W. MacAvoy of Yale reported that companies governed by the strict set of principles advocated by the California Public Employees Retirement System give back to shareholders an extra 1.5 to 2 percent in annual returns.[7]

Although the empirical data are mixed,[8] shareholders strongly believe good governance leads to good results. Two-thirds of institutional investors, who together manage $840 billion, say that they would pay an average premium of 16 percent on a stock of a well-governed company, all else being equal.[9] Study coauthor and McKinsey consultant Jennifer H. van Heeckeren writes: "Institutional investors . . . believe strong boards will help companies correct mistakes, recover from crises, and find, support, and reward outstanding CEOs."[10]

Company boards and leaders like Johnson and Kozlowski have not waited for empirical research to pour in, though. They have acted on their convictions. Kozlowski says that, aside from aiding performance, running an independent, active board is simply the right thing to do. He subscribes to a sort of golden rule of governance: Govern for your shareholders the way you would have them govern for you—if they were the company boss and you were an outsider director or shareholder. "Coming in as CEO, you have the chance to do the right thing," he says. "I did not want to govern an entity I was an autocratic leader of."

At Tyco, one of Kozlowski's first moves was to ask for an evaluation as CEO from the board. He did not want to run without the checks and balances of good governance. The longer a chief executive waits to institute governance reforms, the worse the potential problems, he says. "You can really start believing in your own propaganda," he adds.

So today, with Philip Hampton as lead director, Kozlowski is the only executive on the board, committee heads rotate, Hampton spearheads the CEO and board member evaluations, directors run annually for election in confidential voting, and executives work without management contracts, poison-pill provisions, or golden parachutes to protect them. "We're all here at the will and election of shareholders each year," he says.

Two Essentials

Companies that want to emulate the model created by the leaders will find that recent innovations aim at improving two essentials: director independence and board performance. Both are necessary to enable the board to make unbiased decisions and to stimulate continuous improvement in company performance.

Most companies have started revamping board governance practices by adopting principles that require independence. That means that directors must hail from outside the company and outside the circle of friends and business associates connected with the company and its officers. The principle of independence is easy to place on the board's policy sheet, even though it takes time to implement.

Most of corporate America has gone a long way in improving independence of boards. Institutional Shareholder Services reported in 1997 that 83 percent of the boards of the Standard & Poor's 500 have at least a majority of independent directors. Outside directors sit in more than two-thirds of the board seats. However, boards at smaller firms seem to have missed the message. Institutional Shareholder Services says dominance of insiders at smaller firms is actually growing.[11]

To be sure, even when firms load their boards with outsiders, they may not actually operate independently. That's why many firms have gone further. They nominate new directors solely through the nominating committee and stock that committee solely with outside directors. They also stock all other committees—particularly audit and compensation—solely with outsiders. In addition, the directors stand for election every year. At companies like Tyco and Campbell Soup, they designate a lead director like Philip Hampton to represent the board's contingent of outside directors.

Only about one in five big companies has a lead director today,[12] an idea popularized only recently. By naming a lead director, a board can operate, if needed, unfettered by influence from the CEO. At Tyco, says Hampton, "It did provide the board with a mechanism of independence of organization and a mechanism of convening the board in an orderly way without management."

Lead directors can also set the agenda rather than simply follow it. Hampton convenes a session without management at alternate board meetings, even if he has no particular issue to discuss. In recent years, the directors have talked a lot about the level of Kozlowski's compensation, about recruiting minority directors, about changing the board size, and about the CEO's evaluation. Says Hampton, "We go around and make everyone speak up."

With such independence, boards can bring an extra measure of objectivity to their judgments. Campbell Soup's board went so far in late 1996 to create a selection committee for a new CEO almost entirely independent of chief executive David Johnson. The committee, led by Philip Lippincott, former Scott Paper CEO, met more than two dozen times. It hired Spencer Stuart Associates, the search firm, which recommended seventeen external candidates. In mid-1997, the committee and the board, meeting in part without Johnson, finally selected insider Dale F. Morrison.[13]

The other goal of governance reform, promoting board performance, has drawn just as much attention in recent years. Changes in expectations of performance have actually had more far-reaching impact in some ways because they require directors to spend a lot more time on their board responsibilities.

Search firm Korn/Ferry International in New York found in 1998 that the average director of a big company spent 159 hours on board matters, up 40 percent since 1987.[14] This is one reason that many people believe directors have to strictly limit the number of boards they sit on, often to no more than two. As National Association of Corporate Directors' President John Nash says, "More and more directors know that being a director is a job—and you have to take it seriously."[15]

One of the first changes has been for companies to issue guidelines for the scope of work of directors—two-thirds have done so, according to the Korn/Ferry Study. Campbell Soup, for example, drafted and voted on a list of "Director Requirements" in 1995. The list included an obligation to review succession planning and to critique strategic and operating plans.[16] Such guidelines have made clear that directors have to dedicate renewed effort to the task.

Another of the changes has been a focus on evaluation, a means to constantly upgrade the performance of the board. In three-quarters of companies, the chief executive submits to a regular evaluation, although in less than half of the companies is the review in writing. In one out of five companies, each director submits to a regular performance review.[17] In a handful, the directors even conduct regular reviews of the evaluation process. In any case, the objective is to help the board benefit from the same process of continuous improvement that has become so common in lower levels of the corporate hierarchy.

In the most publicized of governance reforms, companies have reworked director incentives, namely pay and stock awards. They are aiming to encourage directors to think and act like owners. Many companies have required directors to invest a significant chunk of assets in company stock. They have also started paying director fees in stock alone.

During the late 1990s, surprisingly, a broad consensus of the key issues in governance has arisen. The National Association of Corporate Directors—taking the point of view of outside directors—released *Director Professionalism* in late 1996, a document resulting from a commission led by governance expert Ira Millstein.[18] In September 1997, the association of chief executives known as the Business Roundtable published its less prescriptive Statement on Corporate Governance.[19] In spring 1998, the Council of Institutional Investors, an association of 110 pension funds with over $1 trillion in assets, approved a consolidated list of governance policies.[20] With publication of these documents, the notion that board reform has become a cornerstone of modern management has been cemented in place.[21] These documents detail further the model of governance that has become the standard for industry.

Room for Improvement

For all the improvement to date, many companies have a long way to go in developing the level of accountability through governance that will drive performance. While some companies have readily adopted reforms, others have dragged their heels, unsure that reforms make that much difference.

As examples of the spotty progress, only 44 percent of big firms today have more than five independent directors, only 37 percent convene their boards at least sometimes in the CEO's absence, and only 49 percent rely on an independent committee to nominate new directors. These figures come from a National Association of Corporate Directors survey in 1997 of 1,100 chief executives from 8,100 major U.S. companies. Evidently, a lot of directors, though charged with acting freely in the shareholders' interest, are actually acting with strings still attached to management.

Progress on other reforms is more variable. Only 20 percent of boards evaluate their own performance, and only 53 percent are required to own 1,000 or more shares of stock. However, 70 percent of companies pay directors in cash and stock, and 9 percent pay them in stock alone. In one remarkable development in recent years, 90 percent don't offer any retirement plan at all, widely considered a form of compensation with little to no link to performance.

Companies have made a lot of progress in some areas, little in others. Many chief executives hint at stricter practices in the future. In the National Association of Corporate Directors survey, 84 percent of those chief executives responding felt that boards should have a majority of independent directors, and 68 percent felt that the nominating, compensation, and audit committees should comprise exclusively independent directors, including the chairmanship.[22]

To the extent that chief executives are hesitant to move ahead with governance reform, they should think again. In a world where every company is looking for the ideas, intelligence, and feedback to solve the riddles of strategy and competitive execution of strategy, an active, engaged board offers one obvious source of help. The model for proceeding has been created by pioneers like Campbell Soup and Tyco International. Executives need look no further than the Campbell Soup proxy itself for a quick overview of leading-edge governance. The proxy is a veritable case study in enlightened board practices.

THE ACCOUNTABILITY GORILLAS

For executives who don't recognize the future opportunity buried in governance reform, a gorilla stands ready to remind them. This is the powerful animal we mentioned in the last chapter: the institutional money manager. Slow-moving companies may well find themselves facing the intense pressure from such managers, in particular those who run pension funds.

The single actor on the institutional stage who has raised the biggest ruckus in calling attention to governance and accountability is Robert Monks, founder of Institutional Shareholder Services and cofounder of the LENS fund, a specialist in shareholder activism. Monks has spent much of his life arguing for greater corporate accountability. His recent merging of LENS in early 1999 with Hermes Pension Management Ltd. spreads his influence to one of the UK's largest pension management groups.[23] Monks's unvarnished view: "The default setting of corporate power is CEO as dictator."

One of Monks's most celebrated causes was the reform of governance at Sears, Roebuck and Co. In 1992, he spoke at the Sears annual meeting, as the company was faltering (before its latest comeback). In the combined chairman and CEO, said Monks, Sears had "a man who marks his own report card . . . [who] has not met his own goal of 15 percent return on equity once in the last ten years (hardly even come close)." Monks called for reform as a way not only to revive Sears but as a mechanism to juice the value of his considerable Sears holdings. He closed his statement by saying what a lot of shareholders would like to say to a lot of poorly run boards: "Sears has a slogan: 'You can count on us.' We want to hear the board say that to the shareholders. We want to see the board earn that trust."[24]

As a principal of the Hermes Lens funds Monks spends a lot of time at what he calls the "Sisyphean task" of pushing CEOs uphill away from the default position. He believes that companies that don't keep pushing the governance stone uphill risk letting it slide back to the bottom.[25] Monks has shown repeatedly through large shareholdings taken by his fund that when the board starts marking a CEO's report card, performance often goes up.

A classic target of the LENS fund was Stone & Webster, the Boston-based engineering firm. Monks and partner Nell Minow bought a chunk of the firm in summer 1993. At the time, the old-line engineering firm was reporting profits solely as a result of transferring pension surpluses to the bottom line. Otherwise, it was running in the red—a fact difficult for shareholders to discern in the published financial statements.[26]

LENS, a holder of 1.5 percent of Stone & Webster shares, sued over the handling of the pension-surplus accounting, badgered for the replacement of two CEOs and eight directors, pressed for divestment of noncore assets like real estate and an oil and gas division, lobbied for recasting the financial reporting system to separate the pension surplus from operating earnings, and urged management to put the company up for sale.[27] By 1997, as MIT professor Kent Hansen was named lead director of nine outside board members (on the eleven-person board), Monks and LENS could declare victory on their longest-held investment. Not only was governance changed entirely, but company operating profits were up sharply. Between year-end 1996 and 1997, its total return to shareholders soared more than 50 percent, while its heavy-construction industry peer group swooned 25 percent.[28]

Few outsiders evoke the visceral dislike of company bosses that Monks does, but he has helped establish the concept of accountability like no other single person. He also symbolizes the pressure that institutional managers can bring to bear if companies don't voluntarily adopt better governance in the name of accountability. Of meeting a new CEO he says, "He may not like me, but he knows he can't ignore me." Monks believes that in his years of work, originally brought to special attention from his and Nell Minow's 1991 book, *Power and Accountability*,[29] he has made one point clear: "It's well understood that involvement by owners is a good thing," he says. "It adds value."[30]

Company chiefs may not all agree, but many big institutional managers far bigger than even Hermes Lens certainly do. These powerful managers have a variety of levers for prying the corporate doors open. For Sisyphean backsliders, they have a ready cattle prod. For dictators, they remain prepared with the guillotine. The institutions have amassed unprecedented power, and it grows daily with pension money pouring into their accounts to support the retirement of people from every walk of life.

The Muscle of Pension Funds

Institutional investors come in many forms, as pension funds, life-insurance companies, mutual funds, bank trust departments, and so on. No institution is putting more pressure on companies to govern themselves to better serve shareholders than pension funds.

Pension funds have tipped the balance of power Berle and Means wrote about away from the princes of industry and toward the institutions themselves. Total pension-fund equity holdings alone reached $5.7 trillion in 1997.[31] The California Public Employees' Retirement Systems, or Calpers, now manage over $140 billion. Goliath TIAA-CREF, or the Teachers Insurance and Annuity Association–College Retirement Equities Fund, manage over $135 billion. The managers of these single funds control huge blocks of company stock. They no longer swim with the small investor. They rank as leaders of capital investment. Chief executives simply can't ignore them.

The institutions have gained power through a sequence of permanent changes in capital markets. As they have grown into investing behemoths, they have had to completely change the way they trade stocks. Smaller investors, if unhappy with a company, take the Wall Street Walk. They sell out and go elsewhere. The biggest funds—New York, New Jersey, California, Wisconsin, and Pennsylvania—own so much stock that they can't pull out overnight, or even over a week or a month. If they did, they would pummel the price of their millions of shares. So they have, for practical purposes, become too big to sell.

If they can't sell stocks to readjust their portfolio's value, their only alternative is to rearrange the management of the companies within the portfolio. Many institutions did not catch on to this change in their fiduciary role until recent years. Now, however, they don't shrink from the task—they don't have to, given their size. In 1997, the institutions held 59.9 percent of all stock of the largest 1,000 companies. That's up sharply from 46.6 in 1987. More remarkable is that in 1997, institutions held more than 70 percent of the stock of 38.9 percent of the 1,000 largest companies. That's more than triple the level (10.7 percent) of 1987.[32]

Although the institutional dollar has become the lifeblood of the public company, corporate executives and boards have reacted reluctantly to the new reality. Just over half of all large companies (55 percent) have an investor-relations program, but only 10 percent of chief executives actively seek the views of institutional shareholders.[33] The failure to reach out shows. Asked their opinion, only one in five Wall Street star analysts feels boards do a good job of representing institutional investors.[34] Commonsense suggests that executives should spend more time with their biggest suppliers of capital, if only to be ready to handle the discontent when their stock prices fail to keep pace with their competitors'.

The Growing Ownership Instinct

Several events in the last decade have turned on the ownership instincts of institutional managers. Remarkably, the possession of mountains of investment dollars would not have been enough, alone, to switch the balance of power between companies and institutions.

First, in the late 1980s, the U.S. Department of Labor ruled that the proxy voting rights that come with stock are valuable assets and that pension managers have the fiduciary duty to vote those proxies if doing so would enhance the value of the pension plan's investment. Eventually codifying this opinion in a 1994 interpretive bulletin, the Department of Labor put trustees of pension funds on notice that they couldn't continue to ignore proxy solicitations. Nor could they vote, knee-jerk style, with management. They had to think of their pensioners. All of a sudden, trustees had to view themselves as, if not activists, at least involved owners.

Second, executive pay skyrocketed. In 1990, Rand Araskog at ITT took home $11.4 million while ITT stock fell 16 percent.[35] Although Araskog's case amounted to just one data point on a breathtaking, decade-old, skyward trajectory of the value of pay packages, he became the poster boy for outraged activists. What miffed shareholders most was that so many executives pocketed huge sums paid out according to formulas unlinked to performance. The award of seemingly undeserved windfalls of cash and stock put a fire in the belly of activist institutional trustees—a fire that still burns bright today.

Third, in 1992, the SEC changed an obscure rule that had blocked institutional trustees and money managers from freely comparing notes. The rule had required preapproval by the SEC for talking about proxy resolutions with more than ten shareholders, in effect gagging the institutions. Unable to easily pick up the phone just to chat, the institutions couldn't plot coordinated strategy (unless they had plenty of money and lead time). So even a gang of angry institutional gorillas couldn't make an impact. They were caged by an arcane rule.

On October 15, 1992, the SEC lifted the rule. At once, the iron bars of tradition, red tape, and passivity seemed to fall. Less than two weeks later (on October 26), a group of money managers toppled General Motors chief executive Robert Stempel. In January 1993, they deposed three more of Corporate America's most powerful chieftains: IBM's John Akers, American Express's James Robinson, and Westinghouse's Paul Lego.[36] The institutions displayed unprecedented power, and they haven't stopped since, having pressed the boards of one company after another to fire underperforming chief executives.

These three events sent the governance revolution into full swing. Today, the power of institutions is stronger than ever. The biggest players—Calpers, the Wisconsin State Investment Board, TIAA-CREF, and the New York city and state funds—are flexing their muscles like never before. How far their influence will spread is hard to gauge. Governance expert Carolyn Brancato at the Conference Board points out that although pension funds own 47.5 percent of institutional assets, they manage only 19.6 percent. They farm out the rest to professional asset managers. Rarely do the pros care much about governance, especially if they are short-term momentum investors.[37]

The Tools of the Powerful

Although nobody can say how the play of power will unfold in the years ahead, the activist managers are using a variety of tools to force the hands of executives and boards to govern more accountably. Probably the most widespread, though least visible, is relationship investing. By knocking on doors, requesting meetings, and exercising persuasion behind the scenes, the institutions are coaxing change without making a public show of their efforts. TIAA-CREF, known for applying constant pressure for better board governance in all corporations, worked out agreements with thirty-two of forty-five companies it had approached between 1992 and 1996 with various issues (board diversity, confidential voting), without a proxy resolution ever coming to a vote.[38]

Probably the most visible of tactics to force change are media campaigns that drag the power struggle into the open. Institutions have found that such campaigns, although a blunt tool, strike fear in the hearts of directors. The International Brotherhood of Teamsters, which counsels numerous union funds with $60 billion under management, began publishing its report, *America's Least Valuable Directors* in 1996. In 1997, it listed nineteen, including former diplomat Lawrence Eagleburger. In 1998, it listed nine, including Rand Araskog. The Teamsters mainly targeted directors on low-performing companies with high CEO pay, in Eagleburger's case, Comsat, in Araskog's case, Dow Jones and ITT.[39]

The unions haven't been the only ones in this act. The Council of Institutional Investors published a list of "Director Turkeys" at Thanksgiving time in 1996.[40] It has not ruled out plans to publish another. (The Council includes both public pension funds, like the Pennsylvania State Employees' Retirement System, and corporate funds, like the Coca-Cola Company Retirement Plan.) No corporate director wants to see his or her name on such a list.

A lot more attention has been given by institutions to boards as a whole. In 1995, Calpers graded boards of the 300 largest U.S. companies with an A+ through F, according to their governance practices.[41] *Business Week* started rating boards on a scale of 0 to 100 in late 1996. Campbell Soup scored highest in both 1996 and 1997—with a rating of 87.1 in 1997—while Walt Disney fell to the bottom at 10.3 because of director conflicts.[42]

It's a good bet that institutions will continue to try new ways to gain attention for their cause. Given that outlandish CEO pay is often a red flag for poor governance, documented in Graef Crystal's 1991 book, *In Search of Excess,* the AFL-CIO decided to go on-line to apply pressure for reform. The union launched www. paywatch.org in early 1997 to track executive pay—and to allow shareholders to voice their disapproval. Surfers at the website can draft a letter or e-mail message to the company's board, a pension- or mutual-fund manager, or Congress. The AFL-CIO has since issued a report detailing cozy relationships between a number of compensation committee members and the chief executives whose pay they set.[43]

Along with the power of publicity, institutions have pressed hard with the power of proxy. They have submitted hundreds of resolutions calling for a majority of independent directors, yearly elections, confidential voting, repeal of poison-pill provisions, minimum stock ownership, independent nominating committees, and a number of other practices that drive board objectivity and performance. The Investor Responsibility Research Center, which tracks shareholder resolutions for 1,800 companies, reports that of the roughly 700 shareholder resolutions in 1998, over 400 concerned corporate governance.[44]

Data from the Investor Responsibility Research Center shows that advocates of better governance are starting to get more than a token vote from shareholders, too. In contests to redeem or require a vote on poison-pill provisions, shareholders won an average 56.7 percent of the vote in 1998. Poison-pill provisions, via various means, protect managers from hostile takeovers. For confidential voting, shareholders won 45.2 percent in 1998. Confidential voting enables all shareholders, even if they have business interests that company management might threaten, to vote as they see fit. Even for a detail that seems pretty picky to most shareholders—an independent nominating committee—shareholders won 19.9 percent.[45]

Calpers, in an example of one successful vote, scored a clear victory at Reebok International in May 1997. The California pension system, which had named Reebok as one of its ten worst performers in February 1997, sponsored a proxy resolution to destagger terms on Reebok's board. Annual elections, Calpers maintained, would improve the independence of boardmembers. In the final vote, 53 percent of shareholders (including Calpers's 599,000-share block) agreed.[46]

Of course, losing in a proxy vote is not like losing everything in a game of poker. The losers often take some chips with them—in the form of publicity for their cause. The publicity, and the threat of a repeat contest the following year, often pushes management to act. The very submission of proxy resolutions, and the prospect of later publicity, also often spurs management to change without even bringing the issue to a vote. Publicity is the major form of pressure in such contests, especially because most resolutions are not binding on management.

When motivated, though, shareholders resort to tougher tactics. The binding resolution has been spurred into use as activists found companies ignoring even those resolutions receiving a majority vote. In 1996, eleven of the fourteen governance resolutions that passed resulted in no company action. In 1997, nineteen of twenty-two resulted in no action.[47] The poor response from the 1996 votes led union activists in 1997 to submit binding resolutions to redeem or require votes on poison pills at three companies: Harrah's Entertainment, Fleming, and May Department Stores. The Fleming resolutions passed, winning 61.9 percent of the vote. The other two failed but received huge votes—51.4 percent at Harrah's (short of Harrah's 75-percent bylaw-prescribed majority needed) and 43 percent at May.[48] The popularity of the binding resolution has continued to grow since.

When the institutions don't use the proxy, they often use their votes to express their displeasure directly. At Walt Disney, even though chief executive Michael Eisner has performed spectacularly, shareholders came to believe that neither he nor the board was accountable to shareholders. Two events galvanized shareholder displeasure: Eisner received a 1996 options package estimated (present value) at $195 million over ten years, and Michael Ovitz received a $96 million severance payment for only fourteen months of work.[49]

Incensed, and bent on protesting such compensation, 12.7 percent of shareholders, led by two dozen institutions, withheld votes on five board members in 1997.[50] In the ensuing year, encouraged by Calpers, Disney itself sponsored a bylaw amendment calling for annual director elections. It won with 60 percent of the vote in 1998. TIAA-CREF, however, was still not happy with the responsiveness of Disney. It sponsored a resolution at the same time urging the company to reconfigure its board of directors and to create more independence. The TIAA-CREF resolution won 35 percent of the vote, more than double the average 16.9 percent for similar resolutions at thirteen companies in 1997.[51]

Particularly aggravating to investors was that thirteen of sixteen directors on the board, by TIAA-CREF's count, are either insiders (including former executives) or have professional or personal ties to Eisner. The head of the compensation committee in 1997, and a member in 1998, is Eisner's personal lawyer (although he recused himself from voting on Eisner's earlier pay package).[52] Investors felt their gullibility stretched too far to believe the board with only three outsiders was accountable to shareholders. Disney responded that TIAA-CREF's definition of "independent" was excessively restrictive (in contrast to Disney's definition, in which a former employee who has not worked for the company in the previous three years is considered independent).[53]

Institutions don't shy from applying even more pressure by taking their cases to court. In late 1997, Carl McCall, New York State Comptroller and sole trustee of the $90 billion New York State and Local Retirement System, filed suit against Columbia/HCA. New York State and Local Retirement System owns 2.7 million shares of Columbia/HCA stock. McCall alleged gross mismanagement, corporate waste, abuse of control, and breaches of fiduciary duty by members of the Columbia board and senior executives of the company. Soon thereafter a number of other institutions, representing 15.3 million Columbia/HCA shares, joined the suit, including Calpers, the State of Louisiana and the City of Philadelphia pension funds.[54]

Calpers alone owns more than 3.7 million shares of Columbia stock, which declined $50 million in value after reports of Medicare fraud were made public in mid-1997. In its announcement of joining the suit, Calpers stressed allegations that fraud was permitted to flourish because directors failed to ensure that the company had in place adequate information, reporting, and control systems to catch wrongdoing. The message sent by the Columbia/HCA suit, regardless of outcome, is that the board must govern with accountability—or risk far more than embarrassment.[55]

Harbingers of the Future

Although pillorying, proxy fights, and litigation occupy the limelight of the shareholder-activism show, small but significant changes occupy action backstage. These changes show that power continues to slip out of the hands of corporations and into the hands of institutions. Four examples illustrate how the balance of power will never be the same.

In early 1996, TIAA-CREF began regularly screening companies in two dozen governance practices, from board independence and director age to compensation and director diversity. TIAA-CREF has created a data file of 1,650 companies and uses the file to alert its analysts to poorly run boards. Over time, TIAA-CREF expects to correlate its data to corporate performance.[56] The move suggests that one day institutions will be able to screen out stocks based on poor governance practices.

In October 1997, Sarah Teslik, head of the Council of Institutional Investors, submitted a letter to the SEC requesting the SEC amend item 401 of Regulation S-K to replace the paragraph mandating disclosure of director relationships. Through adoption of the new paragraph, the Council wanted the SEC to require even personal friendships—like former college fraternity chums—to be disclosed in proxies.[57] In late 1998, CII amended the letter after talks with SEC staffers, who suggested the demand for disclosure of personal relationships was unworkable. Still, the Council is urging the SEC to require disclosure of relationships involving legal, financial, education, health, medical, therapeutic, cosmetic, and even spiritual services.

Also in October 1997, the AFL-CIO issued proxy-voting guidelines, a book that helps thousands of union pension trustees vote on a range of issues, from board independence to cumulative voting.[58] Veteran activist Bill Patterson also wants to give trustees of the $880 billion[59] in union pension funds standards by which to judge the performance of money managers trustees hire—or, as Patterson calls them, "captive investment professionals that are less than vigorous in representing plan participant interests."[60] Among Patterson's goals is to get managers to invest in companies that adopt union-friendly workplace practices, like training in high-level skills and payment of high wages.

Finally, in 1998, an advisory group to the Organization for Economic Cooperation and Development (OECD) recommended that the OECD's twenty-nine member countries pursue U.S.-style governance reform.[61] While the OECD countries ponder that prospect, the big gorillas like Calpers aren't waiting. Calpers has already begun pressing its global governance principles, drafted in late 1996, in equity markets in the United Kingdom, France, Germany, and Japan.

Other institutional money managers are following Calpers in pushing for better governance worldwide. In a 1998 international survey by executive recruiter Russell Reynolds Associates, 16 percent of U.S. managers and 53 percent of U.K. managers said they had taken four or more shareholder activism steps in the last year (voting for a shareholder resolution, talking to a company board, sponsoring a shareholder resolution).[62]

The Russell Reynolds survey gives unmistakable proof that enlightened corporate governance has become a cause célèbre for institutional investors. Forty-six percent of fund managers in the United States, 32 percent in the United Kingdom, 43 percent in France, and 71 percent in Australia said they agreed with the statement "Corporate governance is a priority even if high return must be sacrificed." Similarly, 70 percent of fund managers in the United States, 64 percent in the United Kingdom, 84 percent in France, and 89 percent in Australia said they have made decisions not to invest in a company because of poor corporate governance practices.

Rewards of Toeing the Line

Does all this activism make a difference? Certainly it has spurred change in board practices. The face of the corporate board will never be the same. Many people question whether it really boosts company performance, however. Studies are mixed on this subject; some actually show that activism does not help.[63] However, enough research shows positive results that institutions believe strongly that their fiduciary duty compels them to continue to rattle board-room cages.

In studies in 1994, 1995, and 1998, Wilshire Associates examined performance at sixty-nine firms targeted by Calpers for corporate activism since 1987. The stock prices of these companies trailed Standard & Poor 500 returns by a total 89 percent (14 percent per year) in the five years before Calpers began badgering them with letters, meetings, and shareholder proposals. Following Calpers action, the firms outperformed average total returns by 23 percent (or 4 percent per year).[64]

Another study, reported in 1995 and updated in 1997, tracked performance at 117 companies that landed on the Council of Institutional Investor's Focus List between 1991 and 1994. These firms presumably became the focus of the Council members' activism programs. Research showed that action among many institutions at the same time had a substantial effect. "In the two years after being listed, firms experienced substantial profitability and share price improvements relative to a variety of control groups," wrote authors Tim Opler and Jonathan Sokobin. "The shareholder value gains are greatest among firms that divested assets and did not announce new acquisitions." Specifically, in the two years after landing on the Council hit list, the targeted firms' stock prices rose a mean of 48 percent compared to 36 percent for the Standard & Poor's 500.[65]

In short, institutions have become convinced that good board governance is a driver of better performance. They are unlikely to back down. What's more, as more institutions take up their fiduciary duties, the pressure will surely increase. The lesson is that good governance has become a core part of achieving full accountability. It is yet one more skill, like quality management, that executives and directors have to learn to be competitive and to meet the pressures of the marketplace for capital.

THE INSUFFICIENCY OF REFORM

The advantage of governance reform is that it restores a process for objective, fact-based decision making at the pinnacle of the company; it restores trust in the workability of the system; and it provides a foundation for running an accountable organization. With such benefits in the wings, it is little surprise that companies have changed governance practices sharply in recent years. To further gain more of the benefits of accountability, they must continue to do so.

It is also little surprise that companies have recognized they have to respond much more actively to large institutions through relationship investing. They must reach out to institutions, meet with fund managers regularly, and work closely with institutions to meet the needs of an outside constituency without a formal process or antagonistic, public brawls.

Still, the advances in governance and relationship investing fall far short of making companies fully accountable. In fact, the governance story is but one chapter in the larger story of companies striving for full accountability. In the next three chapters, we will explore how companies are attacking the accountability crisis on three more fronts: revamping measurement, management control, and reporting practices. Each of these areas of initiative hold huge promise.

Indeed, for all the success in pushing the new governance agenda, many institutions are starting to realize that they may not see the accountability for the desired turnaround in financial results. They have been addressing a process of decision making but are not addressing the content. They can see that a company may run with all the levers and switches typical of a high-performance vehicle, but in the end they may get less than the best performance from the drivers working those levers.

Of the governance movement, the Conference Board's Brancato says, "Corporations are absorbed with designing and redesigning their governance practices in view of rapidly changing corporate governance norms"—namely, implementing the dozens of modern governance practices.[66] That's a good thing. Taken too far, however, it also worries people. The house of good governance may present an edifice so consoling that it stops companies from pushing for steps that foster additional accountability. That would be the most counterproductive outcome of all, in which companies make a good start renovating the portals of accountability but leave the inner sanctum in disarray.

4

Inventing
New Measures

Management by the numbers. Few people would argue the meaning of that phrase or quarrel over its unforgiving overtones. It raises the image of a hard-nosed manager, unbending and implacable, holding people's feet to the fire to deliver the numbers in the profit and loss statement.

But plenty of people might argue over what that phrase *should* mean. These are the people who are breaking new ground as they address the second element of accountability, performance measurement. (See Figure 4-1.) They believe that management by the numbers should evoke a new image. They see an enlightened leader conducting a brave experiment: developing a balanced set of indicators, financial and nonfinancial, to power the performance of the accountable organization.

A few leaders are already conducting that experiment. When Jerry Choate was named chief executive of Allstate in 1994, he faced running the $19 billion business mainly with numbers straight from the financial accounts. They gave a detailed accounting of dollar figures, right down to line items like employee travel. However, they failed to give him a detailed accounting of what he calls "moments of truth," or the most basic drivers of business success.[1]

Figure 4-1
The Second Element of Accountability: Measurement

Moments of truth, the way Choate saw it, came a thousand times a day at Allstate. That's when someone from the company quotes a policy, returns a call for a claim, negotiates with a supplier, or hob-nobs with a city official or legislator. These moments of truth are the instants when Allstate builds rapport with the people who sustain it—customers, employees, business partners, community leaders.

The trouble is, when it came to better managing the perform-ance at these moments of truth, Choate found his toolbag empty. Even though Allstate did track corporatewide customer satisfaction and retention, the financial numbers still reigned. Choate began to realize that the financial accounts were too blunt a tool for manag-ing a company during rapid change.

To build accountability for the long term, Allstate and like-minded companies are revamping their measures. In particular, they are supplementing the financial figures with nonfinancial ones. By measuring performance in new ways, they are trying to empower business units, teams, and individuals to more reliably ex-ecute the strategy and tactics that drive high performance. They are also reassuring boards of directors and company outsiders that they have the measures—the factual basis for decision making—to ensure an accountable performance.

It was in a particularly difficult climate that Allstate revamped its measurement system, led by Choate (who retired at the end of 1998) and chief operating officer Edward Liddy. The year was 1994. Allstate faced 46,000 claims from the Northridge earthquake in California. It faced an industry undergoing a revolution, with markets fragmenting into niches, customer expectations soaring, and competitors offering new products through new channels. It also faced the reality that the company's operating practices were slipping behind those of competitors. Company research showed response times as slow.

Under the leadership of Choate and current CEO Liddy, Allstate created a new measurement system that retains the financial rigor shareholders care about and also yields numbers for managing those thousands of moments of truth with customers, employees, agents, and the community. As Allstate sees it, the nonfinancial and financial variables connect in a complex chain of cause and effect. A well-handled moment of truth produces best-of-class processes, and in time, a well-deserved profit.

For example, Allstate measures frontline statistics like claim contact time, the elapsed time between an auto accident and the involved parties' contact with Allstate. In the company's daisy chain of measures, shorter contact time leads to higher customer satisfaction, higher customer satisfaction leads to higher renewal rates, higher renewal rates to higher premium revenues, and higher premiums to higher operating income and share prices. In a parallel chain, shorter contact time also leads to lower legal fees, lower claims payments, lower loss ratios, and, again, to higher operating income and share prices.

It is this chain of linked measures—including many other measures like employee effectiveness and satisfaction, business-process performance, and even employee skills—that drives success at Allstate. Unlike in the past, "we really go to the drivers," says Choate. "By using a balanced framework, you have the ability to ensure long-term success." Today, Liddy continues to use the balanced set of measures as the core of discussions that take place routinely with each business unit.

As they attack the accountability crisis, many companies have traveled the same road as Allstate. They have created a more comprehensive approach to managing with measures. They are finding that, without expanding the universe of variables with which they gauge themselves, they can't deliver peak performance. With the new measures—many unheard of a decade ago—they are bootstrapping their way out of the accountability crisis. They are harboring no sacred cows, either. Even the measures of financial performance, which stand on centuries of tradition, have come under scrutiny.

ON THE FINANCIAL SIDE

Many companies consider the traditional financial measures as tried and true. The financials have stood the test of time. Managers figure the measures may have weaknesses, as we described in Chapter 2, but at least everyone knows what they are and can work around them. More than a few managers disagree, however. They want to find new ways of measuring financial performance to improve decision making. They have tired of the distortions—rapid increases in real-estate market values not reflected on the balance sheet, or huge increases in intellectual capital values expensed as costs for R&D and training. Moreover, they want to seek a solution to the measurement crisis by tinkering with the financials before turning to the less-tested nonfinancials. After all, if the financials are lousy—too narrow, too historical, too functional, too inaccurate—many managers reason that they should fix the broken measurement dial first, before adding new dials.

Many financial managers in the last decade have poured their attention into better measuring "shareholder value," creating measures that are proxies for, or leading indicators of, share-price advances. This focus on shareholder value was kicked off in 1986 by Alfred Rappaport in his book *Creating Shareholder Value,* since revised.[2] The book has been followed up by a number of others, each with its own refinement, but all driving toward the same goal—trying to develop financials that better reflect the variables that push up share prices.[3]

What has triggered the flurry of activity is an age-old discomfort with how poorly accounting numbers relate to share prices. To an astonishing degree, the correlation doesn't exist. Research shows that 90 to 95 percent of the differences in annual or quarterly stock-price changes are unrelated to reported earnings.[4] "In the 1960s and 1970s, about 25 percent of the differences in stock price changes could be attributed to differences in reported earnings," writes New York University's Baruch Lev, who conducted the research. "But by the 1980s and early 1990s, this figure had dropped to less than 10 percent."[5]

Many companies, searching for something better, have been turning to a measure actually developed years ago: economic profit (book profit minus the cost of capital employed). Equivalent to residual income, economic profit remained largely a sleeper for decades, but recent research showed it correlates much better than does net income with stock prices.[6] Such data lit up more than a few faces in the ranks of chief financial officers. They believed they had found, in a figure derived from the accounting books, an indispensable proxy for shareholder value.

Alas, the latest research casts doubt on the superior correlation of economic profit with stock prices.[7] Nonetheless, many finance officers still find the measure appealing because the behavior stimulated by the measure—getting managers to carefully manage the capital entrusted to them—contributes strongly to efficient capital utilization and cash flow, both critical contributors to financial performance.[8]

Indeed, operating without such a measure, managers at many firms strive to achieve profit and revenue goals unrelated to the amount of investors' capital they employ. Although they have to compete with other units inside the firm for capital, once they get their money, managers treat it as if it were a gift. They feel they have incurred no financial cost. No wonder so many general managers try to solve their business problems by investing in a new plant and equipment. Regardless of how much capital they employ, and how well, their budgeted numbers remain unaffected.

They will find that the shine on their numbers dulls quite a bit, however, when they calculate the economic profit figure. The more capital they use, the more they get charged for it. If the charge exceeds book profit, they spill economic red ink. Of course, companies have long used returns measures—return on investment

(ROI), return on equity (ROE), return on capital employed (ROCE), and return on net assets (RONA)—to motivate managers to deliver returns that account for capital usage. The problem is that few managers, at any level, have clearly understood that those returns have to exceed the cost of capital—the weighted average of debt and equity capital, generally 9 to 15 percent—to create shareholder value.

The economic profit figure makes this message explicit. If the economic profit is positive, managers are *building* value for shareholders. If the figure is negative, they are *destroying* value. No more can they pretend that an ROI of, say, 6 percent is a decent figure.

Sadly, for decades, most companies failed at building value, their main obligation to shareholders. In effect, investors gave managers capital to destroy. The managers often boosted earnings but not economic profit. One of their commonest errors has been acquiring companies that returned less than the cost of the capital to buy them.[9]

That's why so many firms have tried economic profit as an alternative measure of financial success. They tell glowing stories of how economic profit has helped them stanch economic losses and produce economic profit. One story comes from Valmont Industries, the Valley, Nebraska, maker of commercial irrigation systems and metal structures. The former top managers had bought a fluorescent-light component business from General Electric in 1987 for $30 million and had tried to rejuvenate it with $10 million more in capital. The business faltered, and Valmont wrote off $11.3 million in 1991 and another $11 million in 1993 to restructure it.[10]

Shareholders, to say the least, were displeased. The company's stock went nowhere as market averages doubled. Directors looked to a new CEO, Mogens Bay, and a new CFO, Terry McClain, to get a leash on managers' use of capital. Speaking of that era, says McClain, "We didn't necessarily think about the amount of capital it was going to take to generate a dollar of business."

Although the irrigation and structures business performed well, managers weren't getting all the right financial cues. "People were growing earnings, but weren't making the best choices about how and where to grow them," says McClain. "Capital decisions were being made on the basis of too much emotion and too little analysis."

In 1994, Valmont, then with sales of $471 million, decided to adopt a simple economic profit measure, dubbed TVI, for total value impact, calculated by subtracting from NOPAT (net operating profit after tax) a charge for capital employed. They computed this measure for every business unit—and tied people's pay to it right from the start. Managers quickly got the signal that there is a healthy cost to capital. If the cost of capital is 10 percent, say, a return of 9 percent isn't a return of value at all, it's a subtraction.

In the years since making TVI a central measurement and linking bonuses to it, Valmont has kept the focus on capital and gradually watched its fortunes turn completely around. Early on, for example, Valmont's irrigation equipment unit was trying to choose between two capital projects, a new product-development effort or an investment in widening its dealer network. TVI showed clearly what wouldn't have been obvious otherwise—expanding dealers would build far more economic profit.

In the meantime, Valmont executives concluded that Valmont Electric, though nurtured back to profitability by such initiatives as cutting costs, working capital, and warehouse space, could never break the barrier to economic profit. It had to constantly battle pricing pressure in a market where two companies held 40-percent share, while Valmont held only 10 percent. So Valmont divested Valmont Electric in 1997. By guiding all such decision making with the tough discipline enforced by TVI, Valmont reported near-record results in 1997, with a 14.6 percent return on invested capital and sales of $623 million. "Economic profit is like a rudder," says McClain, "keeping people focused in that shareholder direction."

The experience at Valmont shows why many finance managers have become advocates of economic profit: It tells people clearly whether they're adding value, a positive economic profit, or destroying, a negative economic profit. They can't portray positive earnings figures as creating value unless they exceed the capital charge. Economic profit erases the deceit of traditional profit figures. Managers focus on the growth of capital for which shareholders will bid stock prices up.

Other companies have taken more complex approaches to economic profit. Rather than subtracting a capital charge from book earnings, they first adjust the bottom line to better reflect cash flow. Consultants Stern Stewart & Co. have brought the massaging of economic profit to a high art, and even trademarked its concept with the brand name EVA, or economic value added.[11] Stern Stewart advises companies that, before subtracting the capital charge, they make at least a handful of adjustments to better reflect the economics of the business—like capitalizing R&D and eliminating the amortization of goodwill.

One company that adopted EVA is Harnischfeger Industries, the maker of mining machinery and paper-making equipment. CFO Francis Corby noticed during the recession of the early 1990s that as Harnischfeger's profits sagged, managers were not paying ample attention to capital. The managers watched the top and bottom lines, of course, but ignored the balance sheet.[12]

The view of Corby and chief executive Jeffery Grade was that although the company had to live with the cyclical nature of its business, it didn't have to live with excess capital invested in fixed assets and inventory. Corby also felt the company had to move away from a tradition of allocating capital each year based more on the size of a business than on the returns of each project. The bigger businesses often got the most capital.

"We were falling into the trap of spending a lot of money on capital items that, perhaps, we really didn't need," says Corby. Aggravating the problem was that Harnischfeger had no effective system to track whether the capital projects yielded projected returns. People left it to the finance department to worry about capital. The result was that, while fighting a recession, in 1992 the company ran a $100 million EVA deficit.

Harnischfeger executives wanted to change managers' behavior radically. They knew that they couldn't make progress by badgering them to watch days sales outstanding or inventory turnover. So, in 1993, they started measuring EVA and, by 1994, replaced traditional bonus and profit-sharing plans with an EVA-based incentive pay. It was now up to line managers and salaried employees to manage capital better—their take-home pay depended on it.

The results show just how quickly one measure can alter behavior and, in turn, performance. In the first three years of using EVA, capital employed fell from $1.2 billion to $900 million, an astonishing $300 million drop—while sales increased. Managers and employees across the company began to squeeze excess capital from their operations.

At the company's surface-mining unit, managers told executives like Corby that they couldn't sell equipment with a downpayment.

That just wasn't the way they moved big machines like huge strip-mining shovels. However, once they found their EVA measured, Corby suddenly noticed the "advance payments and progress billings" account come to life. "Operating units found they could in fact get a check with the taking of an order," says Corby. Today, the company even gets advance payments for $8 million pieces of machinery.

Helped by economic recovery, Harnischfeger has now earned positive EVA—returns have exceeded its 12 percent cost of capital—since 1995. Corby reports that managers have come to understand how to manage both the income statement and the balance sheet. "Even though we're a cyclical business," he says, "we have to manage well, on the capital side and on the income side, on the down part of the cycle as well as on the upward part."

With all this help from such new financial measures, many executives believe that a single-minded focus on financials as the overriding performance measure can solve the crisis in financial accountability. They believe that a single measure focuses the company best. People throughout the firm then understand one unambiguous goal. They don't have to try to trade one measure off against another, perhaps failing at achieving targets for both. Some executives believe that fixing the measures of financial performance fixes the performance measure rudder.

ON THE NONFINANCIAL SIDE

Many other executives belong to another school of thought. They believe that one, or even several, financial measures still distort decision making and provide a poor basis for accountability. They argue that the financials, even economic profit, still rely too much on book accounting, provide too narrow a view of performance, and fail as leading indicators of performance. These executives have started experimenting with a measurement mixture, financial and nonfinancial, as the route to an accountable organization.

Surveys show just how common this experimentation is. In one survey, by Renaissance Solutions and *CFO* magazine, 59 percent of companies said they use quality measures to set targets, 57 percent use customer satisfaction, and 30 percent use employee satisfaction.[13] In another survey, in 1998, about 40 percent of U.S. and

Canadian firms said they use product, process, or service quality measures for developing and monitoring strategic plans; about half use customer satisfaction and delivery performance measures; and one-fifth use measures like employee satisfaction, turnover, and training.[14]

To be sure, the idea of operating with a mix of measures isn't new. Since the turn of the century, many French managers have run their firms with a "tableau de bord" (dashboard) of mixed measures.[15] Moreover, most plant managers have long used nonfinancial measures to run their operations. Only since the late 1980s have many top managers tried to pilot the corporate ship with a mix— and insist their facility, business unit, and team managers operate according to a set of measures that complements that mix.

A variety of events have triggered these companies' experimentation. Some have sought to extend the thinking of quality management, in which a culture of "fact-based" decision making requires plenty of quantitative performance data. Some have sought a better way to implement the fine details of strategy, which today include nuances financial measures simply can't capture. Some have simply sought higher performance, which calls for precision targets and feedback only numbers can supply. Their stories differ, but together these companies have opened a window on a new world of possibilities. They show the wide range of measurement that can contribute to solving the crisis in accountability.

A Cue from Quality Management

Analog Devices uncovered the importance of nonfinancial measures from its experience with the world of quality management.[16] Recall from Chapter 2 that at Analog, a pioneer in balanced performance measurement, executives had come to argue over the priority of financial versus nonfinancial measures. The solution was to integrate them, creating one of the earliest sets of balanced measures. (See Table 4-1.) Analog's family of measures was also important to the work of Robert Kaplan and David Norton in creating the concept of the "balanced scorecard," which we discuss in the next section.

The Analog scorecard has three parts: financial, product development, and quality improvement processes. The categories reflect the variables that make or break a firm in the intensely competitive

TABLE 4-1

ANALOG DEVICES SCORECARD: TEN YEARS OF EVOLUTION

1987	1997
FINANCIAL	
Revenue	Bookings
Revenue growth	Revenue
Profit	Gross margin percentage
Return on assets	Selling, management, general, and administrative percentage
	Profit
NEW PRODUCTS	
New product introductions	Six quarter window sales
New product bookings	Six quarter window gross margin percentage
Business plan peak revenue	Number of products to first silicon
Time to market	Customer sample hit rate
	Number of products released
	Tape-outs per product
	New product work in progress
QUALITY IMPROVEMENT PROCESS	
On-time delivery	On-time delivery
Cycle time	Cycle time
Yield	Yield
Defects (parts per million)	Defects (parts per million)
Cost	Quality of work environment
Employee productivity	Customer responsiveness
Turnover	Baldrige score

Source: Robert Stasey, "What We've Learned About Using Scorecards," Analog Devices internal document, 1997, 34.

integrated-circuit business, where customers the world over demand leading-edge designs, delivered to meet their demanding manufacturing schedules. As Table 4-1 shows, Analog has learned to maintain consistency while changing measures to meet new competitive challenges. It has kept the scorecard similar from year to year, and it continues to focus on new products and quality, especially on-time delivery. But it has changed the scorecard gradually over the years to keep up with competitive changes. For example, in 1999, it expects to revise its new-product performance measures.

The scorecard at Analog dovetails with *hoshin* management, a Japanese-inspired form of business planning. Each year, CEO Jerry Fishman kicks off planning by setting one or several of the most important companywide goals, or hoshins. In 1997, one of them, in keeping with company strategy, was to improve new-product generation. Managers down the hierarchy then come back and say how they plan to achieve the specified targets, and what measures they'll use to judge their progress. This process goes back and forth. In the end, the scorecard naturally stresses, among other key performance indicators, the vital issues from the planning process.

Over the years, Analog's trail-blazing scorecard has helped managers deliver huge improvements in several dimensions. Late shipments (of individual invoice line items) plunged from 30 percent to 4 percent after the advent of the scorecard. Outgoing defects spiraled downward from 2,500 parts per million to under twenty-five. New-product development turnaround time shrank by two-thirds. Total factory yield has also improved by several hundred percent over a ten-year period.[17] "If we had not made the progress on improving yield . . . we would have required several more plants" to meet current demand, says Director of Quality Improvement Robert Stasey. Each plant costs in excess of $40 million.

If Analog had not achieved such progress—if it had not adopted new practices for planning, new tools for quality management, and new measures to align the workforce's efforts—it could not have turned in superior financial performance. But the managerial changes turned Analog's fortunes around. Between 1992 and 1997, for example, it delivered total returns to shareholders of 764 percent, compared to 403 percent for the Standard & Poor's technology sector and 247 percent for the Standard & Poor's 500.

Another company that opened the door on a new world of measures is Whirlpool. At Whirlpool, the trigger was the company's acquisition of Philips Electronics' European appliance business in 1989. To bring the company's growing global business together with the same management principles, CEO David Whitwam put together fifteen "one-company challenge teams" to unify management practices. CFO Ralph Hake, corporate controller at the time, led a team around the world, to Europe, Asia, and Latin America, to benchmark companies such as Nestle, Fiat, Hitachi, and Mitsubishi. Although Whirlpool practiced quality management like

Analog, Hake was charged with recommending measurements to propel Whirlpool to world-class performance.[18]

As a follow-up to that work, in 1991, Hake and his team devised a "top sheet" of measures—a "state-of-the-business report," he calls it. Every month, the top sheet lists financial and nonfinancial measures, which has evolved as it continues to guide the company.[19] (See Table 4-2.)

In 1997, Whirlpool executives added a refinement to their measurement approach. They concluded that the top sheet was too com-

TABLE 4-2

WHIRLPOOL TOP SHEET (EXCERPTS)

FINANCIAL

Earnings per share
Cash flow
Economic value added

CUSTOMER SATISFACTION

Market share
Customer satisfaction (by survey)
Brand preference for Whirlpool or Kenmore
Satisfaction with service
Trade-partner satisfaction
Product availability
Telephone answering wait time

TOTAL QUALITY

Worldwide excellence (quality) score
Defect levels
Cycle time
Service incidence rates

PEOPLE COMMITMENT

Leadership survey results
Work-unit survey results
Commitment survey results
Diversity survey results
Percentage completion of high-performance culture
    milestones

GROWTH AND INNOVATION

Percentage of new product sales

Source: Author interview with Ralph Hake, CFO, Whirlpool, March 1998.

plex for the average employee to grasp. The innovativeness of managers in creating nonfinancial measures had overshadowed the usability of the measures throughout the organization. "We got a Christmas tree and kept hanging ornaments on it," says Hake.

So Whirlpool devised a complementary "balanced scorecard." The scorecard (borrowing terminology from Kaplan and Norton) divides companywide performance measures into three categories: shareholders, customers, and employees. Each category has only three or four of the most critical top-sheet measures. The customer category, for example, includes only market share, trade-partner satisfaction, service incidence rate, and customer satisfaction.

Top executives still use the more comprehensive top sheet for operations reviews and planning, but the scorecard gets all the publicity among employees. Executives believe it more simply communicates corporate strategy—and effectively, too, especially because scorecard targets are the criterion for calculating all salaried employees' bonuses.[20]

A Cue from Strategic Change

Other companies have reexamined their measurement systems during times of corporate transformation. They have similarly turned to a broad range of measures that help their companies achieve a range of new goals.

CIGNA Property & Casualty (introduced in Chapter 2) is one of those companies. At the P&C unit, President Gerry Isom came aboard in 1993 determined to turn a company pursuing a generalist insurer strategy to one pursuing a specialist one. In a generalist strategy, people chase premium revenue wherever they can find it. In a specialist strategy, they chase income only in selected markets with carefully selected customers where underwriters understand the risk and the company can make good margins.[21]

To effect the transformation, Isom and his team devised a balanced scorecard, a classic case of following the method developed by Robert Kaplan and David Norton.[22] (See Table 4-3.) Isom believed the scorecard would give him a tool not only for detailing strategy but also for aligning everyone with the details. Isom desperately wanted alignment of people's minds with the vision and people's work with the strategy at the corporate, division, and busi-

TABLE 4-3

CIGNA PROPERTY & CASUALTY BALANCED SCORECARD

FINANCIAL PERSPECTIVE

Net operating income
Combined ratio
Premium growth by business
Premium mix by business

CUSTOMER PERSPECTIVE

Loss ratio by producer (agent/broker)
Expense ratio by producer
Producer triangle
Premium run-off rate
Performance against producer plans
Average policy size

INTERNAL PERSPECTIVE

Loss ratio
Expense ratio
Price monitors
Underwriting quality survey
Claims frequency
Claims severity
Severity-control monitors
Loss-control utilization

LEARNING AND GROWTH PERSPECTIVE

Premiums per salary dollar
Net operating income per salary dollar
Competency development plan status
Key staff turnover
Key staff acquisition

Source: Adapted from Richard L. Nolan and Donna B. Stoddard, "CIGNA Property and Casualty Reengineering (A)" (Boston: Harvard Business School, Case No. 9-196-059, 1995).

ness-unit levels. If he failed, people working at cross purposes, or for no purpose, would continue to clobber performance.

Of course, CIGNA Property & Casualty already had a rigorous financial system. Managers were used to its signals. For a company making a ninety-degree turn in strategy, however, the financial figures provided too clumsy a guidance system to ensure success. "Business unit heads in most businesses will spend an awful lot of time on the things they like to do," says Isom. "This [balanced scorecard] causes them to do a much better job of articulating what they should be doing, and then we have a way of measuring against that."

Indeed, the balanced scorecard, along with complementary scorecards in each division and business unit, helped Isom handle subtleties in strategy. Isom wanted every unit to pursue stronger relationships with brokers and agents, for example, but he wanted each one to pursue it differently—by providing more flexible underwriting in one unit, faster underwriting decisions in another, a broader array of services in a third, and more price competitiveness in a fourth. Financial signals alone couldn't begin to define that variability.

The company could have articulated such objectives in terse, narrative statements as it had done before, but using traditional objectives invariably leaves the course of action ambiguous. With the new measures, Isom wagered that managers would get a sharp picture of how strategy should play out in their particular unit.

As an example, one part of CIGNA Property & Casualty's strategy was to build premium growth, but getting profitable growth in different businesses requires different actions—ranging from expanding channels to multiplying segments to broadening product lines. So CIGNA Property & Casualty had to vary the growth measure unit to unit. In some businesses it chose increases in premiums from new producers (brokers and agents); in others, it chose premiums from new segments; and, in still others, new premiums from new-product sets.

The balanced scorecard effort at CIGNA Property & Casualty opened a lot of eyes to the power of new measures. Managers, who formally meet monthly to review scorecards, can now check current results at any time on the company's computer feedback system. Measures hitting target appear in green, those missing target in red, and those on the edge in yellow. The employees have become accountable for success according to an entirely new measurement yardstick. With that new accountability, Isom has turned around the fortunes of the Property & Casualty unit completely, from a $278 million loss in 1993 to a $98 million gain in 1997.

Another company whose story of experimentation with new measures began with strategic change was Mobil Corporation's U.S. Marketing and Refining Division. The change began in 1994. Bob McCool, executive vice president of the $20 billion division, was seeking a means to cement in place a new strategy of targeting and selling to specific market segments. Mobil had grown by marketing a full range of products and services to consumers of all kinds at its fuel and convenience stores, but McCool believed the unit would prosper by appealing to specific market segments.

Mobil's research showed that American gas buyers come in five varieties, which Mobil dubbed road warrior (generally men who drive a lot), true blues (affluent, loyal customers), generation F3 (yuppies on the go who want fuel, want food, and want them fast), homebodies (generally homemakers), and price shoppers. Mobil aimed to focus on the first three, which included 61 percent of all gas buyers.[23] To implement its plan, McCool and his managers decided to upgrade its stations to give fast, friendly service—with, as they said, "speed, smiles, and strokes." They also decided to redesign onsite convenience stores. They wanted to recast impulse-buying convenience stores as destination shops with the right food and snacks for its segments of buyers.

McCool looked for a measurement system to help put the strategy into action and, like Isom at CIGNA Property & Casualty, he adopted the Kaplan and Norton approach. (See Table 4-4.) The measures clarified the strategy in much the same way as at CIGNA, again with the help of each business unit crafting its own scorecard to complement the division one. (Note that in Table 4-4 we have included the objectives as well, showing that the measures don't spring directly from strategy but come from objectives that are fleshed out from strategy.)

One lesson learned at Mobil is that the appropriate new measures may require entirely new data. For example, when it came to delighting customers and getting dealers to build customer loyalty, Mobil managers had no ready source of information. How could they evaluate the quality of the speed, smiles, and strokes? What they came up with was a "mystery-shopper" program. An independent company, buying gas and snacks at each station each month, graded each station according to twenty-three categories,

TABLE 4-4

MOBIL CORPORATION, U.S. MARKETING AND REFINING, BALANCED SCORECARD

OBJECTIVE	MEASURE
FINANCIAL PERSPECTIVE	
Return on capital employed	Return on capital employed
Cash flow	Cash flow excluding dividends
	Cash flow including dividends
Profitability	Profit and loss ($ millions after tax)
	Net margin (cents/gallon before tax)
Lowest cost	Total operating expenses (cents/gallon)
Most profitable growth targets	Volume growth, gas retail sales
	Volume growth, distillate to trade
	Volume growth, lubes
CUSTOMER PERSPECTIVE	
Continually delight the targeted consumer	Share of segment
	Percentage of road warriors
	Percentage of true blues
	Percentage of generation F3's
	Mystery-shopper rating
Improve the profitability of our partners	Total gross profit, split
INTERNAL PERSPECTIVE	
Improve environmental, health, and safety performance	Safety incidents
	Environmental incidents
Product, service, and alternate profit center development	Alternate profit center gross margin/store/month
Lower costs of manufacturing versus competition	Refinery return on capital employed
	Refinery expense
Improve hardware performance	Refinery reliability index
	Refinery yield index
Improve environmental, health, and safety performance	Refinery safety index
Reduce laid down cost	Laid down cost vs. best competing supply—gas
	Laid down cost vs. best competing supply—distillates
Inventory management	Inventory level
	Product availability index
Quality	Quality index
LEARNING AND GROWTH	
Organization involvement	Climate survey index
Core competencies and skills	Strategic competency availability
Access to strategic information	Strategic systems availability

Source: Robert S. Kaplan, "Mobil USM&R (A): Linking the Balanced Scorecard" (Boston: Harvard Business School, Case No. 9-197-025, 1996). Copyright © 1996 by the President and Fellows of Harvard College. Reprinted by permission.

like station appearance and rest rooms. The mystery-shopper rating became a key measure on the scorecard.

Even frontline workers became acutely aware of the new measures, as their pay was tied to performance two years after the introduction of the division scorecard. Employees became eligible for bonuses of up to 30 percent of salary, paid once each year. The bonus amount is based on corporate, division, and business-unit performance, as gauged by the scorecard. Mobil executives are convinced that the link to compensation both improved employee focus and boosted results.[24]

Indeed, with everyone focused on the scorecard, the division's performance soared. In less than four years, the operation went from losing half a billion dollars in cash flow (in 1990) to gaining half a billion. The balanced scorecard focused the units' initiatives and kept them aligned with strategic objectives.[25] By year-end 1997, the division's ROCE had leaped to 12 percent, from 6 percent in 1993.

A Cue from Performance Improvement

The story of invention of new measures at other companies has come simply from an effort to improve performance. These companies show still more the variety of measures.

The story of the Bank of Montreal, the third-largest bank in Canada, begins in 1989. Matthew Barrett had just taken over as chief executive. Although Barrett wanted a tool for a variety of purposes, one of the major ones was to better measure and reverse lagging performance. Bank productivity at the time was dismal. Costs as a percentage of revenues were the highest of all large Canadian and North American banks. (Bank of Montreal also owns Chicago's Harris Bank.) Returns to shareholders were not much better—five-year returns on common shareholders' investment were just 4.4 percent in 1990. As CFO Robert Wells says, "By a number of measures of financial performance, we were in poor shape."[26]

Barrett and his new executive team didn't look to the financial accounts and focus on short-term slashing of costs. Instead, the executives of the $210 billion bank wanted the employees themselves to turbocharge the performance of the bank at every level. The measurement system was the tool to do it. As CFO Wells says, "It's better to manage through communicating what is expected and monitoring results as opposed to a more authoritarian or dictatorial management approach where you tell people what to do and control it."

In a decided difference from Analog, Whirlpool, CIGNA Property & Casualty, and Mobil, the Bank of Montreal articulates strategy and, in turn, creates its scorecard by creating goals and objectives for each of its key stakeholders: shareholders, customers, employees, and communities. In each category, it specifies results measures and drivers. (See Table 4-5.)

The system then became the lever for Barrett to delegate authority and clarify expectations at every level of the company. For example, he set a goal to improve productivity by 2 percent each year. With the measurement system, he could cascade that goal down through the bank to every one of 1,100 Canadian retail bank branches. Each of those branches got its own productivity-improvement target.

In implementing the measures, each branch measured its performance partly with a subset of bankwide measures. One example is the number of accounts per customer, a key indicator of profitability (the more accounts per customer, the more profitable the customer, because the bank can spread relatively fixed service costs over more accounts). However, each branch also devised its own measures, tailored to its own market, to guide it in meeting the target. One branch might focus on boosting the number of new mortgages, while another might focus on cutting administrative costs. By drawing on the corporate scorecard for guidance and by tailoring measures to each unit, Bank of Montreal created unprecedented accountability throughout the organization.

A Cue from Intangible Value

One company that walked a unique path in developing new performance measures is Skandia Group, the $8 billion Swedish financial-services firm. In the 1980s, then-CEO Björn Wolrath and First Executive Vice President Jan Carendi had become dissatisfied with the signals from the traditional accounting system. They felt the strengths of a service business, especially a knowledge-intensive one, lay in people's talent, in relationships, and in Skandia's ability to manage competence. Wolrath and Carendi knew they couldn't build value by managing bricks, mortar, equipment, and inventory.

TABLE 4-5

BANK OF MONTREAL'S PRIMARY AND SELECTED SECONDARY MEASURES

SHAREHOLDERS

Primary measure
  Return on common shareholders' investment

Secondary measures
  Revenue growth
  Expense Growth
  Productivity
  Capital ratios
  Liquidity ratios
  Asset quality ratios

CUSTOMERS

Primary measure
  Customer satisfaction and quality of service

Secondary measure
  Customer surveys for different market and product requests

EMPLOYEES

Primary measures
  Employee commitment
  Employee competence
  Employee productivity

Secondary measures
  Different elements of employee opinion survey
  Different elements of customer service index (regarding employee
    competence)
  Financial ratios of employee costs to revenues by different
    classifications

COMMUNITY

Primary measure
  Public image

Secondary measure
  Different external surveys

Source: Anthony A. Atkinson, John H. Waterhouse, and Robert B. Wells, "A Stakeholder Approach to Strategic Performance Measurement," *Sloan Management Review* 38, no. 3 (1997): 25(13).

They could build value only by getting a grip on the value of intangibles and figuring out how to develop them.[27]

In 1991, Carendi made a leap of faith—that launching a program to understand and build so-called intellectual capital would propel the company's future success. He reasoned that Skandia needed to make intellectual capital a function, just like finance or marketing. He did so, and named Leif Edvinsson director of intellectual capital, the first such position in the world.

Early on, Edvinsson and his team began their work by inventorying hidden value at Skandia; that is, the value that failed to appear in the financial statements. Many Swedish companies were valued on the Stockholm Stock Exchange for three to eight times their book value.[28] (For comparison, the average in the United States in mid-1998 was five times book value, which means the balance sheet reflects only about 20 percent of the value of the company.) Edvinsson's job was to create a way to visualize the hidden sources that made up the difference. The team inventoried a number of items, like trademarks, concessions, customer databases, and alliances. As they worked, they developed a theory: Intellectual capital comes in two varieties—human (people) and structural (systems, procedures, information technology, and alliances).[29] The first walks out the door every night; the second does not.

As they refined their understanding of the sources of value, a critical question came up. Would Skandia use its emerging model for valuation or management—that is, for putting a number on intellectual capital assets or for developing a way to better manage an intellectual capital-intensive business? The answer is that it would do both.

To create a management tool, Edvinsson and his team devised the Skandia Navigator, a balanced measurement system that Skandia created in the same era as the balanced scorecard. The Navigator shows the remarkable variety of measurements companies are developing today. (See Table 4-6.) In the last five years, Skandia has developed and refined Navigators following its unique five-part format. The company has even created PC-based software to enable people to dissect each part of the Navigator, as well as simulate the results of their actions. Table 4-6 shows the Navigator for Skandia's European telemarketing insurance company, Dial.

TABLE 4-6

SKANDIA GROUP'S NAVIGATOR (NAVIGATOR FOR DIAL)

FINANCIAL FOCUS

Gross premiums written
Gross premiums written per employee

CUSTOMER FOCUS

Telephone accessibility
Number of individual policies
Customer satisfaction

HUMAN FOCUS

Average age
Number of employees
Time in training (days/year)

PROCESS FOCUS

Information technology employees/total number of
   employees

RENEWAL AND DEVELOPMENT FOCUS

Increase in gross premiums written
Share of direct payments in claims assessment
   system
Number of ideas filed with Idea Group

Source: Skandia Group, "Customer Value: Supplement to Skandia's 1996 Annual Report" (Stockholm: Skandia Group, 1996).

Today, Edvinsson points out how the Navigator reflects the original concern of Wolrath and Carendi. "The renewal and development focus and the customer focus are the key drivers for your future earnings capability," he says.[30] He explains that the measures highlight a fact of business today: Companies must continually learn and adapt to new market situations. The financials alone don't much help a company adapt, but the broad mix of measures provides the needed "three-dimensional" balance, balance between performance of the future and the past, balance between internal and external, and balance between financial and nonfinancial. We discuss Skandia more in Chapter 9.

SOME TEMPLATES EMERGE

As the experience of Valmont, Harnischfeger, Analog Devices, Whirlpool, CIGNA Property & Casualty, Mobil, Skandia, and Bank of Montreal shows, companies have experimented broadly with new performance measures. Their experience also shows how companies have chosen a variety of measurement templates to get critical issues in the open. The balanced scorecard, as at CIGNA, and stakeholder scorecard, as at Bank of Montreal, are two templates. Other companies organize their thinking around the value chain, developing measures to achieve excellence in product design, manufacturing, distribution, marketing, and other company core competencies and processes.[31] These templates force executives to take a comprehensive view of the enterprise and help ensure they ask all the right questions. Chapter 7 shows that all of these concepts converge as one, and in that chapter we recommend a composite template for the accountable organization.

Whatever the final means to organize measurement, the corporate-level template sets the organization up for brainstorming complementary sets of measures down through the organization. Although we show top-level measures only, managers must cascade measures down through the hierarchy, each tier of management following the rough template of the one above. By taking a cue from the family of measures developed by corporate executives, every unit of the organization attacks the crisis in accountability in a coordinated way. Business units, functional groups, facilities, teams, and even individuals obtain guidance from measures that dovetail with corporate strategy. When peoples' efforts to execute strategy are aligned in this way, a company can expect to join leading firms in enjoying the benefits of increased accountability.

A prime challenge is creating what authors and consultants Geary Rummler and Alan Brache call a "performance logic" among all measures.[32] From the bottom of the organization up, managers must ask, How does each variable measured contribute to some higher-level variable and, in turn, contribute to organizational results? From the top down, What variables drive the economic profit figure and, in turn, what variables drive those variables? The critical step, according to Rummler and Brache, is to configure the wires behind the dashboard so that measures at the corporate, process, function, and team levels connect.

A Deloitte & Touche survey showed company efforts to revamp and broaden measures have met with widespread favor. Although most businesses are dissatisfied with their measures, the study revealed, the level of satisfaction increases at firms using a variety of nonfinancial measures. It also increases as firms use capital-usage measures like economic value added.[33]

Taco Bell is a classic example of a firm discovering the value of nonfinancial measures. The fast-food giant tracks profits daily by unit, market manager, zone, and country. Those profits link tightly to both employee and customer satisfaction. How did Taco Bell discover the linkage? As for customer satisfaction, exit interviews with 800,000 customers showed that stores ranking in the top quartile in pleasing customers also ranked at the top in all other measures, including financial. As for employee satisfaction, it found that 20 percent of stores with the lowest employee turnover rate yielded double the sales and 55 percent higher profits than the 20 percent of stores with the higher rates.[34]

In an example of discovering the value of measures of a far different kind, advertising giant Young & Rubicam has argued for measures of brand value, maintaining that "stronger brands lead to high growth, higher earnings, and higher stock price." Young & Rubicam's Brand Asset Valuator measures leading and lagging indicators, including differentiation, relevance, esteem, and knowledge. That these indicators are useful for both internal and external evaluation of corporate performance is supported by a recent study. Researchers showed that "brand value estimates capture information that is relevant to investors and are sufficiently reliable to be reflected in share prices and returns."[35]

Despite the value of these new gauges of performance, some executives will doubt that managers or workers in an organization can handle multiple measures. They will fret about the risk of too many measures confusing people, about people making improper trade-offs, and about managers suboptimizing their groups' performance. These are real risks, but many managers believe that their organizations have no choice but to fight back the growing complexity of business challenges with a richer set of measures.

In the transformation of Tenneco, chief executive Dana Mead outlined thirteen categories of excellence for which all firm managers were to be accountable. He called these the "baker's dozen": operating-cost leadership, customer satisfaction, profitability, market position, customer base, productivity, capital effectiveness, health and safety, environmental quality, management capital, product development, information systems, and international business. Asked what's most important, Mead is fond of telling managers, "There are no priorities among essentials."[36]

Many executives would agree with Mead. Even many executives who spend more time worrying about analysts on Wall Street than anyone else feel that the financials are just not enough. They recognize that the nonfinancial measures are often the drivers of financial performance. Today's competitive demands require managers to, in effect, keep a half dozen pie plates spinning at once. They can't get away with spinning just the plate filled with financial data.

Of course, spinning the measurement plates like a virtuoso still won't create the accountable organization. The accountable performance requires creating a winning strategy and executing it by adopting all four elements of accountability. In the next two chapters, we discuss the remaining two elements: more tightly integrated management systems and broader internal and external reporting. Weaving the four elements together is the secret to vanquishing the crisis that so many firms face today.

5

Managing
the System

W hen Earnest Deavenport, chairman and CEO of Eastman
Chemical Company, went on a road trip to sell the virtues of his
company to Wall Street in 1993, analysts didn't much care about the
company's most remarkable achievement: winning the Malcolm
Baldrige National Quality Award just months earlier—the first
chemical company to gain that honor. "I would say that over 80 percent of the analysts I talked to had never heard of the award," Deavenport recalls.[1]

What an irony. An award like the Baldrige shows that a company
like Eastman, the $5 billion Kingsport, Tennessee, spin-off from
Eastman Kodak, has been installing the kinds of management and
control systems that make people at every level accountable for
performance, financial and nonfinancial. These systems, albeit no
guarantee of future success, convert strategic planning into frontline action. Many companies today that are trying to achieve greater
accountability are retooling these internal systems, trying to install
just the kind of discipline that Eastman long ago established.

In Chapter 3, we found that companies aiming to build an accountable organization have been experimenting with new board
governance practices. In Chapter 4, we found they have been experimenting with new kinds of measures. In this chapter, we find

Figure 5-1
The Third Element of Accountability: Management Systems

that they are also addressing the third element of accountability, management planning and control systems. (See Figure 5-1.) They are reexamining and renovating internal planning, budgeting, review, performance measurement, and pay structures.

To deliver the growth in earnings that analysts want—indeed to deliver growth in value of any kind—a company must have a system that ensures that signals given at the head of the company flow to each extremity, and back again. Akin to a corporate nervous system, the management planning and control system enables the accountable organization to flex its performance muscles—and deliver premium value.

Note that companies adopting new planning and control regimens are not always inventing new systems. They are often taking a second look at the systems they already have for formulating and executing strategy. Figure 5-2 shows a skeletal view of the succession of steps in management control and planning. The loop demonstrates that managers working on their management planning and control systems to further accountability are plowing familiar—if rocky—ground.

Figure 5-2
The Elements of Planning and Control

From the start, some managers will object to the notion of emphasizing control systems as a part of accountability. "Control" rings a dissonant bell. Managers might argue that such systems drive the creativity and zeal from the hallowed land of innovation. In fact, the reverse appears to be true. In over ten years of research, Harvard's Robert Simons found that "the most innovative companies used their profit planning and control systems more intensively than did their less innovative counterparts."

Simons suggests an explanation for this paradox: Control systems help managers balance the tension between the yin and yang of management—between restraint and freedom, empowerment and accountability, top-down direction and bottom-up creativity, and experimentation and efficiency.[2] The control sought by leaders of accountable organizations is not the command-and-control of the sweatshop. It is the interactive sensing and responding that guides strategy and makes sure everyone in the organization stays on track to deliver it.[3]

MENDING THE SYNAPSES

Many executives complain that the strategic plan they craft with pain and anxiety ends up in the same place every year—on the shelf. They dust it off the next year and perform the strategic-planning drill once more. Companies that practice this annual ritual in such an ineffective manner should take the hint that their management systems for accountability have broken down. If the strategy gets so little attention at the top, odds are that it gets no attention at the middle level and with frontline managers.

This broken synapse at the top of a planning and control system probably mirrors broken synapses elsewhere. The annual plan and objectives are probably not considered in the budget. The budget runs at cross purposes with improvement initiatives. The initiatives match poorly with people's performance plans. The performance plans get little support from pay plans. The result is an unpredictable or confused response from employees to the strategic objectives of management. Full accountability is impossible.

As Arthur Andersen consultant Steven Hronec says, most employees don't know how what they're doing ties to anything else in the organization. "Just go out there and slay dragons for God and country" is the message they get from their bosses, says Hronec. "That's not effective in motivating a workforce in the long term."[4]

Most managers know this already, but leaders of accountable organizations are finding they can operate in a better way. By merging control practices and systems into an interconnected whole, the company can gain the full power of accountability. An integrated system triggers quick reflexes of corporate action, ensures clear planning, precise execution, thorough follow-through, reliable feedback, and even greater worker motivation.[5]

Recall Mobil's U.S. Marketing & Refining Division from Chapter 4. Each tier of management creates a scorecard that dovetails with the scorecards above in the hierarchy. The scorecards connect like links in a chain from the division level all the way to the frontlines. All employees' scorecards link to their supervisors, and to compensation. This helps employees, from truck drivers on up, to understand how they contribute to corporate strategy: specific, measurable objectives and performance plans make the connection clear.

One caveat about management and control systems: Managers and employees can blunt their effectiveness through gaming and dysfunctional behavior. Division employees may push up quarterly revenues by shipping high-value products early—which can hurt customer satisfaction by annoying people buying low-value products. Or engineers may rush products to market to meet cycle-time goals—which can push up long-term warranty and service costs. One division or function may do well at the expense of another. Unfortunately, no company can escape such hazards entirely. Managers must simply take care to design all elements of the management planning and control system to focus employees on achieving the overall corporate strategy—and not achieve just personal or divisional gain.

To ensure that a management planning and control system works, executives must educate employees on the new, accountable approach the company is taking. They must communicate both the goals of the system and the goals of the company. Their objective is to obtain extensive acceptance and participation by employees in making the new system work. Every employee must understand the logic and flow of Figure 5-2, the managerial logic for keeping employees aligned with corporate objectives.

The Eastman Chemical System

An excellent example of a company integrating management planning and control systems is Eastman Chemical, the twelfth largest chemical maker in the United States. The genesis of Eastman's approach dates to the early 1980s, when the company adopted the quality management process at every level of the organization. Unlike so many other companies, Eastman did not quarantine quality fever in the factory; rather, it exposed executives to a full dose.

Today, everyone in the company uses the same plan-do-check-act quality-improvement cycle—including Deavenport's executive team. The only difference for executives is that they subject conceptual processes to the quality procedure, rather than physical chemical production. The executive team then coaches every team that reports to them to hook together their quality management and control processes.

Executives' prime process is "strategic quality planning." The "plan" stage of that process directs executives to create the mission and vision, develop strategic alternatives, select key result measures, and determine companywide improvement focuses like cycle-time reduction. The "do" stage directs them to implement improvement projects. The "check" and "act" stages direct them to conduct regular progress reviews, give rewards, take corrective actions, and document lessons learned.[6]

Once executives have started strategic planning at Eastman, they hand the planning and control job down the chain of command. "Interlocking" Eastman teams then create complementary action plans and interlocking measures; that is, the executive team develops the top measures to gauge strategic success. Each member of the executive team then leads his or her own team in developing his or her own plans and the unit's measures. Each member of that executive's team runs another team, creating another set of measures, and so on down to the frontline. Every team and measure interlocks with the ones above. The goals and measures vary only to remain relevant to each level.[7]

Because of the company's focus on quality, executives chose a stakeholder approach to come up with key result measures. Deavenport explains that, when the executive team came to the point of defining its customers—the people who receive the output of their efforts—the team decided it had five: customers, employees, investors, suppliers, and publics (communities, government agencies). This decision helped clarify the executives' mission: to create superior value for all stakeholders.

For example, one top-level measure is customer value—that is, the value Eastman delivers to customers as measured by surveys. Other measures are employee retention; community satisfaction—how happy plant neighbors are with Eastman's control of pollution and odors; and, the key financial measure, economic profit.

Step into any room at Eastman and you're likely to see the central role the broad mix of measures plays in management. On the one hand, in the control room of a plant, a bulletin board displays a set of hand-drafted quality-control charts. On the other hand, in the executive conference room, wall panels slide back to reveal a raft of corporate-level graphs: Two of the graphs trace safety. Six show a running total of top executives' visits to customers. Four show progress in innovation, from identifying new product needs to new products as a percentage of sales. A network of a dozen more show, in a cause-effect tree, the many key measures that contribute to return on capital (customer satisfaction, sales revenue, labor costs, inventory, and so on).

All of these measures feed and inform Eastman's management planning and control systems. As part of the system, Eastman's executive team singles out several major improvement programs each year. In 1997, they tapped global growth, reducing process cycle time, and a cost-control program called "resource effectiveness." Top managers measure the progress of each of these programs, and every quarter the company posts placards on bulletin boards in every facility showing progress measured.

Eastman includes in its planning and control system a job-development and review process for each employee. Following a similar plan-do-check-act cycle, an employee and his or her "coach" agree on job expectations, the employee later assesses the gaps in his or her performance, and the coach and employee draft an improvement plan. Coaches and employees formally review not only how the plan ties to personal growth but how it ties to the major initiatives that support the company's strategy.

Eastman reinforces the tie to company strategy through the last leg of its management planning and control system, its pay plan. In the early 1990s, Eastman executives decided to no longer base variable pay on different measures for different people in different parts of the company. To gain the broadest possible alignment of effort, they sought instead one measure, and chose economic profit. Every Eastman employee puts 5 percent of his or her base pay at risk every year. If the company doesn't earn the cost of capital, nobody gets a bonus. If they do better, they get up to 30 percent.

Eastman shows how one company has put together, in tight succession, all the links of the chain of management planning and control. The logic is compelling, though certainly not new. Many managers, however, never carry through on it. Their systems let people drop the ball between strategy and budgeting, between devising new measures and using them, or between creating business-unit action plans and connecting them to people's reviews and pay. They need to create systems that help them pick up the ball and keep it moving—toward a winning game.

The Tenneco System

Another company that has installed a tightly linked management planning and control system is Tenneco Inc. Tenneco installed its systems under very different circumstances, as part of a wrenching three-year turnaround campaign. It worked with Val Feigenbaum of General Systems Corp. to build what it calls its MPC (management planning and control). In outline, Tenneco's system mirrors Eastman's, including many interconnected steps that ensure accountability and drive performance, but Tenneco has customized many details.[8]

The Tenneco system begins with long-term strategic planning to lay out the big picture for the company. It then moves to long-term business planning and annual operating planning to lay out a working plan for each business unit. It fleshes out those plans by specifying objectives, measures, and people responsible in a document called a matrix. Finally, it links every employee to the matrix with individual, annual performance agreements. The MPC essentially takes the grand scheme for company strategy and explodes it into concrete, bite-size pieces—each with someone's name on it.

As Richard Wambold, the executive who guided its development, says: "It was all about how you make a commitment and live up to it." As at other companies, Tenneco's goal was first to develop a strategy and then to foster a commitment and structure for driving it through the entire organization.

Three elements in particular ensure that commitment at Tenneco, says Chief Executive Dana Mead. The first is the MPC matrix, which lists objectives, people responsible for meeting them, measures, and performance targets. The matrix, in principle, differs little from the balanced measurement schemes described in the last chapter. The second is the so-called performance agreement, a written understanding of objectives, action plans, and performance measures signed by each employee. The third is a compensation plan that ties pay to performance. More than any of the other features of the management planning and control system, says Mead, these three form the basis for accountability.

"We're trying to emphasize that you are accountable for these goals," says Mead. "All of this created much more management intensity."

The matrix, like a balanced scorecard, quickly became a high-profile guide to action, because, after executives created the first matrix, business-unit and functional chiefs created their own, in the same way as described for companies in the last chapter. The matrixes cascaded downward, each one specifying increasingly refined objectives, measures, and targets, until someone's name became assigned to individual tasks. The cascading ensured that activities at the bottom contributed directly—"in a straight line," as Wambold says—to higher-level goals.

Tenneco followed up with disciplined procedures for reporting results. For executives, Chief Executive Mead holds joint quarterly reviews. The heads of Tenneco's business units (formerly six, now two) meet and actually present their matrixes and results to each other. Such open reporting, in any organization, immediately creates more commitment to delivering results.

CFO Robert Blakely says that the first few meetings back in 1992 marked a sharp cultural change for Tenneco. "As one group, one management team, you'd have to explain what's going right and what's not going right," he says. "Obviously, that raises the bar, raises the intensity . . . creates a lot of peer pressure."

The performance agreement makes that accountability explicit. Everyone in the company has one—even the top executives. In each year's fourth quarter, everyone works with his or her boss to draw up what amounts to a contract of objectives, actions, and measures for the coming year. Blakely, for example, asks those working for him to provide their lists of priorities for the next year. He also asks the board of directors for its priorities for finance. He then prepares a summary memo outlining what items should be in his agreement when he and Mead prepare it. The agreement has both financial targets (working capital, for instance) and nonfinancial (reengineering the cash-forecasting process).

The compensation system cements a sense of accountability firmly in place. The company pays the average executive 50 percent in salary, 50 percent in compensation that varies with performance. It pays top executives only 30 percent in salaried pay, 70 percent variable, based on explicit goals. The executives get rated not just on financial goals but on items like safety, quality, equal employment opportunity, diversity, and leadership. "We dock 'em," says Mead, if executives fall short.

Since the early hard days of turnaround management, Tenneco's system has reversed the company's fortunes. By 1996, the company could report operating margins, return on capital employed, and sales growth at least 20 percent greater than its industry peers in packaging and automotive parts (the two businesses not spun off in its five-year-long restructuring).[9] As evidence of what the company considers key to accountability, it still insists that all acquired firms install its measurement matrix, performance agreements, and pay practices—as well as separate management reviews for quality; strategy; executives; and environment, health, and safety.

Eastman and Tenneco are hardly the only companies that have merged accountability with disciplined planning, budgeting, and reward systems. Companies like Allstate, CIGNA Property & Casualty, Mobil, Whirlpool, and Analog Devices have, too. Although each has customized the system to meet its needs, all report far greater clarity and alignment in executing strategy. They also report rich feedback for organizational learning and continuous improvement. These are the companies that have tackled one of the tougher managerial challenges of the accountable organization.

THE CULTURE OF ACCOUNTABILITY

As managers are building these new systems, they are showing that, to be effective, the accountable organization has to use them appropriately. By appropriate, we mean using them according to a philosophy that is a far cry from that perfected by such financially driven firms as ITT in the 1960s and 1970s. In that era, top executives handed down financial budgets to division chiefs, who in turn handed them down to business units. The finance department ran a control system that measured results and variances—and woe to the manager that couldn't explain and eliminate those variances.

The purpose of that system was to exact accountability. At its best, it did so—but of a very narrow kind, usually for short-term financial results. Managers were creating a culture of compliance to the iron hand of the financial budget. They were cultivating bad-cop accountability.

With the building of management planning and control systems today, accountable managers are trying to *elicit* accountability—and of a much broader kind, too. They want people to help drive the long-term performance of the organization. They are reversing

the modus operandi of the past by creating a culture of commitment—commitment to delivering ever-improving value as measured by a host of variables.

What differentiates the new culture from the old one?

- Accountable managers are encouraging not just continuous
  judgment but continuous improvement. At Mobil's U.S.
  Marketing & Refining Division, Executive Vice President
  Bob McCool remarked in 1996 at how, having adopted the
  balanced scorecard, he had changed entirely the way he ran
  business meetings: "In the past we were a bunch of
  controllers sitting around talking about variances," he said.
  "Now we discuss what's gone right, what's gone wrong . . .
  what resources do we need to get back on track, not
  explaining a negative variance due to some volume mix."[10]
- Accountable managers are insisting that everyone, no
  matter how low in the organization, participate in decision
  making. At Allstate, Assistant Vice President Loren Hall led
  a team of ten people to devise new business performance
  measures. They involved employees, agents, and frontline
  managers to get ideas on how to tune the system.[11]
- Accountable managers are setting an example of constant
  learning, and not just about others but about themselves.
  At Eastman Chemical, executives ask subordinates during
  360-degree performance appraisals (by superiors, subordinates,
  peers, and even customers) questions like: "What is it I do
  that you feel is especially well done? What am I doing that
  you wish I would quit doing? What would you like me to do
  more of? If you had one single piece of advice you could give
  me to improve my effectiveness, what would it be?"[12]
- Accountable managers are insisting on building learning
  organizations.[13] They are going beyond superficial learning.
  They are digging deep and asking probing follow-up
  questions, to foster what Harvard Business School's Chris
  Argyris calls double-loop learning. People must question
  both their own assumptions and behaviors. Too often, in
  companies operating with total quality management,
  managers engage only in single-loop learning. They correct
  the obvious problem—for example, upon identifying a

cumbersome 275-step product-development process, they streamline the number of steps to seventy-five. However, they don't look into the more insidious problem: Why the company culture allowed managers to condone the buildup of the red tape in the first place.[14]

- Accountable managers are communicating constantly, counteracting the all-too-common culture of confidentiality. They are setting a tone of constant, forthright feedback, uncloaking the facts, good or bad. CEO Mead recalls how, when he joined Tenneco, managers would "hoard" and "rathole" information, if only from inaction. Today, he insists that the quarterly reviews become forums for exchanging improvement ideas. The point is not to obsess over variances but to find ways to close gaps. Accountable managers channel their efforts into praising those who relish gleaning lessons from experience. They want to discourage those who would rather simply trumpet their success and their rivals' failures.

In short, accountable managers are dedicated to reducing the emphasis on using management control systems solely as a means to ask, as consultant Chris Meyer of Integral, Inc., says, "Who's in charge? And who do I nail?" They are emphasizing a discussion of what's wrong and how to fix it. Meyer calls financial command-and-control systems a "silent dog whistle" that, despite executives' talk to the contrary, have trained people to manage to short-term budget numbers.[15]

The experience of managers today shows that a precondition for tapping the power of accountability is revamping this out-of-date culture. Leading managers are setting the example by behaving with candor, trust, and openness. They are showing a zest for sharing, learning, and broad participation. They are making decisions objectively based on hard data. Their work is unifying their organizations' action and spurring organizational creativity and personal development.

To be sure, these managers are using the system in a top-down fashion to make explicit *what* people should do, but they are also using the system in a bottom-up fashion to allow people to show them *how* they can best do it. "Strategy has to be executed from the bottom up," says David Norton. "The direction starts at the top, but it has to be internalized at the bottom."[16]

THE INFORMATION TECHNOLOGY IMPERATIVE

Managers are also showing today that information technology can make or break effective use of the management planning and control system. In fact, without the rich inventory of data that computers can collect, process, and disseminate, the kind of accountability we talk about would not be possible at all.

One of the reasons management planning and control systems have long focused solely on financials is that they just couldn't handle anything more. They were constrained even when it came to financial data by the demands of collecting, aggregating, and disaggregating data. No system could have handled the amount of data spewed forth today by everything from activity-based cost systems to environmental management systems.

It is only with the information systems today that managers can build the fully accountable organization. These systems, creating a single digital nervous system, give managers a vast new opportunity. Managers can expand measurement and control to many more categories of performance. They can increase real-time monitoring of business initiatives and strategy. They can drill down from corporate-level results to pinpoint the sources of shortfalls. They can quickly capitalize on winning tactics and strategies validated by rapid feedback. In fact, we are only beginning to see the innovations possible with the new capabilities available.

At CIGNA Property & Casualty, President Gerry Isom shows that these new capabilities can lift management planning and control systems to another level of usefulness. For several years, Isom has been able to turn to his desktop computer to quickly review results in fourteen categories, from operating performance to claims management to improving competence. In 1997, he began to put the company's entire strategic information, monitoring, assessment, and feedback system on-line.

Today at CIGNA Property & Casualty, thousands of managers and employees can view their unit's scorecards, the company's scorecard, or any other unit's scorecard, on their computers.[17] They can study lists of objectives, numerical results, written assessments, and initiatives, each identified by "owner." In effect, they can get a complete picture of where the company and its units' performance is today, as well as its priorities, initiatives, and future goals.

The new system enables people all over the company to take charge of their work. By using the company intranet and browser, they can point and click their way to the specific screens of information they need for their jobs. If they feel unclear about how to support company strategy, they can browse their group's scorecards, study objectives and initiatives, and even read assessments to get a feel for what their bosses want. In this way, says Tom Valerio, senior vice president and transformation officer, the system has begun to answer a question many companies have not yet posed: "How do you connect a strategic tool to the individual?"

As CIGNA Property & Casualty rolls the system out to every employee, it is enabling every person at the bottom to fathom the strategic wishes of Isom and his team at the top. If someone has a question as to how, or if, his or her work furthers the company's strategic thrust, he or she need only grab the computer mouse to find out. If the information isn't available, he or she can send e-mail asking the owner of the initiative for clarification. The system will facilitate two critical obligations of all employees: clarify how their work contributes value to the company and how to align their efforts with the strategy.

Valerio is also counting on the system for one of the most important goals of an accountable organization: unleashing a rich flow of feedback from people throughout the company. On each browser page, employees can click a button to log an idea, complaint, or comment. A claims representative in one unit could read about troubles with an analogous problem in another unit—and in seconds offer lessons from experience that become part of the company's knowledge base. The promise of the system is to significantly shorten the lag time between field learning and management action. "There's more leverage in that dimension [capturing and sharing knowledge] than almost anything else we can do," says Valerio.

Valerio gives an example that shows the potential power of the system. When loss-control engineers recently learned that a scorecard measure was to improve customer retention, they pointed out that they could make an immediate impact. They had once viewed their jobs only as visiting customers, inspecting conditions, and suggesting changes to reduce accident risks. In the process, however, they often get hints of customer discontent before anyone else does. They realized they could help improve customer retention by alerting underwriters when a customer account appears to be turning sour. Though not their prescribed job, customer retention is something the engineers could align their work with. They could then serve the larger corporate strategy.

Other companies that hope to proceed to full accountability will have to similarly hitch their management planning and control systems to advances in information technology, using software from firms like Oracle, SAP, PeopleSoft, Baan, Lawson, and Gentia. One high-tech firm, N.E.T. Research of Belgium, even offers a product called the "management cockpit," based on SAP software. In one room, flanked by dozens of computer screens, a top manager can track the operations of the entire company, the same way Mission Control tracks a space flight from Houston. Screens show internal and external information like profit, customer satisfaction, brand value, project progress, sales activities, quality of staff, and threats and opportunities. Red lights flash at off-target results. A cockpit officer gives regular briefings.

Information technology also enables many new opportunities in performance reporting to company outsiders. On the one hand, the World Wide Web allows companies to disseminate data immediately, at almost no additional cost. That helps address the long-standing complaint by analysts that performance data arrives on their desks far too late for its timely use. On the other hand, computer power, paired with growing network bandwidth, allows companies to give stakeholders a much broader choice of data. With a point and a few clicks, users can drill down through a corporate website to find the spreadsheet of financial or nonfinancial figures that most closely suits their information needs. A website might also include a range of standard reports, from summary annual reports, to reams of business-segment profit-and-loss data, to a narrative of forward-looking statements of strategy and year-ahead projections.

For dealing with data-hungry outsiders, like financial analysts and public-interest watchdog groups, today's computing and bandwidth capacity also enables a new capability altogether: allowing the downloading of *disaggregated* data, which analysts can manipulate as they see fit. Providing disaggregated data would have been cost prohibitive even a decade ago. Today, however, companies can provide raw numbers at little cost, numbers that analysts can enter into their own applications. This would allow the analysts to conduct sensitivity analyses that assess the impact of changes in assumptions—about currency exchange rates, economic growth, segment performance, and so on. In the same way that some customers now tap into corporate computer systems to check on the status of their orders, analysts might tap into corporate systems to obtain the latest data to plug into their personal computers for custom analysis.

To make this possible, and to keep costs down, companies will have to deal with the problem of system inconsistency. They will have to standardize accounting systems and information systems worldwide. They cannot retain old traditions that require manual aggregation of domestic and foreign accounts. They must make the aggregation automatic. They must adhere to new international accounting standards that enable analysts in every major country to readily interpret financial reports. No firm wants to turn off the spigot of foreign capital by failing to harmonize accounts with emerging worldwide accounting principles and practices. Firms want to improve the flow of information across international boundaries, with the promise of increasing the supply of capital and improving firm valuation.[18]

In short, the critical pieces of the organizational infrastructure that companies are putting in place to create the accountable organization include easy-to-use computer systems, networks, and applications; a revitalized management planning and control system; and an accountable culture. Through them, the company can broadly disseminate the information needed for decision making, empower people to pitch in without management prodding, and turn lessons learned into a springboard for improvement. The result is a workforce aligned with and committed to the strategy and a strategy executed with speed and precision.

Yet, once again, even combined with good governance and a new universe of measures, revitalized management planning and control will not suffice to create a fully accountable organization. As we see in the next chapter, companies are experimenting with yet another element to achieve accountability: more complete reporting to people inside and outside the company.

6

Lifting
the Veil

Nobody likes to hang their underwear out to dry—dirty or not. The less exposed the better. The same attitude seems to go for reports of company performance. The less put on display, the more comfortable everyone inside the company feels. This should come as no surprise: few people naturally seek the stern eye of judgment.

However, many managers seeking the benefits of accountability have begun to turn this logic on its head. They believe that hanging their results in the wind of public opinion gives them an advantage. These managers are experimenting with the fourth component of full accountability: combining broad public disclosure with extensive internal performance reporting. (See Figure 6-1.)

One of the executives who has helped lead this revolution is William McGuire, the cardiopulmonary specialist who runs United HealthCare, one of the nation's largest managed-care companies with revenues of $12 billion. In 1993, Chief Executive McGuire directed fourteen of the company's health plans to release quality report cards to the public. The move was unprecedented, in health care or any other industry. United uncloaked vital data on customer satisfaction, quality of care, administrative efficiency, and cost reduction.[1]

Figure 6-1
The Fourth Element of Accountability: Reporting

Executives like McGuire are showing that companies need not limit reporting to just financial figures. They can—and should—disclose results once held as tightly as family secrets. They should reveal both more about the past, including financial, operational, and social information, and more about the future, including forward-looking plans and projections. They should disclose this information to all stakeholders as a part of a corporate communications strategy. To reap the benefits of the accountable organization, they are finding that developing the better governance practices, measures, and control systems described in the last three chapters is not enough. They must take a fourth step: Tell the world in more detail the stories of their performance.

United HealthCare's story stands out. Even by today's standards, the report cards (actually short reports) gave a remarkable view of what most companies would consider their most sensitive, proprietary measures: consumer satisfaction with the quality of doctors' care; claims turnaround times; the rate of "one-contact" customer service; service delivery levels like C-section rates, pediatric-asthma hospitalization rates, and mammography rates.[2] Even more remarkable is that such data, in just five years, have become for many health-care companies the status quo of disclosure.

Such reporting marks the frontier of corporate accountability. On this frontier, managers not only develop more leading and lagging indicators of performance for decision making by themselves and employees, they also develop more for analysis and forecasts by analysts, shareholders, customers, partners, and others. Not a lot of managers care to visit this frontier, but a number of leaders are. They are testing the notion that posting results much more publicly will propel their performance. They believe that future competitiveness will depend, first, on giving people inside the company ample facts and figures to better make decisions as a unified competitive force and, second, on demonstrating that performance to outsiders.

These leaders are opening a new chapter in corporate management. They are gravitating away from embracing a passive, compliance-centered philosophy, in which reporting is a cost of doing business. They are rushing toward an active, communications-centered approach, in which reporting with greater transparency is a competitive tool. They are finding that disseminating the numbers that demonstrate their performance helps them to gain an edge on others in attracting capital, employees, business partners, and community and public support.

Ed Jenkins—long before he was chairman of the FASB—had it right when he said: "External reporting should focus on competitiveness—today it does not."[3]

A few companies are changing that, and rapidly in some cases, as we will see in case after case in this chapter. In health care, a number of executives, long wincing from barbs thrown at them by the public and politicians, have put their organizations at the head of the pack. In issuing their report cards, they have become more publicly accountable for performance than even many of the big U.S. firms they serve.

If the kind of data in the health-care report cards were released in other industries, eyebrows would jerk sky high. Is an auto company ready to tell the world the turnaround time on customer phone complaints? Is a brokerage firm ready to release customer satisfaction data on its retail brokers? The health-care industry has been *voluntarily* giving out this kind of information. No legislation mandated the change (although the Clinton administration sought to do so in the early 1990s).

The journey led by managers like McGuire speaks volumes about a trend cutting across industry as a whole. Like so many other executives, in health care and outside, McGuire sought in the 1980s to radically boost the quality of the service his company provided. He directed his people to measure performance in terms of cost, quality of care, customer satisfaction, and access to care. With the data, he pressed every health plan in the corporate fold to practice quality-management techniques to deliver better care and service. So successful was United HealthCare that, by 1992, members graded its customer service a 94, on a scale of 0 to 100, compared to 79 for health-care delivery systems as a group.[4]

The story of continuous improvement, so common at many companies, took an uncommon turn at United. In 1991, the company began to devise a way to report a cross-section of its results publicly. McGuire wanted to show the world that the health-care industry, under attack as the agent of health deterioration, was an agent of just the reverse. It could tap rich veins of data, feed them back through the quality system, and improve health-care outcomes. The report card, exposing to the outside the performance on the inside, began to win over at least some of the doubters. Says McGuire, "It allowed the people we were trying to serve to recognize that we were working on their behalf."

In other industries, the ramifications of this trend have not sunk in because managers have continued to look at the disadvantages of candid reporting. They have not brought themselves to look at the advantages. If they did look at the plus side, they would view performance information more as a product, aimed at a customer. It requires the same market sensing, product innovation, standardization, and just-in-time delivery as other products. As FASB Chief Jenkins, while chairing the financial-reporting committee of the American Institute of CPAs in 1994, pointed out, a company has to deliver information that satisfies the needs of the *users* of the information, not the producers.[5]

As just one example of how poor a job companies do in delivering that product—even to shareholders—consider the results of the survey of star Wall Street analysts we have referred to before. To the credit of most companies, 91 percent of the analysts believe they get the information they need to forecast future financial performance. In striking counterpoint, only 41 percent feel they receive the information necessary to diagnose or assess the source of problems if the strategy is ineffective.[6]

Leading companies today are on the trail of rectifying this problem, experimenting with disclosing the numbers of accountability to do so. Many managers believe that stakeholders have a right to know more of the data that measures company performance, regardless of whether it helps company competitiveness. This chapter looks at a number of companies that are defying the closed-mouth habits of the past to reveal more about themselves for a competitive advantage. They are disclosing far more information in three broad categories: financial, operational, and social. In so doing, they are betting they can win favor and loyalty from the very people whose support they need to prosper—customers, investors, employees, communities, the public, and even the regulators and politicians who work the levers of mandated disclosure.

FORTHRIGHT FINANCIALS

While many executives complain about having to publish too many financial numbers, others are actually stretching to supply more. They believe that beefing up even traditional disclosures works to their advantage.

Coming Out Early

One means that companies have tried to gain at least some advantage is disclosing financial or nonfinancial data before regulators decide to require it anyway. In 1991, International Paper (IP) took this approach. At the time, the company had been toying with a dilemma many companies faced; that is, when to release an accounting of liabilities for health-care benefits of retirees. Many accountants and analysts believed U.S. firms would eventually announce gargantuan accruals—some might even wipe out the companies' net worths. IP managers worried that the accrual, or investors' worries about it, might jeopardize an anticipated securities offering.[7]

So IP decided to release its numbers early—two years early. In January 1991, it recorded an obligation of a whopping $350 million ($215 million after tax) to reflect the adoption of the new accounting standard (SFAS 106). Despite the huge sum, IP had the financial strength to handle the liability. Executives attributed the subsequent, smooth issue of 9.2 million shares of common stock, raising $650 million, and a debt offering, raising $250 million, to reporting the big number early on. Taking the hit early relieved analyst uncertainty over the size of the liability. It also reassured investors that IP stood tall among the ranks of General Electric, IBM, and other blue-chip companies, who also reported early.

The notion of proactive disclosure is not new, of course. Nor are the benefits. According to Baruch Lev, voluntary disclosure often has a significant impact on stock prices and trading volume. It decreases price volatility and narrows bid-ask spreads, enhancing securities liquidity. Lev maintains that disclosure can change perceptions even in large, active capital markets.[8]

Other recent studies support Lev's view. Firms with more informative disclosures have a wider analyst following, receive more accurate earnings forecasts, and have less volatility in forecast revisions. The research suggests that companies that disclose more have a bigger pool of investors, and maybe even a lower cost of capital.[9]

Going the Extra Mile

Despite the seeming straightjacket of GAAP accounting, firms have many opportunities to get ahead of competitors in disclosing financial information. They can use segment reporting, comprehensive income, current-value accounting, and forward-looking information. Certainly, the owners of the company, the shareholders, want the information. In surveys, roughly two out of three shareholders would like financial statements restated in current values (or replacement costs). About the same number would like reporting of product-line and segment profitability. A remarkable nine out of ten want more forward-looking information about the company's future.[10]

While hardly keen on more paperwork, financial executives certainly see the benefit of enhanced reporting in at least isolated instances. One company that has stepped out is The Rouse Company, the large real-estate development and management firm based in Columbia, Maryland. Rouse reports the value of its properties according to both current-value accounting and mandated cost-basis accounting to banks, credit agencies, and municipalities that want reassurance of the company's value. The market value estimates generally come from present-value calculations of future cash flows from its properties.

Through 1996, the company even reported the numbers in its annual report and form 10-K report. Rouse executives had found a striking correlation between its current value and stock price for nearly fifteen years, until the 1990 real-estate recession. In publishing the figures in side-by-side balance sheets, one representing market values and one mandated cost-basis accounting, executives believed they better portrayed the value of the firm. They used their voluntary disclosures as a way to make sure shareholders got the same picture. In 1996, for example, Rouse reported total assets, at current value, as $5.5 billion, compared to cost basis, as $3.6 billion, nearly a $2 billion difference.[11]

After the real-estate recession, analysts began to value real-estate firms based on current cash flows. Rouse continued the current-value disclosure for more than five years, even as demand for the information slackened. In 1997, however, it ceased publishing the side-by-side balance sheets, and now releases the figures only to those financial-statement users who request them. The company does publish a summary figure for current-value shareholders' equity, which rose from $1.8 billion in 1996 to $2.1 billion in 1997. Rouse executives don't rule out publishing the current-value statements again, when the demands of external users justify the cost and effort.[12]

Another firm that has stepped out with an altogether amazing disclosure compared to other firms is Cambrex Corporation, a $450 million specialty and fine chemical maker headquartered in East Rutherford, New Jersey. In the early 1990s, the firm's executives believed that institutional investors were expecting the worst of Cambrex's share of liabilities for cleaning up polluted sites. At the time, institutions held most of Cambrex's stock. Cambrex certainly didn't want nervous investors, who were well aware that even one Superfund cleanup could run into tens of millions of dollars.

So Cambrex, eager to "diffuse the worst expectations" of institutional shareholders, says Frederick Larcombe, Cambrex's director of internal audit and taxation, opened its books for a surprisingly full accounting. In a unique approach used since 1992, Cambrex discloses an estimate of the minimum-maximum range for potential liability—in 1997, $4.5 million on the low end, $9.9 million on the high. It also shows funds recorded in, deducted from, and added to the liability account—Cambrex moved $1 million out of the reserve in 1996 as the progress of several cleanups clarified its obligations. With the disclosures, Cambrex quelled investors' concern over possible skeletons in its environmental closet. In essence, it published for outsiders some of the same detailed figures the company uses inside.[13]

Good Times and Bad

Of course, many companies naturally want to report more when they have something good to say. But what about when they have bad news? Some managers still believe they should disclose more. The expanded reporting signals that company managers want investors to have a complete and fair view of the financial landscape. Presumably the candor creates more trust, leads to a better understanding of corporate operations and future prospects, and, over time, to a fairer valuation of company stock.

In late 1997, Microsoft went way beyond current requirements to clarify for investors its full liability of stock options issued to 21,000 employees. The irony is rich here, given that many high-tech firms fought the FASB to water down accounting for options, only to have the archetypal high-tech firm volunteer a full market-value-style accounting. Starting with its September 30 10-Q, the company actually calculated the value of all options issued to employees, as if Microsoft had to buy them itself on the open market.

For the quarter ended September 30, Microsoft reported $0.50 per share earnings, but it reported a $0.05 per share *loss* pro forma, the result of the cost of granting 28 million options that would have cost $1.1 billion. Microsoft even prepared a pro forma income statement to make itself clear. CFO Gregory Maffei noted that the options liability was the most important the company had, calculated at $26 billion.[14]

Given that analysts say they want more of this and other kinds of data, companies have plenty of opportunity to provide it. Certainly, analysts are not fooled by companies that are not forthcoming with information when they're not doing well. In surveys, analysts say they believe companies are only about half as likely to come forward with extra useful information during bad times.[15] The blackout of forthright information undoubtedly gives outsiders a more jaundiced view of the information they do get.

Volunteering the Latest and Greatest

A handful of companies have gone beyond the confines of traditional financial reporting altogether. As they adopt new measures like economic profit, they are disclosing the results to company outsiders. Managers at these companies believe that disclosing a figure that shows progress in building shareholder value enriches their financial accounts to their advantage.

One of the first companies (if not the first) to disclose economic profit was Coca-Cola, which routinely lists economic profit in its ten-year financial summary. Coke believes that using and reporting economic profit shows investors a commitment by the company to invest capital only in ways that return more than the cost of capital, which in theory propels stock prices.

Coke has long charted the close correlation of economic profit growth with its stock-price advance. That gives it a rare advantage over other firms: When it articulates how it will build economic profit, it in essence articulates a credible plan for raising stock prices.[16] With economic profit, Coke has created a numerical signal for convincing investors of the promise of future gains.

Although companies can forgo the publication of economic profit figures, they may miss a bet in doing so. Analysts at firms from First Boston and Goldman Sachs to Paine Webber and Smith Barney use economic profit to value corporations. Some analysts even believe that the announcement by a company just to use economic profit sparks a rise in stock price, if only momentarily.[17] Certainly, the subsequent publication signals to investors that managers have narrowed their decision-making calculus to manage shareholder capital more carefully, and that is the point: Managers can appeal to investors and other stakeholders by reconsidering the data they disclose. They do not have to structure their reporting solely around the tangle of mandates of the SEC and FASB. They can structure them around the long-term needs of the market—whether for capital, labor, or customers.

As the SEC and FASB press for more disclosure, more companies are likely to take the tack of Rouse, IP, Cambrex, and Coca-Cola; they will figure out how to use financial reporting to their advantage. They can, like Coca-Cola, build an extremely high level of credibility over time, building that trust year after year with consistent forthright reporting.

EYE-OPENING OPERATIONAL MEASURES

As managers disclose more about their finances, they are starting to reveal more about their operations, as well. Analog Devices periodically publishes on-time delivery performance. Eastman Chemical regularly reports community satisfaction, and periodically releases other data—employee satisfaction and customer ratings. Skandia, a standout we'll discuss more in Chapter 9, releases a wide variety of information as part of its Skandia Navigator. These companies portray the trend toward the fully accountable organization.

Most managers shy from disclosing hard data on operations, however. They are locked into traditional ways of thinking. They believe that operational performance, like trade secrets, is confidential or that potential rewards of such transparency don't justify the risks and costs. This thinking is suspect. As Baruch Lev says, "Those who seek solace in a 'no voluntary disclosure' policy should be aware of a fundamental attribute of information in a competitive environment: *no news will generally be perceived as bad news* [Lev's italics]."[18]

The Tale of Health Care

The story of the health-care industry shows how quickly some managers have changed the conventional thinking. Many health-care firms, for-profit and not-for-profit, are starting to show—with broad, voluntary disclosure—that leaving people in the dark has become a strategy of the past.

United HealthCare, although first with a public scorecard, was hardly the only leader in developing the model for an accountable organization. In the same year, 1993, managed-care giants U.S. Healthcare (now Aetna U.S. Healthcare), Kaiser Permanente, and others also issued report cards. So ardent were the companies' belief in the value of grading their performance that U.S. Healthcare in 1996 bought a full two-page spread in the *Wall Street Journal* to trumpet its data compared to industry averages.[19] Competition on the basis of accountability had come to health care.

The reaction to the new report cards was swift. At United HealthCare, Lee Newcomer, United's chief medical officer, reported that the company got 1,000 calls of support. Employer and labor groups—United's key customers—loved the idea.[20]

The release of the report cards was a momentous event, loaded like a freight train with implications. First, the report cards' release demonstrated that continuous improvement counted big in health care. Managed-care firms could show they had a method for improving care and for transferring best practices. The mere fact that United spent so much money preparing the report card delivered a powerful message. The software and methodology took 11.5 people working full time two years to complete.[21] "Measurement is a tangible way for people to see what's going on," says McGuire. "The fact that you have disclosed it . . . should help drive people to be cognizant of its value and importance."

Second, the report cards showed that a huge New York Stock Exchange-listed company had committed itself to voluntary reporting of hard-edged operational data for decision making by *outsiders*. Consumers could see what percentage of United members would recommend their plan to others—and how that percentage stacked up against the figures at other organizations. They could see the eye-exam rate for diabetics, and again how that compared with the rate at other health organizations. They could see the number of days people generally had to wait for a physician's appointment, and once again how others stacked up. In short, they could assess value for dollars spent, and they could shop around. "Just because people are happy in their ignorance isn't an appropriate endpoint," McGuire says.

Third, the risk of not reporting was greater than that of reporting. Executives knew full well that politicians could mandate new disclosure regulation. Third-party agencies could jump in and impose disclosure standards without industry involvement. Consumers could coerce disclosure on unfavorable terms. A key provision of the 1993 Clinton plan was national measurement standards. By acting early, United HealthCare and other leading organizations influenced the debate, set an example of giving out critical information before people asked for it, and presumably helped to fend off the strictures of regulation. Public reporting of a new set of data was a huge investment in the future—an investment McGuire was confident would pay off.

A Story Destined to Repeat

The health-care industry marches to its own drummer to some extent, but the forces that have borne down on health care are the same ones bearing down on all industries. Competition is stiffening relentlessly. Regulators are digging deeper into company affairs. Lawmakers are riding herd on pet issues of public welfare. As a result, the evolution of disclosure in health care foretells in broad outline a more transparent future for many other industries.

The report cards marked the first step of the evolution. They required companies to develop wholly new systems and measures internally to drive improvement. They required new strategies and methods for reporting externally. They demanded new means to handle the tide of data that external feedback provided. This was no small step. Within just a couple of years, accountability through public reporting had gone beyond a single-company story. It became an industry story.

The second step in the evolution of reporting in health care was standardization. Once the leaders in the industry set an ad hoc standard, managers across the industry sought consistency. The group that emerged to spearhead the standardization efforts was the National Committee for Quality Assurance (NCQA), an independent nonprofit managed-care accrediting institution. The NCQA produced the Health Plan Employer Data and Information Set (HEDIS). Today, nearly every managed-care company follows the HEDIS standards, including United HealthCare. (See Table 6-1.)

The third step in the evolution was that the NCQA standards, updated several times, reached near-universal acceptance among managed-care organizations. NCQA then announced that it would begin to *require* compliance with the standards. Starting in July 1999, any managed-care organization that wants accreditation by NCQA, the premier accreditor of health-maintenance organizations, *must* supply audited data on key measures like mammography screening rates and member satisfaction. The act of reporting,

TABLE 6-1

UNITED HEALTHCARE REPORT CARD, EXCERPTS FOR
UNITED HEALTHCARE OF NEW ENGLAND

KEY INDICATORS	UNITED HEALTHCARE OF NEW ENGLAND	COMPARATIVE DATA
EFFECTIVENESS OF CARE		
Mammography rate	72%	60%
Cervical cancer screening rate	60%	85%
Prenatal care in first trimester	96%	90%
MEMBER SATISFACTION		
Overall member satisfaction	84%	86%
Thoroughness of treatment	95%	88%
No delays in care while waiting for approvals	92%	80%
USE OF SERVICES		
Acute care days/1000	212.3	187
Average length of stay: C-section	3.6 days	3.3 days
Cerebrovascular days/1000	3.2 days	2.6 days
Cardiovascular days/1000	1.9 days	1.7 days

Source: 1997 United HealthCare report card for United HealthCare of New England.

Note: Although an excerpt, this is actual data. The full report card, which conforms to HEDIS 3.0 standards, includes a number of additional categories.

once largely a voluntary affair, had become in most competitive markets, essentially mandatory.

The evolution is likely to continue at a quick pace, if only because the standards makers aren't sitting still. They are constantly raising the bar. The NCQA requires the reporting of fifty-three measures for 1999, but the number is likely to climb as the organization tests new measures. Moreover, key industry groups are working with the NCQA to advance the standards. One of those groups is FACCT, the Foundation for Accountability, a coalition of consumer groups and buyers. FACCT devises new, state-of-the-art measures to contribute to the standards. Another is JCAHO, the Joint Commission on Accreditation of Healthcare Organizations. Long the major accreditor of hospitals, JCAHO has created standards of its own for both hospitals and managed-care organizations. The three organizations, along with the American Medical Association, came together in 1998 to begin measurement standardization across the health-care industry.

The momentum of the reporting effort has become unstoppable. Health-care managers now fully recognize that they will have to repeatedly rise to new, higher levels of reporting. NCQA is applying intense pressure to make this happen. In 1999, the group will start publishing managed-care organization report cards on its website. Consumers will be able to compare the performance of all health-maintenance organizations in their region in five categories (access and service, qualified providers, staying healthy, getting better, living with illness). They will also be able to view HEDIS-based NCQA accreditation status (excellent, commendable, accredited, provisional, denied). The NCQA report cards won't be complicated, either. They will all follow the same familiar format, a one- or two-page summary table similar to those published for merchandise assessments in *Consumer Reports.*[22]

The frontier of reporting in health care is now advancing so fast that all organizations must rush to keep up. No organization can fight the trend toward ever greater accountability. What's remarkable is that despite the swiftness of change, some organizations are moving even faster—staying ahead of the standards setters' curves. Long a leader in quality improvement, Group Health Cooperative of Puget Sound, a Seattle-based health plan with 363,000 members, publishes a full HEDIS report detailing performance in every category, along with adding a few of its own. Group Health customers can read such segmented data as Group Health's senior flu immunization rates. They can even call up all of the data on Group Health's website at www.ghc.org. Most organizations publish only a summary of the HEDIS data.

Minneapolis HMO HealthPartners not only publishes its HEDIS data on the web, it launched a program with publicly announced targets in 1994 to improve care in eight specific categories: breast cancer, childhood injuries, dental cavities, diabetes, family violence, heart disease, immunization rates, and infant and maternal health. Chief executive George Halvorson publicly set the targets—such as cutting by 50 percent the cases of breast cancer that reach an advanced stage before being detected. He publicly reports on results each year. For example, to meet the breast-cancer detection target, HealthPartners has set a goal of 85 percent mammography screening, at least biennially, for women fifty to seventy-four years old. In 1998, Halvorson could declare HealthPartners had surpassed its goal. Ninety-two percent of the fifty- to seventy-four-year-old group was getting the called-for screening. Overall, HealthPartners was detecting 90.3 percent of all breast cancers in early stages.[23]

For all the progress, industry outsiders might conclude that the health-care industry had reached some sort of maturity in accountability, but the reverse is true. Most insiders believe that measurement and reporting remains in its infancy. Standards are likely to advance for years to come. The biggest gap? Reliable reporting on how well patients recover from illnesses and injuries. To a patient, that sounds like logical data to have. Consider, though, that's like asking a manufacturing firm to report how well its products improve its *customers'* productivity. The challenges are huge.

Although the evolution in health care has a long way to go—as organizations improve data gathering, prove validity, set standards, establish comparative benchmarks—the message to managers outside the industry should be clear. This pattern of reporting practices could be on the verge of repeating in many other industries. The question of whether to build an accountable organization may not be a matter of *if* but a matter of *when*.

The health-care story suggests that any company can use public reporting as a gigantic lever to boost performance. What is encouraging about the story is that the myriad measurement and reporting efforts are all voluntary initiatives. True, the Health Care Financing Administration, the administrator of Medicare and Medicaid, now requires HEDIS data disclosure. However, no government body, like the SEC, swept in to create quality standards for performance reporting. Leading companies, and an industry under pressure from customers, fashioned the response. Now not only are the companies benefiting, so are consumers and buyers.

Even financial analysts are benefiting. They can use the measures as leading indicators of the managed-care firms' financial performance. As *Barron's* noted in first recognizing the implications in a 1996 cover story: "Outcomes [published according to emerging standards] aren't opinions, they are facts. And these are the fundamental facts that will eventually affect share prices."[24]

THE FIGURES OF SOCIAL RESPONSIBILITY

If managers are hesitant to reveal operational performance measures, they are perhaps even more reluctant to reveal those for social performance—for employee treatment, environmental protection, community giving, and so on. Yet a number of leading managers have started to do so. Some of these managers make such disclosures as part of a business philosophy, as at Ben & Jerry's and The Body Shop. But others, as at Royal Dutch/Shell, have begun to report on socially responsible management as part of building mainstream, high-performance accountable organizations.

Aside from their charitable leanings, leading managers have recognized that many issues long considered part of corporate social responsibility, and as a source of costs, are today foundations of future long-term profit. At the same time, they have recognized they don't have the information they need to make decisions regarding these issues. They need a broader set of measurements for enlightened internal decisions. They are also recognizing that stakeholders will want this added information for their analysis and decisions about the future prospects of the firm.

Equal Opportunity, Community, and Society

One good illustration of using social data to demonstrate superior performance is the use of equal employment opportunity information. Most U.S. companies are particularly secretive in handling the equal employment opportunity data. In some ways, this is peculiar. The data are readily available. All but the smallest companies compile the data and submit EEO-1 forms to the Equal Employment Opportunity Commission. Federal contractors—just about all big companies—also submit the data to the Department of Labor's Office of Federal Contract Compliance Programs, which even releases the data under most Freedom of Information Act requests. Yet only about 10 percent of big firms make their data public voluntarily.[25]

The reluctance of some firms has given an opening to others to stand out. One company taking advantage is Allstate, which has award-winning programs for diversity education and affirmative action. The company, spurred by the initiatives of the recently retired CEO, Jerry Choate, ardently pursues a strategy of managing diversity for competitive advantage, and today reports that 21.2 percent of executives and managers are minorities, compared to 11.8 percent nationally.

Allstate's strategy is to make the workforce reflect the customer base, and the company aims not only to attract a diverse pool of workers for positions at every level of the firm but to show them they have the opportunity to get ahead. Among Choate's moves was to begin publishing summary EEO-1 data in the annual report showing race and gender makeup for all equal employment opportunity job classifications. "The annual report is not just for investors; everybody reads it, our employees read it," Choate says. When the company operates with the advantages of a diverse workforce, he adds, "sometimes you have to be able to demonstrate that and show it visibly to your people and to the outside world."

According to independent research, Allstate is the largest insurer of African Americans and Hispanics in two of the three major insurance lines (auto, home, life). Executives believe the diverse workforce gives the company the skills and expertise to attract and retain additional minority customers. Choate says that reporting the equal employment opportunity data and emphasizing the data inside the company helps ensure that managers train and promote a diverse, winning workforce. The external reporting then tells a strong story to investors. "We want our shareholders to understand that we're not just focused on today," he says, "but we're building what we think is a very strong resource with our employees."[26]

In internal documents, Allstate even takes pains to point out how its superior equal employment opportunity links to the bottom line: Expanding career and advancement opportunities for women and minorities drives employee satisfaction; employee satisfaction drives customer growth and retention; and customer growth and retention drive profitability.[27] This is just another of the chains of causation that Allstate monitors to deliver high performance. It is also one of the chains that has helped Allstate deliver a total return to shareholders from 1993 through 1997 of 369 percent, compared to 240 percent for the Standard & Poor's 500 and 237 percent for Allstate's insurance-industry peers.

Another good illustration of using social data to demonstrate superior performance arises in a very different area, albeit more specialized: community reinvestment in banking. Thousands of banks in the United States fall under the legal mandate to reinvest in the same parts of the community in which they take deposits. But few take the lead in making a show of their performance as a way to attract business.

The Community Reinvestment Act requires that banks create a public file with a report from bank examiners on their performance. The examiners evaluate every bank in twelve categories. Then they give the bank a rating, from outstanding to substantial noncompliance. Once again, with the data at hand, banks can use their community reinvestment performance as a way to distinguish themselves—but few have done so.

Bank of America is an exception. While devising innovative financing arrangements that turn a consistent profit, it forthrightly discloses results. In recent years, Bank of America has rated "outstanding" for every unit subject to the Community Reinvestment Act rules. When Bank of America and NationsBank merged in 1998, executives announced an unprecedented $350 billion, ten-year commitment to community-development lending and investment, roughly equal to the combined total of all commitments by the rest of the banking industry since 1977, the year the Community Reinvestment Act became law.

The new BankAmerica fully intends to use its community lending commitment as a way to hone its image as a bank with which depositors want to do business. (NationsBank had also earned a consistent "outstanding" rating for its Community Reinvestment Act activity.) The merged bank has set specific lending and investment goals for affordable housing ($115 billion), small business ($180 billion), consumer lending ($30 billion), and economic development ($25 billion). As part of its commitment, the bank will acquire, build, or rehabilitate 50,000 affordable housing units. Starting with year-end 1998, the bank reported its progress annually; it also began holding annual meetings to discuss results with community organizations.

By distinguishing itself so clearly, executives say that the bank realizes more than community favor. It prevents people from using the provisions of the Community Reinvestment Act to hold up mergers, acquisitions, and divestments. During such transactions, anyone can file a complaint with regulators attacking a bank's Community Reinvestment Act record. If regulators believe the complaint has potential merit, they can hold up the transaction for weeks. When that happens, the meter keeps ticking for attorneys and investment bankers hired for the transaction.

Over the years, BankAmerica has gotten few complaints. Two key deals in 1996, including the acquisition of brokerage Robertson Stephens (divested during the merger), went through without any Community Reinvestment Act delay at all. In another case, a community leader in Chicago filed a Community Reinvestment Act complaint, but the Office of the Comptroller of the Currency dismissed it because the bank could readily demonstrate a stellar record. During the merger with NationsBank, 173 people gave testimony to four Federal Reserve officials, about half in favor and half against the merger (not always related to Community Reinvestment Act issues). The Federal Reserve approved the merger with only minor conditions. BankAmerica's earlier achievement of multibillion dollar Community Reinvestment Act commitments no doubt blunted the attack of critics.[28]

Stepping out with the Equal Employment Opportunity Act or with the Community Reinvestment Act is straightforward, if not easy, because the banks already have the data to demonstrate the capability, competence, and performance of management. However, even when companies don't have the data as a byproduct of running the business, many are finding ways of voluntarily disclosing social information to their advantage.

Grand Metropolitan, parent of Burger King, Pillsbury, and International Distillers and Vintners, issued a remarkable ninety-two-page 1997 report on corporate citizenship. The company, now merged with Guinness and renamed Diageo, maintains that building relationships with six constituencies—investors, government, consumers, business partners, employees, and communities—builds value for all. Along with case studies and company policy, the report details a variety of measures of performance to demonstrate its commitment to this approach. It lists items varying from charitable giving and public-opinion-survey standing to in-kind contributions and social impacts.

A table in the Grand Metropolitan report actually matches social and business impacts. Under employee volunteering, for example, the company notes that $20,000 and time spent by 1,200 Pillsbury volunteers on 193 community projects will aid in attracting, retaining, and developing "great people" while enhancing morale, teamwork, creativity, and pride. Under cause-related marketing, it notes that the £350,000 ($595,000) spent on its J&B Care for the Rare program to save rare animals helped twenty-two species while boosting duty-free liquor sales by 37 percent, and earned the company lots of good public relations value as well.

The clearest measure of Grand Metropolitan's overall performance is perhaps its Corporate Community Involvement index, showing a zero (lowest) to 100 (highest) rating in eight categories. According to the index, developed by a group of six major U.K. companies, Grand Metropolitan rates a 75 in leadership and management, a 77 in community benefits, a 70 in external communications, and a 68 in measurement and evaluation. (Note that Diageo is continuing to develop Grand Metropolitan's social reporting efforts and will publish a 1999 report on corporate citizenship.)[29]

As companies increasingly take a higher-profile role in building social value, such reports are sure to increase. They demonstrate the company's dedication to building value for the people contemplating relationships with the company. One question naturally comes up, however: Will the companies continue to report their performance when it looks lousy? That remains to be seen. Many companies get started in good times. No company has, say, a ten- to twenty-year record of consistent reporting to stand on. But managers are well aware that the value of such reporting depends on making it a part of corporate communications for the long term, building credibility with shareholders, analysts, and all other stakeholders. Royal Dutch/Shell, for example, recently published plans, through 2002, to integrate financial, environmental, and social management systems, including a full reporting on each area.[30]

The Tale of the Environment

The story of change in environmental reporting, just a decade in the making, is as instructive for the future of social reporting as was the story of health care for operational reporting. It shows just how fast a company's inability to demonstrate performance can turn into a liability—and how fast candid, extensive reporting can turn into an opportunity. Once a bastion of proprietariness, the storehouse of environmental performance data has become almost an open book.

Changes in social values have turned the tables on many corporations' way of dealing with the environment. For decades, businesses routinely "externalized" their environmental impacts. They gained value by allowing society as a whole to bear the burden of costs like water pollution and habitat destruction. Today, however, the public believes that companies should bear the costs and hassles of pollution. With this change in attitudes, managers recognize that they have to demonstrate accountable environmental behavior to stakeholders. Otherwise, customers may hesitate to buy, and regulators will knock on the door more often. They also recognize that by examining environmental costs more carefully, they can actually come up with solutions that reduce impacts and save their companies money.

Perhaps the triggering event of change in environmental reporting came in 1986. In that year, Congress passed the Emergency Planning and Community Right to Know Act, also called SARA Title III. By law, U.S. plants suddenly had to report toxic releases of more than 300 chemicals. For many companies, this set off alarm bells. At the time of the passage of the law, many companies couldn't have disclosed the data if they wanted to—they didn't have the data or couldn't compile it consistently across the company. When the first data did come out, in 1989, the media gave it big play. Nobody had ever seen data aggregated for entire companies, states, and the country. The numbers were gargantuan. Not only was the public aghast, so were executives, few of whom knew themselves the extent of companywide toxic emissions.

In the first report (calendar year 1987 results), DuPont alone reported releases of nearly 200 million pounds of waste to the air, land, and water. Among the pollutants were millions of pounds of air toxics and carcinogens like benzene, cyanide compounds, and chloroform. That's when former DuPont Chief Executive Ed Woolard, naming himself "chief environmental officer," hit the speaking circuit to reverse age-old assumptions about corporate environmental management. "Nobody likes sitting around the dinner table at night with their kids saying they've heard at school that DuPont is destroying the ozone and asking why we are doing that," he said. "They want to be a part of a company that's doing something good for society."[31]

Along with DuPont, many other companies were scrutinized by the media in the late 1980s, including Polaroid, based in Cambridge, Massachusetts. Polaroid, long known for an unwavering commitment to employees, became a punching bag of environmentalists over its environmental record. Greenpeace, in particular, campaigned against the company in 1987, claiming it was the worst toxic polluter of Boston Harbor.

In response, Polaroid carved out a strategy that many firms would later follow. It countered the attacks on its record not by barring the doors of disclosure but by opening them. The basis of Polaroid's effort became the toxic use and waste reduction program. Unique to this day, the program measures not only the output of pollutants but also the input of toxic materials. The result is a score for reducing hazardous substances at both ends. In 1988, Polaroid became the first U.S. company to start reporting on its environmental efforts. Since then, it has issued an annual environmental report that ranks among the best in the world. Few companies are so candid.

Polaroid learned its lesson. As MacAllister Booth, Polaroid's chief executive at the time, later recalled: "You've got to measure and you've got to publish." The public expects no less. "We don't like to publish it, but publishing it does make us accountable."[32] Indeed, by the end of 1995, about the time Booth left, Polaroid had cut releases to the air of seventeen key toxic chemicals targeted by the Environmental Protection Agency by 66 percent.

Today, the commitment continues. Outsiders widely consider Polaroid a leader in reporting. No doubt the company, like others today, wins acclaim for publishing results whether encouraging or disappointing. In late 1997, for example, along with better pollution figures, it reported ten chemical spills for the year before, far worse than the previous two years. It also reported payment of $100,786 in penalties under the Toxic Substances Control Act.[33]

Companies like DuPont and Polaroid developed reports that each year became more and more revealing. Within just a couple of years, in the early 1990s, DuPont, Polaroid, and other companies locked themselves into an ongoing battle of one-upmanship in producing both better environmental performance and better reports to chronicle that performance. As the reports became part of the competitive game, they became cemented in place at many big companies as almost a de facto requirement. By 1998, more than 600 companies produced reports,[34] up from just a handful in 1990.

As in health care, a variety of efforts emerged to push companies to report in a similar way. Industry groups like the Chemical Manufacturers Association have promulgated extensive codes, recognized worldwide, to profile and report on environmental performance. Government bodies representing the likes of the European Union have prescribed standards for public reports, which are required for each company site registered under Europe's Eco-Management and Audit Scheme or EMAS. Standards organizations including the International Standards Organization (ISO) have crafted worldwide guidelines under the ISO 14000 standard to illustrate the kinds of measures companies should consider for reporting.[35] Independent organizations like CERES have created standardized templates for reporting.

The CERES format was the first effort at bringing standardization to reporting. CERES now requires all companies endorsing its principles to comply with its 110-question form. In late 1997, CERES launched the latest step in pushing standardization: a global organization, the Global Reporting Initiative, to bring business people, accountants, and reporting advocates together to standardize not just the reports but the measurements within the reports. The group is creating guidelines destined to enable people to compare the same measures company to company, like total emissions per pound of product, or the ratio of emissions to raw materials used.[36] In 1998, the World Business Council for Sustainable Development, a business coalition, also started a project to develop standard measures of eco-efficiency, expected to at least include measures of waste generation and material and energy usage.[37]

The state of standards will evolve probably for years to come. Still, with companies aiming to simplify the reporting task, and outsiders seeking consistent and comparable data, reporting seems sure to head, as in the health-care industry, toward standards that companies will feel obliged to follow. Already, many pressure groups believe the CERES principles offer enough of a standard that they routinely file shareholder resolutions calling on companies to adopt them. In 1998, groups like United States

Trust Company of Boston, Progressive Securities, Franklin Research & Development, and the ICCR filed thirty resolutions asking company executives to adopt the CERES principles.[38]

Experience suggests that the principle of going the extra mile with voluntary environmental reporting will remain a means for companies to distinguish themselves. In a unique move of this sort, Bristol-Myers Squibb translated the International Chamber of Commerce's sixteen-point Business Charter for Sustainable Development into its own sixteen-point Codes of Practice, detailing corporatewide requirements for each. The company rigorously tracks—and publicly reports—progress in improving each element of its management system. "We wanted something that could be measured, demonstrated, and quantified," says Thomas Hellman, vice president of Environment, Health, and Safety.[39]

Novo Nordisk, the world's largest supplier of insulin and industrial enzymes, took the same step in 1997, asking an external organization to assign the ratings. Novo also lists targets and notes whether they have been achieved or not. It discloses reams of environmental data for eighteen manufacturing sites in eight countries, from Bagsværd, Denmark, its headquarters, to Araucária, Brazil. Spreadsheets quantify everything from water and energy consumption to hazardous waste and sulfur dioxide emissions to "impact potentials" for global warming and eutrophication. A series of graphs disclose the data for four "eco-productivity indexes," which measure the company's efficiency in using energy, water, raw materials, and packaging. What's surprising is that these indexes also happen to be proxies for normally ultra sensitive figures on manufacturing efficiency.[40]

E.B. Eddy Group, a Canadian pulp and paper maker acquired in 1998 by Domtar, Inc., went beyond a report of environmental performance to "sustainable development"—or caring for the health of the economy, environment, and community. It reported progress in bettering performance in six aspects of sustainable forestry—preserving biodiversity, caring for forest ecosystems, managing soil and water conditions, and the like. It also reported progress in better performance in seven aspects of sustainable manufacturing—resource use, conversion efficiency, waste generation, and socioeconomic impacts. It reported spreadsheet after spreadsheet of data to quantify its results, from sawlog conversion efficiency to solid wastes landfilled.[41]

As with most reporting, the benefits of disclosure are hard to separate from the benefits of the actions the reports represent. But the leaders in reporting environmental performance have become convinced that with greater transparency they're gaining an edge. Sun Company was the first big corporation, in 1993, to sign the CERES principles. When it did, according to Robert Banks, vice president of health, environment, and safety, the company began to receive a flow of letters from people saying they bought Sunoco gas precisely because of the commitment. One of the major Protestant church denominations even ran a story in its newsletter lauding Sun on its commitment. It read like a pitch for the company, and even included Sun's toll-free number for credit-card applications.[42]

"It's hard to put a dollar value on it," Banks admits. Still, he feels candid reporting helps curry favor not just with righteous customers but with investors, business partners, community groups, and the press. He notes, for example, that it gives Sun "a seat at the table in a variety of meetings . . . with environmentalists, religious groups, social investors, regulators, academicians, and the press." Indeed, Sun contributes directly in ongoing CERES meetings to discussions that determine reporting standards for the future. That's a big plus for Sun. As Banks says, "Public accountability and public disclosure is here—it's only a matter of time before voluntary reporting is standardized."[43]

Some would argue that the expanding demands of disclosure won't last or won't affect small and mid-sized companies. Indeed, twenty years ago, numerous academics and companies tried to develop a methodology called "social accounting" or "social audit" to report on corporate social performance. It failed to last because it was never institutionalized in organizations. Companies never made it a part of strategy making, costing, capital budgeting, performance evaluations. In short, managers never used the methodology in day-to-day decisions. So external social reports were, in many cases, well-meaning statements of intentions, often used for public relations.

Today, however, managers *are* integrating equal employment opportunity, environmental affairs, community commitments, philanthropy, and a host of other issues into the fabric of strategy. They are making them a part of budgeting, performance measurement, and personal appraisals. They are reporting publicly on their results to demonstrate their prowess as accountable organizations.

The recent appearance of a social report from Royal Dutch/Shell is a harbinger of the future. It provides details on general business principles, performance according to those principles, and even a report from the company's external auditors, KPMG and PricewaterhouseCoopers. Along with financial measures, such as return on average capital employed, the report covers topics like child labor and bribes, customer value, employee rights, and environmental impact.[44]

No longer are leading executives asking outsiders to take their word for delivering performance based solely on financial figures. They are painting a picture with hard numbers of all kinds, financial, operational, and social. As E.B. Eddy chairman Ted Boswell wrote in December 1996, the guiding notion is summed up in a credo from the Roman poet Virgil, in the epic the *Aeneid:* "Experto credite"—"trust one who has proved it."[45]

With this new forthright reporting, we begin to see how the four ways companies have attacked the accountability crisis are fitting together. Managers are trying governance. They are trying measures. They are trying management control systems. They are trying much broader internal and external reporting. Clearly, none of these works alone. They work together. A synthesis, as we describe in the next chapter, is required for full accountability. Full accountability brings with it the promise that society will readily give corporations the license to freely operate. It also brings the promise of the highest possible levels of corporate performance and competitiveness.

PART THREE

THE
NEW ORDER
OF ACCOUNTABILITY

7

The Accountability Cycle

T he four parts of our story—the four elements of the accountable organization—now come together: good governance, broad measurement, management planning and control, and candid disclosure. Managers have pursued them all, and they have enjoyed rich rewards. In the future, they can enjoy even more rewards as they put the four together into one system, which we call the accountability cycle.

The accountability cycle is the essence of accountable management. (See Figure 7-1.) A company running with the cycle operates with a robust management planning and control system, built with a broad mix of measures, exposed to the eyes of many stakeholders, and overseen by an enlightened board of directors. The cycle shows that managers need not address accountability piecemeal, as we have in Chapters 3, 4, 5, and 6; they can address it in a unified way.

The accountability cycle embraces the best of old systems while creating a new, more encompassing one. The old accountability systems ran on financial numbers. The new run on nonfinancials as well. The old generated results only for reports to privileged managers. The new report results across the organization for everyone to make decisions. The old released data only as far afield as the

Figure 7-1
The Accountability Cycle

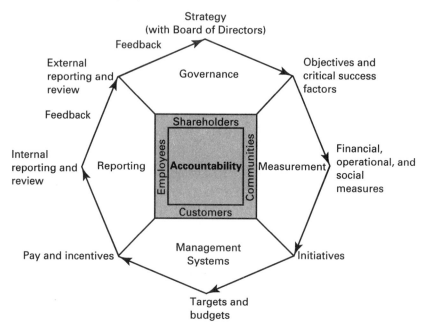

board of directors. The new release a vital cross-section of information to the public.

The old systems, in short, delivered only a meager accountability. The new, tying together these four islands of initiatives, can deliver much more. To the extent that old systems operated with the sophistication of a sextant, the new run with the precision of a global positioning system. They enable executives and managers to guide their organizations in executing strategy more precisely and in delivering results more confidently.

The accountability cycle is an integrated management planning and control system. The difference from old systems is that new measures inform it, a revitalized board digs into it, empowered workers and managers draw new intelligence from it, and stakeholders become involved in it. The cycle is a closed loop, so that information wells up constantly from one part of the organization to feed learning in another.

Of course, many managers have already installed individual pieces of the accountability cycle, as we've seen in preceding chapters. But few have installed them all in one company, and even fewer have linked them together to help deliver breakthrough performance. The most progress in furthering accountability has come in establishing practices for corporate governance and for management planning and control. The most work remains in expanding measurement and reporting. For this reason, we devote much of the rest of this book to these latter two topics.

COUNTING WHAT COUNTS

Measures have great power, almost like genetic code, to shape action and performance. Whether at the equivalent of the cell level, the organ level, or the systems level, measures become the directional device that influences or even dictates the shape of the enterprise. Change the measures, and you change the organism.

Measures have always had the power to shape a corporation's destiny, but the focus on financial figures alone limited their utility. Management accounting of the past forced managers to build world-class organizations with a truncated set of chromosomes. Today, though, with the help of revitalized cost accounting and nonfinancial measurement, managers can develop a full set of instructions—financial, operational, and social—for the enterprise. Those instructions give them the capability to create accountability they never had before.

A balanced family of measures can evolve into a powerful system for executing strategy.[1] The measures help to define the strategy, communicate it to the organization, and direct its implementation at every rung of the hierarchy, from the corporate level to the individual. They also keep everyone's efforts aligned, because they link strategy to budgets, to resource-allocation systems, and to pay programs. In the best of cases, they route such high-quality feedback through the organization that executives can make critical, midcourse adjustments in strategy.

Counting on Stakeholders

Deciding what to measure begins with a look back to strategy. From the strategy come objectives. From the objectives come critical success factors. From the critical success factors come the measures. The measures, embedded in the accountability cycle, enable managers to convert the language of strategists into the action of people throughout the organization.

In formulating a new family of measures, a big question arises: How should executives structure their thinking? The answer is to break out measures that, on the one hand, gauge the performance of stakeholders in helping deliver strategy and, on the other, gauge the performance of the company in helping deliver on promises to stakeholders.

The rationale for this approach is that, in today's world, strategic execution relies heavily on tight, trusting, innovative, lasting relationships. These are the types of relationships that are critical to creating and delivering innovative products and services. Capital, labor, technology, and know-how now move across global borders with ease. Companies can no longer gain a lasting advantage through these resources alone. They must gain advantage through relationships uniquely structured to give strategic advantage.[2]

Customers will give a lasting advantage to a company when they quit buying transaction by transaction and provide a loyal, long-term stream of purchases. Employees will give a lasting advantage when they climb out of the rut of clock-punching compliance with preassigned duties and commit to great service, innovation, and reliability. Shareholders will give a lasting advantage when they quit dumping their stock at each dip in quarterly earnings and provide long-term, patient capital.

Because gaining advantage through stakeholders has come to drive strategic success, the appropriate way for accountable managers to create measures is to first break out the key stakeholder groups that most help drive the strategy and, second, devise measures to fit these groups. For every company, the stakeholders most responsible for helping a company deliver on its strategy are shareholders, customers, employees, and communities.

If there is any doubt about the value of stakeholders, research by John Kotter and James Heskett confirms that companies that stress shareholders, customers, and employees, along with leadership from managers at all levels, outperform firms that do not. "Over an eleven-year period," the authors write, "the former increased revenues by an average of 682 percent versus 166 percent for the latter, expanded their workforces by 282 percent versus 36 percent, grew their stock prices by 901 percent versus 74 percent, and improved their net incomes by 756 percent versus 1 percent."[3]

When the accountable organization frames top-level thinking in terms of the stakeholder view, the labels on the company's measurement categories match, one for one, the critical categories of relationships the firm depends on for strategic execution. This ensures that the company makes no mistake about its number one job: building strong relationships with the people who, in a grand collaborative effort, run the processes that create value for the enterprise.

Chief Executive Matthew Barrett recognized this fact when he took the reins of the Bank of Montreal in 1989. That's when the entire executive team began to organize all corporate strategic planning around the four stakeholder groups that later appeared in its set of corporate measures, as discussed in Chapter 4: shareholders, customers, employees, and communities. "It was a fundamental belief [of top management] that you had to do well on all four stakeholders" to succeed, says CFO Robert Wells.[4]

The Bank of Montreal executives have whistled the stakeholder tune ever since. Whether at the bank's branches in Montreal, at its Nesbitt-Burns investment firm, or at its Harris Bank unit in Chicago, all employees know they have to please the four constituencies. They get scored on their performance in a document called the *figure of merit*. Their pay depends on that score, right down to the teller at every window. If surveys show a bank branch's community image has slipped, the branch tellers' pay takes a dip, too.

This orientation has the distinct advantage of forcing executives to take both a close-up and a wide-angle view of the enterprise, of internal and external demands, and of cross-enterprise and cross-functional processes. Executives' thought processes then embrace all the financial, operational, and social aspects of the business. By singling out customers, executives ensure that they measure product innovation to deliver high-value products. By singling out employees, they ensure that they measure workforce training to attract and retain the best and brightest. By singling out communities, they ensure that they measure citizen concern over pollution or traffic or noise that might unpredictably disrupt company operations. This approach also dovetails with concepts of reengineering, quality management, and organizational learning.

Of course, executives must customize their approach to address the most relevant company relationships. Bank of Montreal singles out four stakeholders. Eastman Chemical singles out five: shareholders, customers, employees, suppliers, and various "publics," including the community. The choice of stakeholders depends on strategy—how much, in the long term, will stakeholder groups influence our success? It also depends on philosophy—how important should we make them?

Certainly every company will first stress shareholders, customers, and employees, but executives should at first cast their net wide. They may embrace regulators, creditors, environmental and social activists, the general public, or even the media. This is not to say that, when all is said and done, they should operate with a kaleidoscope of both critical and trivial measures relevant to all conceivable stakeholders. On the contrary, they should ultimately narrow their choice of measures to retain focus. They should simply start by taking the broad view.

Cautions in Counting

When some people hear the word "stakeholder," they think "altruism" or "management run amok with shareholders' money." Former Sunbeam Chief Executive Al Dunlap popularized this view. In just one of his comments, while successfully restructuring his former employer, Scott Paper, he said, "Shareholders are the number one constituency. Show me an annual report that lists six or seven constituencies and I'll show you a mismanaged company."[5] Whatever Dunlap's track record, his point should at least be taken as a caution. The stakeholder philosophy could become a cover for errant management.

A company committed to accountability, however, has no choice but to deal with stakeholders. Not only do executives have to manage the contributions of stakeholders, they have to demonstrate to those stakeholders that their relationships are win-win (or at least not win-lose). Such a demonstration of value is the only way to inspire the loyalty of the constituencies that a firm needs to execute strategy with commitment and drive. In a sense, a company has to pay stakeholders what they're worth—give them a fair deal. Otherwise, they will drag their feet, look for a free ride at company expense, or worse.

In the past, stakeholders did not have as much power to affect company fortunes, but they are getting more power all the time. Power through the media. Power through a culture of consumerism that ratchets up expectations each year. Power through increased access to corporate intelligence. And power through their increased leverage in more competitive, global capital, labor, and product and service markets.

To be sure, corporations are the most powerful institution on the planet, but they operate fettered by complex partnerships with their stakeholders. One company may be a competitor, joint-venture partner, customer, and even supplier of another—and all at the same time. That's why, in adopting measures according to stake-holder-driven strategic planning, managers don't automatically give one stakeholder group priority over another.

At Eastman Chemical, executives make clear that stakeholders are all equal. At the Bank of Montreal, Chief Executive Barrett makes clear that shareholders prevail. He actually assigns a weight to each of the four groups. In calculating a total score for bank performance, he gives shareholder measures a weight of 40 percent of the total, customers 30 percent, employees 20 percent, and communities 10 percent. Says Barrett, "We have a stakeholder strategy because we believe it is the most effective shareholder strategy."[6]

Philosophies vary, of course, as discussed in Chapter 1. Many companies that rank shareholders above all others still implicitly follow a strategy of providing shareholder value through the efforts of other highly valued stakeholders. Coca-Cola is an example, and many companies that wave the shareholder flag force decision making relating to all other stakeholders through a process that requires both financial and nonfinancial analysis. A measure like economic profit, for example, can simultaneously improve capital-investment decisions, which shareholders care about, and environmental management decisions, which local communities care about.[7] Regardless of the formal treatment, a company that proposes to win through accountability must take the broad, holistic perspective that the stakeholder view provides.

The Corporate Family of Measures

One effective way to come up with measures is to brainstorm with the help of a matrix similar to that shown in Figure 7-2. This matrix suggests that a set of measures has two powerful purposes: On the one hand, it serves, as would a musical score for players in a symphony, to guide the performance of everyone in the company. When managers and their subordinates look at it, it answers the questions: What are my strategic priorities in dealing with each stakeholder? And how do I align my efforts with everyone else in the company to perform financially, operationally, and socially? On the other hand, when filled in later with results, it serves as a report card. It answers the questions: Did the company deliver on its promises or not? Did it (we) make its (our) numbers?

In building such a matrix, managers must begin by asking, Which stakeholders are critical to executing strategy? For convenience and thoroughness, we divide the matrix into four stakeholder groups. In practice, the number of groups is different for each company. Managers should choose those three to five that allow them to both clearly guide strategic execution and clearly measure results. Some companies might include suppliers as a fifth group. Others might include regulators.

With the matrix in hand, managers must ask the next question: *How* is each stakeholder critical to executing strategy? They should consider this question broadly—precisely the reason for breaking out the financial, operational, and social perspectives. Their answers will help them articulate, first, a set of objectives for the company's relationship with each stakeholder, and second, measures for gauging whether the company meets those objectives.

Figure 7-2
The Corporate Family of Measures

	Financial Measures	Operational Measures	Social Measures
Shareholders			
Customers			
Employees			
Communities			

For example, when managers ask how shareholders are critical to the strategy, they are likely to answer that shareholders can supply loyal, competitively priced capital for growth. The company's objective, then, is to maintain performance at a level that attracts that capital. In choosing measures, managers must ask, How can we gauge performance to show that we're delivering the long-term value shareholders want to continue their relationship with us?

Managers will ask similar questions for each stakeholder group. In response, for the customer group, they will conclude that the objective is related to attracting profitable, frequent, long-term buyers. In devising customer measures, they might then ask, How will customers signal that they believe they are getting promised value that prompts repeat purchasing? For the employee group, the objective will be related to stimulating brains and brawn to deliver on the promise of value to customers. So managers may well ask, How must employees develop skills, foster innovation, and create and run critical processes to keep customers coming back?

Note that in considering each stakeholder category, managers should brainstorm the measurement question from both sides of the stakeholder coin. What can the stakeholder do for the company, and what can the company do for the stakeholder. This assures that managers think through their strategy and measures from the inside out and from the outside in. Immediate strategic execution relies on the delivery of stakeholder value to the company, but long-term health relies on the company's delivery of value to the stakeholder.

The kinds of measures managers will put in each cell of the matrix will overlap among categories, but during brainstorming managers should not be concerned about the duplication. The broad mix simply makes sure that the company surfaces all elements essential to executing strategy and demonstrating success.

In practice, as managers later separate the measurement wheat from the chaff, they will find that a handful of measures often both elucidates strategy and demonstrates results. As an example, at Eastman Chemical Company the main measures for customers are customer loyalty, an indication of repeat business, and customer value, the perception by customers of the value Eastman delivers. For employees, the main measures are employee satisfaction, safety, retention, and recruitment success. For suppliers, they are on-time delivery, supplier innovation, and—a measure in the works—gauging the value Eastman brings to suppliers (such as innovative practices or technology). For shareholders, the main measure is economic profit. For communities, it is perception of value.[8] Eastman actually asks communities to rate its performance in controlling air and water pollution and odors. Taken as a package, Eastman's measures cleverly balance both an inside-out and outside-in view of the business.

Note that by breaking out the financial, operational, and social aspects of each measure, the matrix encourages managers to consider both leading and lagging indicators. Most often, the financial measures, like earnings and returns on investment, are lagging indicators. They measure past performance. Management can extrapolate from them, but it cannot reliably *forecast* from them. The operational and social measures, such as factory defects, new-product development, or toxic emissions, are leading indicators. Managers can forecast from them how the financials will turn out in the future, a critical advantage of a balanced set of measures. While Analog Devices measures key results, like revenue and gross margin, it also measures key process measures, like "time to silicon" and parts-per-million defects.[9]

As managers begin to devise a balanced set of measures, they will find that some leading indicators are lagging indicators at the same time. This will seem confusing at first, but in fact makes perfect sense: Remember that all measures should—indeed must—be embedded in a performance logic, as we discussed in Chapter 4. Customer satisfaction is a leading indicator of financial performance, but it is also a lagging indicator of on-time delivery. Each measure is one part of a larger strategic support structure.

At many companies, economic profit is the capstone of the corporate pyramid of measures. The many other measures in the company—at the business-unit, functional, process, team, and other levels—are the building blocks below it. These building blocks, financial, operational, and social, are the performance drivers. Ferreting out the proper drivers, developed through an understanding of each stakeholder's contribution to strategic execution, becomes the spadework that later determines the strength of the entire pyramid.

The work of devising measures, though easy to describe, is hard to do because the set of measures that sends the right signals and prompts the right actions takes hours of soul-searching to figure out. Robert Howell summarizes six objectives of measures. They should (1) make strategic objectives clear, (2) focus on core cross-functional processes, (3) focus on the critical success variables, (4) act like early warning signals for problems ahead, (5) identify critical factors going awry, and (6) link to rewards.[10] Howell prefers to call measures "indicators," stressing their value in managing future performance.

Several other critical things about the choice of a family of measures include the following. First, managers should mix input, output, and process measures. Input includes the money and people put into a process; output includes results achieved; and process includes performance of the systems that deliver the output. In R&D, an input measure is R&D spending; an output measure is number of new products; and process measure is number of change orders per product during manufacturing. Of course, the ultimate output measure is the contribution of these new products to corporate profitability.

Second, measures should address the three dimensions of cost, quality, and time—in comparable terms. When we say comparable, we mean comparable over time, comparable with each other, and comparable with other companies' measures. In the best of all worlds, managers would translate quality and time into dollar-based measures. That way, the company can easily aggregate results, make tradeoffs, and identify excess costs to remove. An excellent example is Tenneco's cost-of-quality measure. Although a lagging indicator, the cost-of-quality number captures all failure costs (warranties, scrap) in dollars, making it easy to track, compare, and weigh the value of quality-improvement initiatives against other investment options.

Third, managers should strive to keep the number of corporate-level measures to a small number. The total number of corporate-level measures should stay under a dozen, or perhaps under twenty. At some point, as managers increase the number of measures, they get decreasing marginal returns. After all, data collection and processing cost money. People in the organization suffer information overload, disregarding what they can't absorb. And the measures lose meaning when they represent only a fraction of people's performance commitments, whether at the corporate, division, team, or individual level.

One guide to minimizing the number of measures is seeking those that "tell the whole truth and nothing but the truth." That means striving to make each measure both complete and controllable. Complete means it sums up in one number all the performance issues managers care about. At the highest level, long-term financial returns are the most complete measure of corporate performance. Controllable means that people using the measure can completely control its improvement. The team assembling a computer peripheral can fully control assembly defects. Obviously, in practice, no measure both tells the whole truth (completeness) and nothing but the truth (controllability), but managers should search for this fit, however difficult this makes the task.[11]

Perhaps one of the most important factors in creating workable measures is making sure they serve not just management but the people that have to execute the strategy, no matter what level of the organization they work in. That's why top management must involve people throughout an organization in choosing the measures. If executives are searching for a process-quality measure, they should ask, say, an assembly-line worker to come up with ideas. As Arthur Andersen's Steven Hronec says, a new performance measurement system must help individual employees to succeed in their work. "Otherwise, it's just another failed exercise with a coffee cup attached to it."[12]

Counting Down Through the Organization

Setting the top-level measures is only the beginning. To benefit from the new measures, the company must wire the headquarters measures to the rest of the organization. Top managers must challenge business-unit heads to create families of measures of their own, aligned with the top-level set. Business-unit heads must challenge their people to create measures, in turn, aligned with all those above in the hierarchy.

Every team and operating unit needs a family of measures to motivate workers to act in concert with the strategy developed for the whole company. The idea is to cascade the measures down through the organization so they logically connect one to the next. Each group of employees must customize their own measures. Sometimes the measures are the same as corporate measures, sometimes entirely different. In any case, they both come from a global strategy and serve local needs.

Consider just one stream of this cascading process at Eastman Chemical, the one that concerns employee safety. At the top, safety falls under the employee stakeholder, for which Eastman measures employee satisfaction, several safety indices, and recruitment and retention. The Tennessee Eastman Division measures items like consecutive work days worked safely and number of serious incidents. The Tennessee division's Acid unit measures items like total injury rate and documentation of near misses. The Acetic Anhydride Department measures items like safety concerns identified and corrected and the number of safety projects per crew. The department's crews measure safety concerns identified and safety improvement projects.[13]

One final note about measures: They run down. Marshall Meyer and Vipin Gupta call this the "performance paradox." In time, their research shows, all measures lose their variability. One reason is that people's performance improves and the difference between the high and low ends of the measure narrow sharply. Another reason is that people learn to game the system. They boost earnings per share by increasing leverage, for example, rather than increasing profitability. Over time, the utility of measures declines, and lose a once-valuable gauge that distinguished good performance from bad. They also lose a means to set stretch targets.[14]

Meyer says that at a few big companies, customer satisfaction and quality measures have already become so widely used, and now exhibit so little variability, that executives are casting about for new yardsticks of performance. Meyer's message is that managers can't cast measures in stone for all time. They have to change them. His prediction for companies in the future: "A world in which we'll cycle through measures with ever greater rapidity. No performance measurement is immutable, especially nonfinancial measures. They're always changing." The conundrum for managers is to reconcile peoples' need for consistency with the firm's need for continuous change.[15]

Analog Devices is one company that has actually created a system to manage its measures. Analog executives evaluate the set of measures for weaknesses each year. They then rejigger their scorecard.

The firm's measures change little each year, but over several years they change dramatically because of rising customer expectations and standards of performance. (See Figure 4-1.) One change in recent years has been to add measures for quality of work environment and customer responsiveness.[16]

REPORTING WHAT COUNTS

As powerful as measures are within the organization, they offer even more power when released to the outside. Disclosure energizes the accountability cycle by broadcasting corporate strategy, eliciting employee commitment, and increasing strategic feedback. It also cements stakeholder relationships more firmly in place. If new financial measures like economic profit help the company better track value creation inside, they also help attract capital from the outside. If measures of employee well-being help executives cultivate a committed workforce inside the company, they also help attract committed talent from outside. If data like on-time performance help run processes better inside, they also reassure customers and business partners on the outside.

The largest accounting firms have been competing vigorously for employees on the basis of reporting performance of employee treatment. Suffering from a shortage of talent and turnover exceeding 20 percent, the firms vie to appear at the tops of best-employer lists. They also impress their recruits with generous family-friendly work arrangements, like flexible scheduling.[17] The best and brightest of Generation X is watching very closely, and the accounting firms are trying to strut their stuff.

A Communications Strategy

Accountable managers must change their approach to public reporting. First, they must develop a new philosophy of reporting. Next, they must change the substance of what they report to the outside. In short, they need to create a communications strategy based on greater transparency.

The tradition of management has been to hold most information close to the vest. That was a good strategy when high-level performance information gave a company a competitive advantage.

However, keeping that high-level data secret today works just as often in the opposite way: It blocks the deepening of business relationships, stanches stakeholder commitment, and suppresses feedback that promotes improvement.

For years, most reporting has been based on mistrust. Managers mistrust outsiders to handle corporate information responsibly. Outsiders mistrust managers to give them information with value. This legacy has led outsiders to lose faith in the key information managers provide, namely annual reports. It is hardly surprising that half of analysts believe that managers purposely write in obscure language when their companies are not doing well.[18]

Accountable managers should base their communications philosophy on trust. If they release more information, and release information that gives a fair appraisal of the company, they will create a reservoir of credibility to draw on later. That reservoir can even tide a company over during a temporary stall in performance. Shareholders won't bolt at an earnings dip if they trust that management will learn from the dip, has a plan for a comeback, and will report honestly about progress.

As Thomas A. Lee at the University of Alabama recommends, "Get rid of the implicit idea that it is your information, and you can decide what is or is not good for the consumer. Taking a proprietary approach to managing this product [the corporate report] is not a good idea."[19]

Perhaps because that proprietary attitude prevails, only one in ten companies has a formal written policy for managing disclosure. Even fewer, one in fifteen, regularly conducts surveys of analysts to find out what that constituency wants to know.[20]

Most managers view reporting as an exercise in following the rules. They think of it as mandatory. They should instead view reporting as an exercise in rewriting the rules. They should think of it as voluntary. They also should think of it as a strategic opportunity. This is neither an investor-relations exercise nor a public-relations exercise. This is an exercise in building firm value through building credible relationships.

If reporting is about rewriting the rules, no company should retain a narrow focus on traditional accounting. GAAP accounting, by itself, too often tells little about whether a company will excel in the future. Many high-technology companies trade for ten or more times reported book value. Surely their GAAP accounting doesn't give a leading indication of the future. Sometimes, it doesn't even give a fair representation of the present. "More and more people realize that the financial report is trivialized by irrational accounting practices, such as the immediate expensing of acquired R&D, the pooling method of corporate acquisitions, or big-bath restructuring costs," says Baruch Lev.[21]

Top management must create a strategy for telling their story via numbers. That strategy should address each venue of communication, from analyst meetings to press conferences to formal documents. One of the few jobs that top executives alone perform is communicating the corporate story to outsiders. They must not only take this job seriously but also manage it like any other corporate function.[22]

Corporate communication should give outsiders a view of the company "through the eyes of management."[23] How do executives view the business, the market, and the strategy? Is the company delivering on its objectives today? How does it measure up compared to competitors? What does the future look like? The old accounting measures, based on bookkeeping principles now 500 years old, won't suffice in today's competitive markets.

The Case of Bank of Montreal

At Bank of Montreal, executives have taken an unusually forthright approach to financial reporting. A flyer that comes with the annual report details the bank's nine financial performance measures: shareholder value, earnings growth, profitability, revenue growth, productivity, asset quality, capital adequacy, liquidity, and credit rating. The flyer also graphs Bank of Montreal's performance against the top Canadian and North American banks, actually ranking the bank's standing with that of twenty-three other North American financial-service giants.

Inside the report, Bank of Montreal has turned its Management Discussion & Analysis (MD &A) section into an in-depth look at the same nine key indicators. Gone is the standard MD &A that drones on about standard measures of performance. In has come a through-the-eyes-of-management report. "We wanted to use MD&A as a vehicle to show how we manage the bank," says CFO

Wells. "We had a belief that shareholders would give more value to an organization that is transparent."[24]

As if anyone could miss the message that bank executives like Wells and Barrett consider accountability paramount, the 1997 report summarizes the bank's performance ranking in all nine categories the same way *Consumer Reports* summarizes the performance of cars and toasters—with empty, blackened, or partially blackened dots indicating top tier, above average/average, and below average compared to competitors. Although financial analysts could make the same assessments on their own, the bank invites shareholders to comparison shop for bank performance.

Wells maintains that the executive team established a philosophy early on that "there was nothing management knew that we weren't willing to disclose to the outside world." He notes that when new employees start working for him, they often ask for a synopsis of bank strategy. "I give them the annual report," he says. "They think it's a front," a sort of shareholder snow job. So they ask again for a document about *real* strategy. Wells replies, that's it! There is no other document. This is through-the-eyes-of-management reporting.

Of course, neither Bank of Montreal nor any other company releases all details. In fact, many of the detailed numbers that Bank of Montreal releases are already public; the bank simply reports them in an unusually candid way, developed to serve the decision-making needs of outsiders. However, every management team should share publicly at least a broad subset of the detail given to the board of directors. The board meanwhile should be asking for critical data across the stakeholder spectrum. Only then can the board play its role in guiding corporate direction.

Objections Overruled

A myth makes the rounds that broader reporting will hurt companies. The primary objection, referred to earlier, is that it will hurt competitiveness. This is unlikely when a company weighs the risks of disclosure against the advantages of adopting the accountability cycle. Most companies already know more about their competitors' strategies than do even their competitors' employees. Ford executives surely know more about GM's strategy than do most stakeholders. So a broad reporting of stakeholder-based performance measures is unlikely to hurt companies' competitiveness.

Many executives today believe that an understanding of a company's high-level strategy won't give other companies an advantage, anyway. The advantage comes from knowing details of the execution of that strategy—that is, the fine brush strokes the company uses to fill out the big picture. After all, many companies have opened their doors to benchmarking already, implicitly admitting that the benefits of sharing are worth the risks.

Another myth that makes the rounds is that broad reporting will cost too much. Again, as part of the accountability cycle, the reporting should be only the caboose on a long train of internal data compilation and reporting. If the company prepares the right data to run the company internally and then prepares it to enable the board to play its oversight role, the added cost of disclosure externally should be small. This objection to expanded disclosure is hard to justify against the benefits.

Yet another myth is that extra reporting will make a company a target for litigation. As mentioned in Chapter 1, we believe this is a specious argument. The facts simply belie the fear. The vast majority of disclosure-related lawsuits relate to "failure to disclose" and "inadequate disclosure." Some relate to "misleading disclosures." For all practical purposes, companies cannot be held liable for disclosing too much, but they can be held liable for disclosing too little or disclosing in ways that do not present financial conditions fairly.[25] The best defense against litigation is a documented, disciplined process for forthright disclosure of both leading and lagging indicators. In today's litigious society, some shareholders will sue management when the stock falls precipitously regardless of the degree of disclosure. Increased disclosure of management information to shareholders, however, can often act as a substantive defense.

A New Reporting Look

We don't propose that disclosure follow a new format. It should simply include entirely new measurement information—information that should already exist in well-managed companies. The annual report is a fixture on whose credibility managers should build. After all, two-thirds of portfolio managers and half of security analysts say that annual reports are the most important document a public company can produce. Eight in ten portfolio managers and 75 percent of security analysts say they use annual reports when making investment decisions. Of individual investors with portfolios totaling more than $5,000, 70 percent say they consult a company's annual report before risking money with the business.[26]

Traditional reports, familiar, credible and long-standing, offer the vehicle for full accountability. Adding leading indicators and new results measures need not require dozens of new pages. The focus should be on pertinent numbers and on the same explanations that should be in reports today—of strategy, initiatives, why performance hit target or didn't, and what the company is doing to improve. The annual report should contain more of the candor and numbers of an internal management report.

This is what the American Institute of Certified Public Accountants recommended in the so-called Jenkins report, discussed in Chapter 2. The Jenkins committee recommended keeping the current format but adding critical new information: segment performance, high-level operating data and performance measures, analysis of trends and changes in operating data and performance measures, more forward-looking discussion of management plans, critical success factors, opportunities and risks, and comparison of performance to previous forward-looking information.[27]

The committee's report documented widespread criticism of traditional financial reporting. Critics charged that the traditional reports had lost their relevance, that the quality of the information product was not good, and that "customers" failed to express delight. When former SEC Commissioner Steven Wallman proposed a new reporting structure in 1996, as mentioned briefly in Chapter 2, he was suggesting a product that would serve many of the unfulfilled needs noted by the Jenkins committee. Wallman's model had five layers, to report both financial and nonfinancial information in a declining order of certainty and reliability.

In Wallman's model, the top layer would more or less represent today's report—a compilation created from formally recognized accounting events, standardized, and highly reliable. The second layer would include hard-to-value items like R&D, advertising, brands, and spending on customer satisfaction. The third would include nonfinancial information like customer satisfaction. The fourth would include items like risk sensitivity analysis for derivatives. The fifth would include items that cannot be reliably measured, like going-concern value and intellectual capital.

One way to meet the goals of expanded disclosure would be to structure the report—and not just the thinking process for coming up with measures—around stakeholders. Some experts have suggested this approach.[28] Along with a report on current financials, an expanded or supplemental report would separately report performance of interest to customers, employees, the community, society, and others. Companies like Northern Telecom have gravitated toward this approach, which is discussed in Chapter 10.

Our view is that the annual report should not become a special-interest group report. The stakeholder notion should structure strategic thinking. It should ensure that management takes a 360-degree view of the network of relationships that support world-class company processes and results. It should become a checklist of thoroughly covering all issues, a prompt to be sure that executives don't let key issues fall through the cracks.

The report, however, should disclose—in a consolidated way—the performance of the company in creating value for all constituencies together. It should show that, despite tradeoffs, managers have made decisions that provide benefits, and create value, for all stakeholders simultaneously. After all, many measures interest multiple stakeholders. A healthy financial condition should cheer not just shareholders but employees who value their paychecks, communities who value tax revenues, and customers who value uninterrupted service from a healthy company. Any employee working for a faltering company, and worried about layoffs, knows just how relevant quarterly earnings releases are.

Managers and stakeholders work in a web of mutual interest. The report should reflect that web, not simply isolated intersections of stakeholder self-interest. Management's job in an external report, as in an internal report, is to clarify, map, and measure for stakeholders the complex set of indicators that drive value. The report should show that management grasps the value drivers, understands how one feeds another, and candidly discloses performance. In broadening reporting, many firms have issued special reports, for environment, equal employment opportunity, philanthropy, and other issues. However, the segregation of these reports from mainstream reporting ultimately sends precisely the wrong message—separate and unequal.

That's not to say, for the sake of addressing key constituencies, that managers shouldn't publish documents specifically for target audiences the same way they produce products for target markets. But a model of reporting for an accountable company should first integrate, not fragment, the mosaic of critical measures that management uses to create value. The president's letter, management discussion and analysis, financial statements, and notes, along with other voluntary disclosures, should offer a holistic reporting that represents the performance of a business whose interests are integrated into the world around it.

We propose to add the following to the annual report:

- Management discussion and analysis: corporate and functional strategy; objectives; corporate-level financial, operational, and social measures; reporting on achievement of previous objectives; and forward-looking projections
- Financial information: standard financial statements supplemented by more thorough breakout of relevant data, such as current values in a real-estate development firm
- Notes: notes supplemented with more segment information and options and derivatives data

In outline, our recommendations will not change the annual report very much, but the report will contain a succinct presentation of data simply unheard of today.[29] In keeping with our view that a small set of numbers, publicly disclosed, is the basis of the accountable organization, the actual number of pages devoted to fuller accountability need not take up more than a half dozen additional pages in even a large company.[30] Managers will probably offer additional information, as they do today, in supplemental special-interest reports.

Much of the voluntary detail in many reports, thanks to the internet, need not be published on paper. The report should contain the key measures and related narrative to tell the corporate story. For detail, serious users can delve into a corporate library on-line. The published annual report should remain crisp, with the salient—and required—narrative and measures.

Many companies have taken the first step toward fully accountable reporting. They boldly disclose strategy, measures, and targets.

Often, they do this just as a new chief executive takes over. The vast majority, however, never follow up. Each year's annual report follows with a new theme, the thread of accounting for past promises left hanging. It is not surprising, then, that only one in five shareholders finds the documents "very useful."[31]

THE ROLE OF ACCOUNTANTS

Of course, to put all the pieces of the accountability cycle together, senior managers must engage the hearts and minds of the finance and accounting staff. These staff members must see their jobs as taking the high ground in improving measures and reports. Their job is to communicate, internally and externally, both the organization's financial position and its operational results. The measures they develop have to reflect both economic reality and operational reality, as well as how the company fits within society.

In the past, accountants have supplied mainly the most basic accounting figures for internal decision making. They have produced financial reports that meet no more than the minimum requirements. They must change their view of their jobs, however. Accountants should become uncomfortable with the problem described in Chapter 2: Conventional accounting, especially GAAP, measures primarily tangible assets, focuses inwardly on products, waits passively for action to precipitate accounting entries, and confirms the rigid hierarchy and stovepipe functional organization of the firm.

Accountants need to expand their goals. They must supply broadened accounting and performance measurement information for internal and external decision makers. They must produce reports that both meet the demands of the market and give decision makers an advantage over competitors. To meet these goals, they must join the movement to full accountability.

Accountants' skills have long resided in compilation, analysis, interpretation, and reporting of financial information required for management. These are critical skills that must not be lost, but accountants must now apply them across a broader range of performance measures and decision-support tasks. Information technology has rapidly reduced the time accounting and finance executives have to spend on traditional accounting transactions. These executives must now view their role as critical members of the senior management team. Among other duties, they now have to master a whole new field: communication. They have to ask themselves: What does it take to communicate the corporate story, through performance measurement, to a broad range of constituencies?

In many ways, accountants have fallen behind the times. For years, they have suffered from the "expectations gap"—the difference between what people expect of them and what they deliver. As part of a long debate circulating in courts, in a 1984 Supreme Court decision in *United States* v. *Arthur Young*, Chief Justice Warren Burger stated that accountants perform a "public watchdog" role "transcending any employment relationship with the client." In public reports, he added, "the independent public accountant performing this special function owes ultimate allegiance to the corporation's creditors and stockholders, as well as to the investing public."[32]

This is a broad prescription, instructing accountants to serve the commonweal. Many people don't subscribe to it. Nor has the judiciary come to broad agreement on just what the role of accountants is. For the sake of corporate accountants today, however, the ethical, philosophical, and legal issues are becoming moot. A broad view by accountants, and skills and practices that contribute to broad reporting for the accountable organization, has become a business imperative. The corporate manager of the twenty-first century must face not only decisions driven by internal facts and figures but also decisions driven by the world outside.

Of course, the accountants' role starts with providing information to spur good internal decision making. Many finance organizations have not even taken on this role, however. As Robert Kaplan says, there are two kinds of CFOs, those determined to stick to their knitting of conventional GAAP and those who view their role broadly as providing information for the business— based on activity-based costing, a balanced set of measures, shareholder value analysis, and so on. "In the longer run," he says, "the financial people that take the narrow view of themselves will be confined to a middle management role."[33]

Because many stakeholders do not trust management, executives have to press the accounting community to rethink its auditing role as well. Audited statements give users much more confidence than unaudited ones. Outsiders may not trust management, but they do largely trust auditors. They want auditors to verify both more items in the current annual report and more that other stakeholders would like to see in the annual report. Most companies fall short in disclosing even prosaic items that shareholders have long asked for—unasserted legal claims, current value accounting, and budgeted income statements.[34]

Some large auditing firms are positioning auditing more strategically. They are determining both the information needs of external users and the assurances these outsiders require from auditors. They are also recognizing that audits have to be completed with a more thorough understanding of company strategy and business operations. Some accounting firms believe audits could cover leadership skills, business strategy, customer satisfaction, cost of quality, corporate culture, environmental management, technology management, logistics, social performance, and a number of other areas.[35] PricewaterhouseCoopers has even developed reputation assurance. The firm helps companies institute a process for evaluating corporate social responsibility, provides external performance benchmarks, and provides outside verification of results.

Although some executives believe the expansion of audits is merely a way for accounting firms to attract new business, the audits can also help firms realize the benefits of accountable management. People widely accept that auditing of financial statements lowers the cost of capital. The auditing of a broad set of financial and nonfinancial data, by lowering investor uncertainty, could lower the cost even more. In any case, the auditing, and a release of elements of the audit to stakeholders, should become an integral part of the accountability cycle. Third-party attestation can markedly improve confidence in management.

In the end, executives would do well to remember that if they fail to take the initiative to seize the benefits of accountability, they will lose their chance. As SEC Chairman Arthur Levitt says, "Disclosure is the optimal tool for assuring fairness while fostering competition. Disclosure enables us to keep our hands off, but our eyes open."[36] Managers should take Levitt's words as an offer to solve the accountability crisis on their own. Neither the government nor the stakeholders need step in to fill the breach. The choice is up to management as to whether to lead the way or to follow.

The next three chapters show how managers can lead with entirely new measures—first, financial; then, operational; and, finally, social. With a mix of such measures, managers can access the full potential of the accountability cycle. They can then guide their people in building the capabilities of the fully accountable organization.

8

Financials
Revisited

The mark of the financially accountable organization has changed. Once upon a time, standard accounting measures like earnings per share were the gold standards of performance measurement. No longer. Traditional measures today, if used in isolation, raise a red flag. They signal to investors that managers may be reporting their performance reflexively—as slaves to tradition, rather than as leaders of a well-wrought financial and business strategy.

Every company has to follow GAAP accounting for mandated financial reporting, but none has to restrict itself to GAAP conventions in choosing measures to gauge and boost performance. Executives must choose yardsticks, traditional or new, that drive value at every point along the accountability cycle. The board of directors, employees, shareholders, and other stakeholders deserve and expect no less.

Monsanto shows just how much the right choice of financial measures can influence accountability. The company measures financial performance not just with traditional numbers. It bets its business on two other measures that gauge its contribution to long-term shareholder value: economic profit and cash flow return on investment. So convinced are Monsanto executives of the value of their system that, in 1997, they were willing to send two very risky signals to Wall Street.

At most firms, the two signals would have savaged stock prices. Chief Executive Robert Shapiro and then-CFO Robert Hoffman announced that they would cut the quarterly dividend of the St. Louis chemicals and drug giant from sixteen cents per share to three cents per share. They said further that earnings-per-share growth would slide from 20 percent annually to next to nothing— and would not pick up again for two to three *years.* [1]

Shapiro and Hoffman worried less than you might think. They told analysts that Monsanto was pouring cash from foregone dividends into blockbuster investments. In 1997 alone, the company would fund five promising compounds in costly late-stage clinical trials, including a breakthrough arthritis drug that came to market in 1999. The market for just the arthritis drug is gargantuan: Twenty million people in the United States suffer from the illness.

Of course, analysts are skeptical about promised payoffs from R&D, but Hoffman had run the numbers to create a convincing case for Monsanto's decision. Behind the scenes, he had two different profit-and-loss statements for 1997 through 1999. One met SEC rules for accounting profit; the other met new rules Monsanto had adopted for economic profit. The economic profit figures, adjusted by capitalizing heavy R&D expenses and major prelaunch drug expenses, showed that even while reported earnings growth might sag, economic profit would climb.

"The whole process that we implemented allowed us, with some peace of mind and conviction, to take the right approach in managing the company," Hoffman says.

The numbers showed that Monsanto's actions would contribute to shareholder value, so Shapiro and Hoffman went ahead with their plans despite the risk to the stock price. The proof that they were right: After the announcements, the price of Monsanto stock went *up,* and within a few months it climbed by roughly 25 percent. "This whole methodology," says Hoffman, "gives us a way for dealing with people that harp on things like earnings per share."

In the first half of this book, we recounted the stories of the many companies experimenting with different approaches to measuring performance. In this chapter, we begin to answer the obvious follow-on

Figure 8-1
The First Element of Performance Measurement: The Financials

question: Which approach works best to drive high performance throughout the accountability cycle?

We begin to answer this question with a look at financial measures. (See Figure 8-1.) In the next two chapters, we cover operational and social measures. In each chapter, we follow the same approach: We suggest the kinds of measures managers should consider. We then show the capabilities that these measures enable when applied throughout the accountability cycle. These capabilities give managers the leverage they need to deliver value far beyond what they have produced in the past, financially, operationally, and socially.

COUNTING THE FINANCIALS

When it comes to financial measurement, a lot of companies are hungrily eyeing shareholder value measures like economic profit. They envision managing like Monsanto, or reaping the astonishing gains of Coca-Cola, one of the earliest adopters of economic profit.

However, the answer to the question of which financial measures work best deserves a different answer for each company. No prescription works wonders for all, notwithstanding the appeal of economic profit.

GATX, the leasing giant in Chicago, argues that economic profit won't work for valuing a company with extremely long-term leases. Economic profit doesn't adequately take into account GATX's cyclical surges in investment or constant replenishment of assets like rail cars and aircraft.[2] On the other hand, Terry McClain, CFO of Valmont Industries argues that economic profit, without adjustment to NOPAT (net operating profit after taxes), creates all the right signals for his company (see Chapter 4). Valmont and GATX have created a model of how their particular businesses create value, and they have created measures accordingly.

The lesson is that executives have to choose measures that promote the specific behaviors and help with the specific financial objectives of their organization. There are always a number of measures that offer some merit. The important point is to make a conscious choice that balances the two factors discussed in the last chapter: completeness and controllability.

To make that choice, executives must first take a broad view. Which measures drive both strategy and local decision making? Which ones give leading and lagging indicators of financial performance? Which give a clear reporting of value inside and outside the company? Which measure the health of stakeholder relationships in financial terms? In keeping with conventional reporting, executives should include among the financial measures more than just dollars-and-cents numbers. Some measures that have made up the traditional financial report card, like credit rating, are appropriate as well.

After this brainstorming, executives should have come up with a matrix like that in Table 8-1, except it will probably run longer to accommodate the innovative ideas that come from brainstorming. They should then winnow the list to a handful of the most critical measures, those that drive financial excellence throughout the accountability cycle.

Executives should expect a list of financial measures to naturally focus on shareholder interests, the stakeholder most sensitive to financial performance. However, the financials should also take into

TABLE 8-1

SAMPLE FINANCIAL MEASURES, BY STAKEHOLDER

STAKEHOLDER	MEASURE
Shareholders	Earnings per share growth
	Cash flow per share
	Return on assets per segment
	Return on invested capital
	Economic profit
	Cash value added
	Growth in current value of assets
Customers	Earnings
	R&D spending
	Credit rating
Employees	Pension funding
	Salary levels
	Employee benefits
	Productivity (sales per employee)
	Salary as a percentage of earnings
Community	Taxes paid
	Total payroll
	Charitable and community
	contributions

account the performance delivered to other stakeholders involved in generating value. This does not necessarily mean coming up with entirely different measures for each stakeholder category. In practice, the measures appropriate for shareholders may also be appropriate for others because of stakeholders' intersecting interests.

GETTING THE POWER OF THE FINANCIALS

As managers create new financial measures, they must use them to deliver greater value at every point in the accountability cycle. Financial measures are among the most powerful of all measures. People simply watch dollars more carefully than other units of measure, especially if their pay depends on it.

To Improve Financial Decision Making

Executives' number-one job in driving financial accountability is to choose or devise the financial measures that provide appropriate decision-making information internally, at every step in the management planning and control process. They have to renounce complete reliance on measures that have led to value-destroying decisions in the past. They have to open their minds to fresh thinking.

In the 1960s and 1970s, many executives equated value with earnings growth. They often acquired companies as a way to grow earnings. They built a varied set of business units, if not conglomerates, but they often didn't build profitability. In the 1970s and 1980s, many other executives, often looking over their shoulders at corporate raiders, focused on returns (on equity, sales, and investment). They cut costs and boosted productivity, so much so that they sometimes stalled investment in profitable new growth.

Neither strategy consistently contributed to shareholder value. A study of 2,700 companies in twenty countries by McKinsey & Company reveals the dismal record: Only half of all companies in the 1985–1994 period created shareholder value (that is, yielded returns exceeding the weighted average cost of capital). Even in the United States, where raiders cast a shadow like nowhere else, only 55 percent of companies did so. Over twenty years, the record is even worse. Only ten of the largest fifty U.S. companies—including Coca-Cola, Merck, Pfizer, and General Electric—earned more than their cost of capital.[3]

Shareholders came away sorely disappointed. They expected managers to deliver returns commensurate with the risk of the investment, or their opportunity cost, the thirty-year Treasury rate plus (more or less) a three- to six-point risk premium. In half of all companies, however, investors never saw their capital so profitably handled, as McKinsey found. Many executives destroyed value year after year—shareholders would have done better investing their money elsewhere at the same risk.

It is little surprise that a survey of 241 firms from 1987 to 1993 revealed that chief executives of companies that earned below the median economic profit were more than twice as likely to leave the job as those at companies that earned above the median. More precisely, one out of five of the chief executives in the poorer performing firms was replaced, compared to one out of ten in the better performing firms.[4]

Most managers outside the executive suite didn't even know their companies were taking value-destroying actions—actions that stunted the growth of cash flows, discounted at the cost of capital, that ultimately enlarge a shareholder's investment. Financial managers may have harped on capital efficiency, but no financial performance measurement told managers that they hurt shareholders by bringing on-line excess factory capacity, building expensive inventory, or allowing overgenerous payment terms.

Investors, reading between the GAAP accounting lines, saw economic reality, however. They were assessing future cash flows, not earnings. In a study by Alfred Rappaport and LEK/Alcar Consulting Group of the 1995–1997 period, sixty-five Standard & Poor's 500 companies that reported falling earnings per share achieved total shareholder returns as high as 40 percent. Sixteen companies with growing earnings per share returned negative shareholder returns. During the same period, the Standard & Poor's 500 soared 31 percent per year. As Rappaport, former Northwestern University professor and pioneer of shareholder value measurement, says, "Cash is a fact, earnings an opinion."[5]

One company that learned that lesson the hard way was Briggs & Stratton, the $1.3 billion Milwaukee maker of small gasoline engines, mainly for lawnmowers. The company grew steadily through the 1980s. Revenues rose 24 percent between 1980 and 1989. But the stock price fared poorly, meandering around $15 per share during most of a decade when stock prices exploded.

Briggs suffered partly from fighting Japanese competition and partly from a weak yen, at 240 to the dollar. Kawasaki stole the company's John Deere contract. Suzuki made off with Toro business. Fuji made inroads at Snapper.[6] But Briggs suffered far more because it had become a poor steward of shareholder capital. During the 1980s, the company had tripled the capital invested in operations. Cash flow, however, had hardly budged.

In 1989, a drought plaguing the lawnmower-engine market knocked the company on its financial back: Briggs suffered a $20 million loss.[7] The red ink, the first in sixty years, galvanized executives into setting a new course. They consolidated the product line, revamped manufacturing practices, divided engine operations into five divisions, and called in Stern Stewart & Co. to help install the EVA performance measurement system. Through the 1980s, cash flow had remained stuck around $1.75 per share. By 1993, however, as the company finally pierced the barrier to economic profit, cash flow rocketed to more than $4 per share.

With the benefit of hindsight, executives could see that better financial measures would have sharpened their internal decision making early on. Briggs's EVA had plunged into negative territory in 1986 and stayed there in 1987 and 1988. The poor financial showing stemmed from slipping capital efficiency as Briggs persisted with 1960s-style inefficient manufacturing—typified by excess capacity, intensive vertical integration, and batch-manufacturing practices. Briggs had also earned disappointing returns on new investments in automation and expansion into a premium engine line. Meanwhile, retailers like Kmart and Wal-Mart pressured suppliers to cut prices.

Yet Briggs & Stratton executives didn't have the data to clarify the cause of the company's malaise. Their main internal yardstick for financial performance was earnings. They had no internal decision-making criterion to set off alarm bells as the company stood ankle deep in economic red ink. Executives, middle managers, and frontline supervisors did not have the measures to do the "right" thing. Up to 1989, says John Shiely, president and chief operating officer, "Nobody was really accountable for value creation below the level of president."

Guided by what Shiely calls the "capital discipline" of the EVA brand of economic profit, Briggs & Stratton managers began to make both strategic and day-to-day decisions with a new sense of accountability for shareholders' money. Under guidance of CEO Frederick Stratton, the company's fortunes reversed completely. The stock, mirroring the turnaround, finally shook itself out of the doldrums, climbing to over $50 per share in 1998 from around $15 in 1989.

Today, economic profit guides company decision making like a taskmaster. It forces all managers to reap more profit from shareholder capital and to find new ways to sow investments for economically profitable growth in the future. EVA has become a key criterion for internal decision making, from product introductions and supplier arrangements to capacity additions and capital structure.[8]

In 1997, Briggs sold its gray-iron foundry, its flywheel source, to a Milwaukee entrepreneur. The sale released capital for use elsewhere, while a long-term agreement guarantees a reliable supply.

In 1998, the company allied with Hero Motor of India to develop a new generation of four-cycle engines for scooters and mopeds. The venture allows global expansion under a regimen of capital thrift. In 1997, it conducted a Dutch-auction tender and open-market purchase program to buy back 3.6 million common shares. Combined with a $100 million debt offering, the auction cut the cost of capital, which in 1997 stood at 10.9 percent, the lowest in years. Through this discipline, Briggs has achieved one of the foundation goals of the business: fulfilling its obligation to return more than the cost of capital to shareholders.

Of course, financial measures can improve decision making by means other than just taking into account the cost of shareholder capital. Other factors excluded by conventional accounting include inflation, valuing many intangible assets, and accounting for externalities (costs created by the company but borne by outsiders). Executives who believe that these factors distort decision making should factor them into their measures—through inflation adjustments, intangibles accounting, and full-cost environmental accounting. If, for example, executives want to highlight the return on investments in such intangible assets as R&D, brands, and employee training, they should capitalize those costs and calculate the return on the investment in them.

Often, costs that appear to be externalities today actually become a part of corporate costs in the long run. Executives would be remiss—even if they have a single-minded financial focus—not to take appropriate externalities into account. If, for example, lawmakers eventually require companies to take back and recycle their products, managers would need to know how that will affect costs. Companies operating in Europe already must routinely take products back. It behooves executives elsewhere to track such trends and start calculating costs appropriate to informing decisions about such issues today.[9]

To Accelerate Feedback and Learning

A second critical role for executives is to use the chosen financial measures to power the feedback loop of the accountability cycle. In most firms, accrual accounting fogs up the feedback channel. Executives have a hard time getting a reading on whether the chosen strategic and tactical courses are returning the benefits expected.

Monsanto took an ingenious approach to sharpening the transmittal of insight through the feedback channel. CFO Hoffman actually sought a means to infer from the stock price what level of returns shareholders were demanding. He then sought measures to help Monsanto businesses make decisions that would meet or exceed those expectations. This proactive approach required several financial measures, including economic value added, cash-flow return on investment, and total business return.

To understand Hoffman's approach, consider the position of Monsanto when he took the CFO position in 1994. The company had been using ROE as its main measure of financial performance. ROE had performed superbly over a number of years to help the company cut costs and weed out less-profitable businesses. From 7.6 percent in 1991, ROE surged past former Chief Executive Richard Mahoney's 20 percent goal by 1994.[10] Despite better returns on equity, however, Monsanto's stock price had closed in 1994 only marginally higher than in 1991, $70½ versus $67⅞.

Hoffman thus began looking for a way to take the company to a new plateau of financial performance. As a yardstick, ROE didn't take into account a number of variables that influence shareholder value—investors' opportunity costs of capital, inflation, future investment requirements, and the residual value of investments. Nor could Monsanto correlate ROE gains closely with stock price. So, after a search by his finance team, Hoffman adopted new measures, which changed entirely the way executives looked at their businesses, giving them a way to differentiate between the value of businesses with varying amounts of capital, growth rates, and cash requirements. Knowledge of the interaction of these variables was critical to developing strategies to increase shareholder value.

That's when, along with economic profit, Monsanto began to use two new measures, called by the Boston Consulting Group internal total shareholder return, or internal TSR, and cash-flow return on investment, or CFROI. The internal TSR incorporates three components of financial performance: profitability, as measured by CFROI; growth, as measured by cash invested; and free cash flow, measured as the cash flow passing internally to or from the business unit.

CFROI measures the cash-on-cash return, cash flow compared to cash invested, adjusted for inflation and off-balance-sheet assets like operating leases. CFROI essentially tells managers the business's internal rate of return. Although most companies use internal-rate-of-return logic strictly for capital investment, companies like Boston Consulting Group and HOLT Value Associates have taught firms to also use it for measuring the performance of ongoing operations.

Monsanto figured the internal TSR for each of its businesses. By adding them together, it could forecast its theoretical *external* total shareholder return, the sum of actual capital gains plus dividends that shareholders can expect. This is where the most ingenious use of the measurement came in. Calling its version of internal TSR "total business return," or TBR, Monsanto calculated backward from the current stock price to infer the CFROI investors expect. Hoffman then asked managers to come up with the mix of actions that would yield the returns and growth to meet investor expectations.

Hoffman and his team found the CFROI number especially helpful because hundreds of institutional investors use CFROI to estimate future company financial performance. Thus, by using TBR first to gauge the returns shareholders were demanding, Monsanto aligned its measure of financial performance with that of many of the world's most sophisticated money managers. In effect, Monsanto set the targets necessary to obtain returns that would produce shareholder satisfaction.

One strategic decision guided by the new measures was the spin-off in 1997 of Solutia, Monsanto's former chemical business. Executives believed in the wisdom of spinning off Solutia, a maker of nylon fiber and other products like chemical intermediate acrylonitrile, precisely because the unit could not supply the CFROI growth to satisfy the shareholder appetite for gains incorporated in the stock price. "It was a counterintuitive move," says Hoffman—but the numbers showed it was the right thing to do.

What was so counterintuitive is that the chemical business was hardly a dog. Its ten units, with sales of $3 billion, were yielding an economic profit (earning a bit more than their cost of capital). They also pumped huge amounts of cash flow—$334 million in 1996—into the company. Few executives would normally eye positively the prospect of losing that cash flow, but, at Monsanto, the business couldn't contribute to the level of financial growth required by stock-price expectations. The TBR numbers gave the undeniable feedback: Solutia contributed about one-third of sales, but only one-tenth of market capitalization.

So Monsanto spun it off. To be sure, Monsanto executives could have justified the spin-off as part of a strategy to focus on life sciences businesses, like plant biotechnology, but the TBR calculation provided objective financial signals as well. "It has given us the courage to do it," says Hoffman.

The move was the best for both businesses, too, because each has such different product, market, and research needs. Moreover, because the chemical business was lower growth, Monsanto had diverted most of its cash to feed drug and biotech businesses. "We were starving the low-return business," admits Hoffman. "We were suboptimizing both of them [Monsanto and Solutia]."

Although Monsanto used TBR and CFROI as tools for sensing shareholder expectations, providing feedback for strategic changes, and translating its plans into future stock-price targets, it still used economic profit for focusing Monsanto line managers and employees on creating shareholder value—for day-to-day budgeting, reporting, and setting annual targets. Hoffman, like most financial executives, deemed CFROI as simply too complicated to motivate most managers. Because both measures are based on the principles of cash flow, Monsanto aligned cash-flow assumptions to get the same answer via both measures.

The lesson is that economic profit ensures capital accountability. It simplifies the financial measurement system to give most employees a focused, understandable figure to pay attention to. This, of course, is a key factor in making new measurements work, using a gauge in which actions that create positive economic profit generally create shareholder value. CFROI and economic profit work like two multitalented partners, one the astute analytic, the other the garrulous communicator. Although they can both run the show on their own, together they provide the extremely rich financial feedback a company needs across its divisions throughout the accountability cycle.

To Clarify and Communicate Strategy

While using new financial measures to inform internal decisions and improve feedback, managers must use them as well to cement in everyone's mind a clear, crisp financial objective. In too many companies, executives communicate only one fact clearly: the profit-and-loss numbers rule. Often, they communicate this fact by default, not by design. Because all managers have a budget to keep, they are expected to keep it well—regardless of provisions in the strategic plan and for meeting other corporate goals.

Executives must not lapse into communication by default. They should instead single out and tout the metrics on which their business strategy depends. The measures should ring true with the strategy, and long-term value creation, not just with objectives of short-term investors. Everyone in the organization can then harmonize with them, and commit to them, from the top of the company to the bottom, from the beginning of the accountability cycle to the end.

Note that the shareholder value measures sold by legions of consultants won't work to communicate the right financial message for every company. Again, it all depends on the strategy—and on the sophistication of managers. A young company with new products to establish in the market might choose revenue growth as its premier financial measure. A mature firm facing plenty of competition and shareholder demands for returns might choose return on capital (ROC), which communicates that what matters most is efficient use of fixed assets and control of working capital.[11] Whatever the measure, as Robert Kaplan and David Norton say, "The scorecard should tell the story of the strategy."[12]

Still, for many established companies today, shareholder value measures are one of the best ways of telling the story of financial strategy. They have the distinct advantage of merging into a single figure aspects of both growth and profitability. Among the hundreds of companies that have adopted economic profit, many find it communicates better than any previous measure the message that capital matters. With a little education, everyone from the mail clerk on up the chain of command can see that he or she can help boost share prices. All they have to do is get more out of company capital, whether it's tied up in equipment, bricks and mortar, work-in-process inventory, receivables, or long-term leases.

At Eastman Chemical, executives actually publish and post, quarterly, a placard that trains people's attention on economic profit. As a Baldrige National Quality Award winner, they put the measure in familiar terms, of course. At the top of the placard, they list two measures that gauge whether the company is exceeding customer expectations: a value index (Eastman compared to competitors) and customer loyalty (based on surveys). They next list measures that show whether the company is succeeding with its major improvement initiatives. The measures include sales and new capacity investment for global growth, percentage of new initiatives supporting business strategy on schedule, and percentage of cost reductions from 1995 average costs. At the bottom of the placard, they remind people of the company mission of creating "superior value in all we do," as measured by ROC minus the cost of capital (economic profit). They then publish the estimated payout from the economic-profit-linked bonus plan.[13]

The message to Eastman employees couldn't be clearer: They must preserve shareholder value before getting back the 5 percent of pay they all put at risk. They must do much better to get the maximum 30 percent payout.

Through such communication, the company has gotten its message to everyone. When the company decides how to spend cash—right down to a decision like patching potholes in the parking lot—employees wearing capital-steward hats raise their hands eagerly to second-guess management. In one incident, when the Kingsport sales office relandscaped, employees came out not just to smell the flowers. They went straight to the office of the president of the marketing organization to ask why he was taking money out of their bonus and putting it into landscaping.[14]

To Implement Corporate Strategy via Plans and Budgets

Managers must also use financial measures to drive strategic implementation, at each step in the accountability cycle. In effect, the financial measures (integrated with the operational and social) can wire together the planning, budgeting, reporting, and pay systems. These linked systems then send identical signals that reinforce the strategy, once again aligning all company efforts. Executives should not make the mistake of adopting only a measurement veneer. A glitzy facade spruces up the mission of the organization, but it often fails to gain substantive follow-through.

At Briggs & Stratton, executives have spent years integrating the EVA brand of economic profit into their operations. So much a part of the Briggs culture has economic profit become that executives announce the company's cost of capital quarterly. People in the hallways can recount the figure to a decimal place. EVA targets start right at the top and flow down into every plant.

When Briggs opened its Ravenna, Michigan, cast-iron foundry in 1995, General Manager Ed Bednar injected EVA into plant-floor vocabulary and training right from the start. To make clear how workers could affect the plant's EVA figure, he first identified the key drivers of economic profit, a step essential at all companies using economic profit as a guiding measure. Bednar found that three drivers contribute more than anything else to economically profitable results: molding efficiency, scrap rework, and attendance. He then measured work teams' performance in each, and he posted team performance monthly around the plant.[15]

Ravenna workers caught on quickly, especially because EVA triggered the payouts in their bonus system. They could earn up to 12 percent of their salary as bonus if they did well, 30 percent based on the three EVA drivers and 70 percent on resulting EVA performance. In one case, two melt workers noticed that liners on the induction furnaces were costing too much per ton of iron produced. By changing the geometry of the lining form and altering the linings' composition, they extended liner life by 25 percent. Shiely glories in such examples of workers taking ownership.

Briggs executives peg their own pay even more rigorously to economic profit. In a formula-driven calculation, they get paid their full annual bonus, in effect, only if they boost economic profit to the point where it exceeds half of the previous year's excess over target plus a required improvement of $4 million. This is a far cry from the negotiated targets at most companies. Likewise, they earn a profit on out-of-the-money stock-option awards only if they increase economic profit by at least the cost of capital for *five* years. Briggs's executives wanting to share in the ballyhooed payoff of stock options have to earn their economic spurs—and then some—each year.[16]

Briggs executives do not make the mistake so common elsewhere: running traditional planning, budgeting, reporting, and pay systems on autopilot. They have chosen not to operate with a control panel composed only of conventional figures from the profit-and-loss statement. Instead, they have integrated into the closed-loop accountability cycle the specific measures they have chosen to gauge strategic success. Once in the budget, once reported broadly to peers and the public, once linked to pay, these measures provide tremendous leverage to move the company to achieve the desired financial strategy.

The result of executives more actively managing measurements is they can avoid micromanagement of operations. The more precise the signals they fire into the circuits of the accountability cycle, the more they can retreat from the burden of command and control. At National Semiconductor, CFO Donald Macleod and his team evaluate company strategic plans and acquisitions with the same TSR and CFROI tools used by Monsanto. However, when the company was decentralized under the former chief executive, Macleod also used TSR to calculate the contribution of each of nine business units to the company's stock price. Every unit chief understood his or her contribution. That actually gave general managers the information needed to take steps to earn the cash-flow returns to meet the share of TSR in their plan—and, in turn, to help National deliver desired shareholder value for the entire company.[17]

To Demonstrate Performance and Inspire Loyalty

Few managers today use public reporting, a critical opportunity to practice accountable management, to its full benefit. They may deftly choose measures to get the most from the principles of accountability internally, but they fail to go on and use the measures to get the most from them externally.

Given the rigor of the report card required by the SEC, most executives today figure they already go overboard in demonstrating their company's financial performance. As we have seen, however, the required report card may not reveal the most compelling measures of company value. Instead, that reporting may flummox stakeholders' understanding of financial value. Companies that rely solely on traditional accounts risk driving away investors—and thus driving up the cost of capital. Investors are wary of the alternative truths produced by accounting discretions. After all, they know that GAAP reporting allows accountants to apply varying principles to everything from cash, receivables, securities, and inventories to plant, equipment, intangible assets, long-term liabilities, revenues, and cost of goods sold. Two identical companies, with identical results, can report opposite results, one growing income, the other shrinking.

Just how crazy reporting has become was demonstrated by Bear Stearns in 1997. The SEC had announced reporting requirements for comprehensive income, which must include adjustments for foreign-currency translation, minimum pension liabilities, and unrealized gains and losses on debt securities. Bear Stearns calculated, as just one example, that while General Electric reported income growth of 10 percent in 1994, 39 percent in 1995, and 11 percent in 1996, it would have reported comprehensive income growth of −33 percent in 1994, 162 percent in 1995, and −20 percent in 1996.[18] Investors could not be faulted for feeling, after looking at comprehensive income figures, that companies give them, at best, a quixotic measure of financial performance.

Many executives argue that, by applying accounting rules consistently, comparable year to year, they minimize confusion. They argue further that by delivering "quality" earnings—by adopting accelerated depreciation, last in, first out inventory accounting, an income pattern reflecting cash flows, and so on—they publish a reliable appraisal of their achievements. They are right that the perception of earnings quality may, in an investor's analysis, rival the importance of the earnings numbers themselves.[19] However, companies cannot credibly defend an aged accounting system as producing great information when they have means to give a much clearer picture of their financial health and prospects.

Other executives argue that efficient capital markets adjust to the fickle ways of financial reporting. After all, don't analysts adeptly crack the code of accounting discretions, translating all the confusion into clarity? Again, the logic is suspect. Analysts and sophisticated investors simply don't figure everything out. Recent research in Australian markets, where firms can revalue assets, shows share prices responding to revaluations.[20] In Denmark, where banks use mark-to-market accounting, stock prices track book values more closely than in those countries that don't report it, despite the volatility of reported asset values.[21] The evidence is that investors don't deduce value so efficiently after all—until the company gives them more information.

Of course, different accounting principles don't fool investors and analysts *that* much, but the question is, Why would a company risk hurting shareholder value with an accounting that gives investors a headache? Recent research shows that poor disclosure can increase the cost of capital.[22] Recognizing this, Cambrex Corporation (see Chapter 6) aimed to improve investor following by releasing additional data on environmental liabilities. International Paper (see Chapter 6) aimed to facilitate a stock issue by adopting postretirement benefit accounting rules early. As Stanford's Mary Barth points out, "If you impose information risk on investors, they're going to charge you for it."[23]

Investors feel that risk keenly. Recall from Chapter 2 that investors widely pan the contents of annual reports. They particularly struggle with some of the most relevant financial sections. One-third of them have trouble understanding the cash-flow statement.[24] Analysts don't give annual reports glowing evaluations either. One-third of them have trouble understanding footnotes. Ninety-three percent want more information on product-line profitability, and 85 percent want more information on key risks, financial liquidity, and competitive strategy.[25]

The first task of executives should be to comply with the existing standards—use the mandated reporting framework to more fully explain their performance—but if they want to win loyal stakeholders through financial accountability, they have to go much further. They need not necessarily publish a lot more information, which CFOs endlessly complain about. But they need to voluntarily disclose the few key metrics and explanatory detail that show if the company is working to create value.

David Johnson certainly set an example of the accountable approach when he took over as chief executive of Campbell Soup in 1990. Declaring shareholders as first among stakeholders, he backed up his commitment with a three-prong financial target: 20 percent earnings growth, 20 percent ROE, and 20 percent cash return on assets (CROA). (CROA, like CFROI, is a cash-on-cash measure.) He then published results of this triad each year, setting a standard for financial accountability. By 1993, he had exceeded all three goals—and then gradually raised them.[26]

Demanding accountability through measures was a pillar of Johnson's management. Inside the company, he kept a scoreboard of Campbell's performance compared to that of peers in the food industry. He took advantage of the commitment to high performance that the scoreboard engendered, particularly when shared publicly. Unlike many company chiefs, who boldly and publicly name targets in their first year and then forget about them, Johnson followed up every year. He provided a model of using the lever of accountability, internally and externally, to lift performance to levels the company had never experienced. "Numbers tell it all," he often said.[27] And he told all, with the numbers outsiders care about most.

Briggs & Stratton executives follow a similar approach to using EVA at every point along the accountability cycle. Briggs publishes a page in its annual report devoted to performance measurement. Good or bad, the company details cash flow, capital employed, economic return on capital, and cost of capital. In 1997, readers could see that Briggs's cost of capital was 10.9 percent, its return a superior 11.7 percent. The return, though down from 17.6 percent in 1995, still showed Briggs building shareholder value. Though just one page, the performance report is the most telling disclosure of Briggs's financial performance. As Shiely says, "In many ways, it's the only valuable piece of information in the annual report."[28]

Shiely maintains that publishing the figure serves several purposes. It holds management's feet to the fire to deliver shareholder value. It shows employees management's commitment to capital discipline and shareholder value. It demonstrates to lead-steer investors Briggs & Stratton's commitment to pushing up the stock price. "We publicly commit ourselves to capital discipline and shareholder value," says Shiely." That kind of commitment we believe is appropriate in the annual report."

The publication of new financial measures is a capstone. It comes after managers have engaged the power of financial measures at every other step of the accountability cycle. More executives should make this their goal. When they achieve it, they will have squeezed a level of advantage from accountability that they had never thought possible. What will remain for them is only to expand their measurement embrace further, to operational and social measures, as we discuss in the next two chapters.

FINANCIAL REPORTING OR ELSE

Some executives may hesitate to voluntarily report more financial figures. They may not believe in the benefits of fuller financial accountability. But they will not escape the ongoing pressure for greater disclosure. Analysis of disclosure trends, which we first touched on in Chapter 2, show that most recently promulgated standards require companies to describe and measure more unrecognized items and to give information for comparing results year to year, and between companies.[29] The SEC's order in late 1997 that companies disclose likely costs for year-2000 computer adjustments is just one example of the detail that regulators want to see reported.[30]

As SEC commissioners continually thump the podium about disclosure, and as the agency continues to send filings back for amendments, executives can be sure that regulators remain unsatisfied. SEC Commissioner Levitt made that clear in two hard-hitting speeches delivered in late 1998 (see Chapter 2). Although Levitt was addressing details of traditional accounting, he could just as well have harked back to 1989, when the SEC issued a Financial Reporting Release that called for better reporting in the Management Discussion & Analysis section on trends, uncertainties, and other forward-looking information. The fact is, many companies still don't offer the kind of forward-looking information that complies with the SEC release.

The hesitancy of some companies to disclose more forward-looking information has not stemmed from a lack of ongoing concern by the SEC. The agency made explicit in the early 1990s the kind of reporting that falls short of requirements. Caterpillar, the SEC charged, had not reported in its 1989 annual report that a quarter of its $497 million profit came from Brazil, where the company expected political changes to hammer earnings in 1990. Although executives had told the board about the upcoming earnings hit in February 1990, they hadn't told the shareholders—even in the first-quarter 1990 report. The SEC finally settled an enforcement action with Caterpillar in 1992.[31]

The Caterpillar case punctuated the drumbeat of new standards flowing from a regulatory machine bent on fuller accountability. The current project at the Financial Accounting Standards Board to follow up the 1994 Jenkins report (discussed in Chapters 2 and 7) is undoubtedly a sign of agency climate. Among other things, the report urged companies to disclose far-reaching information on segment profitability, derivatives, off-balance-sheet liabilities, and fair values.[32] Executives can expect more regulatory requirements to come down the pipeline soon.

Executives intent on competing through accountability should take the FASB's activities as a harbinger of competitive reporting in the future. They could fight the maneuverings as more red tape, but they might do far better to look beyond the current fracas to how accountability can help them compete more vigorously in capital markets.

The reality is that investors simply want more information— almost nine out of ten, according to surveys, want the Management Discussion & Analysis section expanded to include more forward-looking information, like budgeted income statements.[33] Because investors are now looking at investing their money globally, executives can gain from using the Management Discussion & Analysis section to show their accountability to gain credibility.[34] That regulators force the issue at every turn is a sign of business followership; businesses should take the leadership instead, connecting external disclosure more closely to internal management and control systems.

As a signal that even public pension-fund investors care about new financial measures that demonstrate value creation, Calpers added a new feature to its yearly hit list of poorly performing companies: a calculation of economic value added.[35] In a sign that small investors will wise up, too, the *Wall Street Journal* began in 1996 to publish an annual shareholder scoreboard that grades companies from A through E on total shareholder return. As the *Journal* said in launching the scoreboard in 1996, most rankings of companies are flawed: "They omit the answer to the basic question: How well did the corporation reward the people who furnished the money to nourish it?"[36]

In recent years, researchers have begun to produce evidence to show what they had once only theorized: that voluntary disclosure of the information financial analysts care about can boost value. One study at the Harvard Business School looked at how the market reacts to firms that increase their disclosure. The researchers gauged disclosure according to ratings by the Association of Investment Management Research, which assigns higher grades for more segment disclosures, more discussion of operations and financial performance, more candid discussion of company prospects, and so on. The results showed that better disclosure—even when controlled for earnings increases—is accompanied by better stock performance, more institutional ownership, more analyst following, and greater liquidity.[37]

"There's no evidence that you're going to get hurt" by reporting more, says Krishna Palepu, one of the 1998 report's authors. The lesson is that managers should stop fretting over the drawbacks of disclosure and, instead, worry about the drawbacks of *not* disclosing." Disclosure is a fundamental tool," he says, "one way to distinguish yourself."[38]

In practice, many managers routinely show they believe in this concept. Studies of voluntary reporting at 1,880 companies in the 1980s showed that during periods when firms tap equity markets, they more often issue earnings forecasts.[39] Executives should adopt this posture continuously, currying favor in capital markets by choosing measures and reporting results that communicate the nature and success of their model of value creation. Such an approach can reduce uncertainty in the markets and provide executives with a fairer price for the company's shares. It can also provide owners of those shares, along with other stakeholders, the information they want to monitor and analyze corporate performance. In short, forthright reporting should not come as a temporary campaign for capital but as a permanent fixture of best-practice management.

As Shiely says, "Whatever it is that you are doing to drive value, you owe it to the organization to institutionalize that formula." That means incorporating the most appropriate financial measures into every step of the accountability cycle across the organization. In the final step, as executives develop consistent, credible reporting, they will realize that they have built a new gold standard for financial accountability.

9

Beyond
Financials

T he classic business cartoon: A chief executive stands before the board of directors, pointer in hand, jabbing at a flip chart. A single profit line, graphed in bold, plunges downward (or rockets upward, or snakes sideways). With the right punch line, this cartoon makes us laugh. Too bad the single line has become obsolete.

Not for cartoons, of course, just for running a real business. Financial measures of performance, alone, won't create full accountability. They are too unreliable as either a clear gauge of success or a clear sign of the future. To drive success at every step of the accountability cycle, managers must supplement financial measures with nonfinancial measures.

The first supplement is operational measures. (See Figure 9-1.) By operational, we mean mainly nonfinancial, including measures of quality, speed, learning, innovation, and stakeholder satisfaction (although some operational measures look decidedly financial, like productivity). The second supplement, which we leave to the next chapter, is social measures. To deliver top-tier performance over the long term, managers must integrate both the operationals and socials into the accountability cycle.

This may seem pretty far out, but one business is already supplementing that classic cartoon line. Not figuratively. Literally. In a pilot

Figure 9-1
The Second Element of Performance Measurement: The
Operationals

in 1997, American Skandia Life Assurance created five business trend lines. The five, each in a different color, give President Gordon Boronow a multipart index to trace the strengthening or deterioration of his business in five categories: financial, customer relationships, business processes, employee capabilities, and "renewal and development" activities like training and product development.[1]

Given terrific market conditions, no crisis forced Boronow to embrace the new lines. In 1989, when Sweden's Skandia Group launched his unit, the total U.S. variable annuity market, the unit's core segment, amounted to a modest $8 billion in assets. By 1997, it had soared past $80 billion. So, says Boronow: "We've been focusing primarily on keeping up with this burgeoning business . . . we've got this tiger by the tail."

With all the good fortune, you would think that Boronow would mostly concern himself with counting the money and hiring new people. After all, American Skandia has grown from thirty-five employees when Boronow started to more than 650. Assets have spurted to $13 billion. However, the soft-spoken, unassuming president is looking to the future. That's why, in 1997, inspired by Intellectual Capital Director Leif Edvinsson, he sat down with Jan Hoffmeister, his vice president of Intellectual Capital Management, to weight each measure in the unit's Navigator, or balanced set of measures. (See Chapter 4.) With the weightings, he pioneered and created an index for each of the five categories, which Skandia has trademarked as the IC-Index. And with the annual index, he graphed a trend for each over a three-year period.

Today Boronow counts not just the money but the leading indicators that help American Skandia build behind-the-scenes capabilities to grab competitors' business. He regularly tracks, at the company level, such data as new contract processing time and share of gross premiums written from new launches.[2] On a more detailed level, he tracks attitudes and knowledge of customer-service representatives. Such measures make the Shelton, Connecticut-based unit, like many Skandia units around the world, an unusually accountable organization.[3] They also help explain the units' rise from being an unknown to capturing seventh place in U.S. market share in less than ten years.

Other companies hoping to develop a similar level of accountability must similarly develop a host of operational measures. They should rethink these measures in the same fashion as the financial ones, and they should then use these measures across the accountability cycle to drive high performance.

COUNTING THE OPERATIONALS

To create operational measures, managers should brainstorm a list in the same way as for financial measures. The list they end up with would look like that in table 9-1, except it would run much longer to reflect the immense number of operational issues a company faces.

As with financial measures, operational measures often relate to two or more stakeholder groups. After all, the measures that demonstrate long-term value to one stakeholder often demonstrate value to one or several others as well. (Shareholders hate high employee turnover almost as much as employees do.) The point, again, is not to correctly allocate measures to different groups but to sur-

TABLE 9-1

SAMPLE OPERATIONAL MEASURES, BY STAKEHOLDER

STAKEHOLDER	MEASURE
Shareholders	Productivity
	Cost reductions
	Defect level (or scrap rate)
	Cycle time
	Customer retention
	Employee turnover
	Percentage of new product sales
	Process errors
Customers	Repair incidence
	Product quality index
	On-time shipping
	Customer satisfaction
	Customer retention
	Customer loyalty
	New product inventions
	Share of wallet
	Market share
Employees	Occupational Safety and Health Administration recordables
	Employee satisfaction
	Absenteeism
	Employee turnover
	Empowerment index
	Grievances
	Training time per year
	Competence levels
	Salary levels
	Benefit levels
	Family-support services
	Percentage of flexible schedules
Community	Safety record
	Salary levels
	Community satisfaction
	Legal actions

face all the important measures of creating value through multiple stakeholder relationships.

Unlike the financials in the last chapter, most operational measures are leading indicators. When they improve, an improvement in the financials follows, albeit often indirectly, and with a time lag.

Pitney Bowes Mailing Systems, for example, found that customer satisfaction as measured by the rate of one-call resolution of complaints about bills was a leading indicator. By improving that rate, and invoice accuracy (invoice dollars and customer address data), Pitney Bowes customers paid faster. Faster payment cut days sales outstanding and thus working capital. Not long after Pitney Bowes started using the measure, it cut three days from days sales outstanding, saving itself more than $12 million in accounts receivable.[4]

Note also that the measures mix internal performance indicators (cycle time, competence levels, lost workdays) and external ones (customer satisfaction). They also combine input measures (R&D spending), process measures (process errors), and output measures (productivity). Taken together, the family of measures gets at all the critical success factors at running the company backstage, and at the factors that prepare the company—via strategy, people, systems, processes, and so on—to mount a winning performance weeks, months, or years in the future.

There is no end to the number of measures a company can include in a matrix of this sort. A team of Pitney Bowes people originally cataloged over 550 possible control, operational, and strategic measures in 1993. The team used a Pareto (priority-ranking) analysis to winnow the list to fifty-five. The company has since cut the number to a handful. Managers in other companies must pare the final list of corporate-level measures similarly, to not more than a dozen or two, but not before brainstorming broadly to capture the most critical measures of performance and strategic execution.

The output of this brainstorming is not the only reason for engaging in it. The process itself forces managers to raise issues too often left undiscussed. To come up with measures, managers must articulate their notion of how the firm creates value. They must also think about all the impacts of the company's products, services, and activities. Even though they will choose not to measure every source of value and every cause of impact, raising the issues can expand everyone's view of how the enterprise works. That expanded view can only help over the long term to improve the quality of decision making.

Managers should tailor their approach to equip the organization with what quality guru Joseph Juran would have called "the vital few" measures for executing strategy and boosting performance. That is, after all the brainstorming, managers have to settle on the measures that, as a group, provide the critical information for running the organization. The stakeholder approach widens the field of view at the brainstorming level to include all issues that help the company become a fully—internally and externally—accountable organization.

Managers should not view any template, however, as a straightjacket. Skandia's Navigator, for example, has five parts, but only three address stakeholders directly (shareholders, customers, and employees). The remaining two categories are called process and renewal and development. Leif Edvinsson, who frequently stresses the latter, says, "Those organizations that don't focus on renewal and development don't create shareholder value over time."[5] Edvinsson is the near-legendary father of the Skandia effort.

GETTING THEIR POWER

Once managers have devised operational measures, they must leverage them along with the financials at every point in the accountability cycle. They will find that, for many people in the organization, the operational measures are the most powerful. Usually nonfinancial, the operationals are articulated in the language of middle management and the frontlines. They relate much more directly to people's jobs and daily decisions than do financial measures.

To Improve Operational Decision Making

As with financials, managers must first choose operational measures that will help improve decision making. They will find that the measures add tremendous insight to people's thinking at each step of the accountability cycle, from strategy and planning to reporting and pay.

Financial facts remain critical, of course, but they are insufficient. Dollars-and-cents results rarely alert managers early of strategic success or failure. Recall from Chapter 2 how Analog Devices had trouble boosting quality. When it came to investigating the problem of late shipments, managers found employees focusing on margins and profits. Managers solved the problem only by getting people to focus on new indicators like on-time delivery.

Dow Chemical demanded another kind of measure to inform decision making. In Dow's markets, value often comes from product or process patents. As part of a strategy to create "value growth," or growth in innovation, Dow managers sought a better way to measure these intellectual assets. Today, at the corporate level, the company tracks patent utilization. Gordon Petrash, formerly global director, Intellectual Asset & Capital Management, says that the utilization rate helps foretell managers' ability to generate patent-protected value that competitors cannot readily duplicate.[6]

Dow began its effort in 1994. It first purged its portfolio of 29,000 patents, getting rid of the ones with little or no value. That gave it, in 1998, a 16,000-patent portfolio to leverage. Its utilization rate in early 1998 was 42 percent (up from the 20 percent of the 1994 unpurged portfolio). As Dow collects data over the next few years, executives will get hints, from the patent-utilization rate, as to how well company engineers are building value for the years ahead. If the engineers are not building value through patents, the value may not be sustainable.

Dow is "trying to predict the future," says Petrash, one of the pioneers along with Skandia's Edvinsson in valuing and managing intellectual capital. "Rather than . . . guesswork, [Dow is] trying to add some quantification."

Dow's top-level measure of patent utilization complements a number of initiatives lower in the organization. For example, Dow analyzed how owning patents in each of its five product-development phases, from concept to market introduction, can influence future value. Patents in some stages either ultimately save or generate more money than patents in others. So Dow measures patents applied for and received in each stage. A patent covering an entirely new process has more value than one on the details of implementation. Dow eventually will use its research to model the chances of success of individual R&D projects at different stages.

To make sure managers incorporate the new measurement information into the business, the company named "intellectual asset" teams in each business unit. These teams, staffed by plant superintendents, patent attorneys, R&D directors, and product managers, make sure units leverage their intellectual assets, which include patents, trade secrets, copyrights, and critical know-how. They also make sure the units pinpoint gaps in their knowledge so they can develop intellectual assets to fulfill their business strategies. Guiding the teams are measures like those in Table 9-2.

TABLE 9-2

Dow Chemical Company Intellectual Asset Measures

Value Targets (Results Measures)

- NPV of value growth and value preservation attributable to intellectual assets
- Percentage of current sales protected by intellectual assets
- Percentage of patents "business will use" not aligned with technology plans
- Percentage of "new" business initiatives protected by intellectual assets
- Percentage of business-relevant competitive intellectual assets that requires specific response
- Value contributed to the business by significant or extraordinary intellectual asset-management actions

Measurement Indicators

- Projected costs until patent expiration
- Percentage of annual intellectual asset management costs of R&D budget
- Ratio of NPV apportioned to intellectual assets to net present cost of R&D per period
- Percentage of competitive samples analyzed that initiate business actions by purpose (e.g., enforcement, benchmarking, product development)
- Percentage of patents business is using
- Percentage of patents business will use that are more than five years since priority filing
- Qualitative value classification as a percentage of projected costs (e.g., what percentage of portfolio costs are for defensive cases? potential license cases? key cases?)
- Classifications completed (of patents, trade secrets, know-how)

Source: Author interview with Gordon Petrash, January 1998; and Wendi R. Bukowitz and Gordon P. Petrash, "Visualizing, Measuring and Managing Knowledge," *Research & Technology Management* 40, no. 4 (July/August 1997): 30.

"Am I creating value?" is the question managers constantly try to answer, says Petrash, now a partner with PricewaterhouseCoopers. This is the basic question that all employees at all companies ought to be asking. Too few managers ask that question or sensitize employees to the importance of the answer. At Dow, the information to ponder that question was unavailable in the past. Now the company gathers a host of information, which gives managers fresh insight on where to target new research efforts. That helps Dow provide a foundation for fulfilling its value-growth strategy for years to come. Other companies must similarly choose measures that give them the foundation to create value.

As managers leverage measures for decision making internally, they may fail to take the next step. They may stop short of enriching the entire accountability cycle with more decision-making performance data; that is, they may not supply operational data to the stakeholders to make *their* decisions. At first blush, releasing information to help outsiders make decisions might strike managers as irresponsible. Yet such release, in addition to fulfilling stakeholders' right to know a circumscribed set of data, can benefit a company.

Most companies have actually crossed this conceptual bridge already, at least at the middle management level. Companies that benchmark each others' practices, or form tight supply-chain links, often share the most sensitive kinds of data. In some cases, the boundary between a company and its suppliers, alliance partners, and customers has blurred into oblivion. Employees from each company share offices, desks, computer systems—everything but the logo on their paycheck. To work together so closely, they must share everything from shipping data to new-product development plans and progress.

Dow Chemical's polyolefin business, a leader even at Dow in measuring its intellectual assets, parlayed its self-knowledge into a joint venture with DuPont. Dow had invented a new catalyst technology for elastomers, plastics with rubbery characteristics, bouncy, heat resistant, oil resistant, and so on. The polyolefin business's process for codifying and "visualizing" intellectual assets provided part of the basis for putting together a new alliance called DuPont Dow Elastomers.

Though few companies now disclose corporate-level operational measures, many have accepted the competitive necessity of at least some sharing. Sometimes they have no choice, as when a big company like Wal-Mart requires an audit of supplier fitness. They must move further and recognize the advantages of giving third parties a freer look at their operations. At the least, the data make companies' value clear to joint-venture and other potential partners.

To Clarify and Communicate Strategy

One of the most powerful ways for managers to use operational measures is to clarify and communicate strategy. For too long, executives articulated strategy with bulleted phrases—if they articulated it at all. The bullets were often too vague, however. They didn't elicit accountability for the chosen strategy.

As the earlier stories of CIGNA Property & Casualty revealed, stating a strategy and delivering on it are two different things. Not until President Gerry Isom attached quantitative measures to the "specialist" strategy did managers comprehend what it meant. They got the message quickly when one of their performance measurements became percentage of premiums from new segments. They also got it when Isom began measuring the quality of Property & Casualty relationships with brokers in segments the company targeted for growth.

At American Skandia, employees similarly got a clear message from their performance measures on how to execute strategy. American Skandia has built its business by cultivating deep relationships with the 800 firms and 16,000 financial advisors that sell its annuities, mutual funds, and other products. President Boronow has long kept track, via the five-part Navigator, of the number of brokers with whom the company works—a rough measure of the stable of relationships that underwrite the firm's future success. (See Table 9-3.) The Navigator has served the business well during rapid growth.

To lay the groundwork for the future, Boronow refined the measures to further his relationship strategy.[7] In 1996, he broke the customer-service staff into teams. He focused each customer-service team on one region. He also focused each team on one of three channels: securities houses, bank broker dealers, or financial planners. Each team got its own Navigator, and each Navigator measures four levels of relationships: new brokers, regular brokers, top producers, and superstars. The company rates each broker relationship

TABLE 9-3

AMERICAN SKANDIA NAVIGATOR

FOCUS	MEASUREMENT
Financial	Return on capital employed (%) Operating result (net income) Value added per employee
Customer	Number of contracts Savings per contract Surrender ratio (%) Points of sale (brokers, etc.)
Human	Number of employees, full-time Number of managers (total) Number of managers (women) Training expense per employee
Process	Number of contracts per employee Administrative expenses per gross premiums written Information technology expense per administrative expense (%)
Renewal and development	Share of gross premiums written from new launches (%) Increase in net premiums written (%) Development expense per administrative expense (%) Share of staff under forty years old (%)

Source: *Skandia Group, "Human Capital in Transformation: Intellectual Capital Prototype Report"* (Stockholm: Skandia Group, 1998), 20.

on a scale of one to eight and tallies the number of relationships in each category for each quarter.

With the measures, Boronow explicitly encourages his people to build stronger relationships. In one quarter, for example, he could see that the average customer-focus team had 382 new brokers, 358 regular ones, 90 top producers, and 11 superstars.[8] With such numbers, he and everyone else had a running tab on a fundamental indicator of future value—relationship quality. Boronow uses the measure to keep people aware of their responsibility to push relationships to the superstar level at the top of the pyramid.

"What we try to do is get to a number that people can see," says Boronow. "The power of it is that it becomes a way to keep everyone informed and focused." Along with other measures like contract-accuracy rates, people at American Skandia know precisely where to spend their time and energy to execute the organization's strategy.

Operational measures especially help organizations in the throes of change. The stories of Tenneco and CIGNA are two good examples. As Harvard's Robert Simons notes, measures are a powerful tool to *instigate* change. They can help executives overcome organizational inertia and gain allegiance to a new agenda. They can also generate uneasiness with current performance and teach an agenda for strategic renewal.[9] In other words, executives can use them as a tool for prying individual and collective behavior out of one mold and reshaping it to fit a new strategy.

"It's a different way of running a company," says CIGNA Property & Casualty President Gerry Isom. "This creates a precise vehicle for getting critical success factors on the table."[10]

To Revitalize Planning, Budgeting, and Resource Allocation

Accountable managers must also use the operational measures, along with the management planning and control system, to execute strategy. The measures not only clarify plans, they also provide precise guidance on how to budget money, move people around, and spend capital.

When Dana Mead came to Tenneco in 1992, he found that goals at the top often translated poorly to budgets just one level down, the business-unit level. At one point, one of his unit chiefs reviewed a strategy with him to expand globally. A month later, the same executive submitted a capital plan without any money for the expansion. "The money wasn't going where ostensibly the strategy was," remembers Mead.[11]

Today, Tenneco aligns business objectives top to bottom. Managers at each level bat measures back and forth to make sure everyone becomes an owner of the scorecard that will guide their work. The measures become the management code that directs the planning and control systems. Richard Wambold, the executive who headed the team to come up with new measures, remembers that Tenneco made the classic mistake with strategic planning: The process ended when, once a year, executives put a book on their shelves. There was often "zero relationship" between the budget and the plan, he says. Managers had objectives but no measures related to them, and, if managers did have measures, they didn't necessarily link to anyone else's measures above or below in the hierarchy.

With the new approach, Wambold, now executive vice president of the specialty and consumer packaging business, says that he's managing one of his biggest development projects, entering a new packaging business, with hardly any financial measures at all to put the plan in place. "It's more like taking an engineering approach to running a business," he says. Measures mostly relate to marketing, human resources, capital spending, and so on.[12]

To Accelerate Feedback and Learning

Executives must also use measures to investigate their successes and failures. Unlike financial measures, operational ones provide far more insight into the source of performance gaps, or jumps. This information gives clues as to how to refine strategy or improve strategic execution. The faster a company can learn from mistakes or successes, the more competitive it can be.

With operational measurement data, managers can trace problems to their roots. They can essentially follow the same root-cause analysis used in total quality management, familiar to all managers today. They also can push the fact-based problem-solving technique beyond the plant floor, where many companies have corralled it, and bring it to middle and executive management levels.

Top managers have often persisted in the belief that, if only they could more finely dissect the financial numbers, they could gain insight into most operational problems. However, the wellspring of feedback, and the source of a tremendous amount of learning, is not the financial ledger at all, but a nonfinancial one. It provides fodder not just for continuous improvement but for breakthrough thinking. The measures offer the basis for rapid organizational learning, as advocated by many authors today, as the means to create new capabilities and knowledge that competitors have trouble matching.[13]

In the health-care industry, executives have leaned heavily on measures of quality and access to deliver both tactical and strategic performance. At PhyCor, the $1.1 billion Nashville-based managed-care company, executives have developed a number of strategic priorities. One of the priorities calls for delivering better care through "economies of intellect," essentially a system of picking the brains of physicians to establish best practices in health-care administration and delivery. Unlike other health-care firms, PhyCor aims not to "manage" the care of its 28,000 affiliated physicians; it aims to have the physicians do the managing. "Instead of doing it from an enforcement aspect," says Ronald Loeppke, vice president and chief medical officer, "[we] do that from an empowerment aspect."[14]

Although many managed-care organizations ask doctors to call "1-800-MAY-I?" as Loeppke says, PhyCor helps empower the doctors with the tools and systems to make the decisions themselves, keeping physicians at the center of the health-care system. Note how this philosophy differs little from that at firms dependent on professional and knowledge workers. The people doing the work provide and act on feedback. "We . . . have that accountability locally," says Loeppke, "and should have it locally."

In one effort, PhyCor, which serves over 2.5 million managed-care patients, created five Care Management Councils, comprising doctors from around the PhyCor system. The councils study conditions in five categories: diabetes, asthma, lower-back pain, cardiovascular, and oncology. They review data on patient outcomes (how well people recover) and then adjust care guidelines to treat people more effectively. The frontline "knowledge workers" feed back the data to execute corporate strategy.

The physicians in its diabetes council, reviewing twenty variables, found two striking features. First, up to 50 percent of patients tested positive for susceptibility to depression—three to four times the 10 to 12 percent of people who suffer from depression in the population at large. Second, the health of diabetics suffering from depression was worse than for those who did not—in how well they tolerated pain, functioned physically, interacted socially, and so on.

With the data, the PhyCor Diabetes Care Management Council revised its diabetes treatment guidelines to include the screening, diagnosis and treatment of depression. Given that more than 70 percent of depression cases can be effectively treated, PhyCor hopes physicians will see a positive impact on patient self-efficacy in managing diabetes. In one of the diabetic treatment centers of excellence, hemoglobin A1C for the diabetics fell from 10.9 in mid 1996 to 6.6 in early 1997. (This is a big improvement; the A1C is a measure of diabetics' long-term control of their blood-sugar levels.) The comprehensive diabetes care management program focused on patient education and empowerment, and resulted in a $500,000 savings during that year.

Interestingly, PhyCor found the same sort of link with depression in asthmatic patients. Through implementation of focused asthma care-management initiatives, one PhyCor clinic cut days asthmatics spent in the hospital by 77 percent, and it cut emergency-room visits by 58 percent. The data confirmed the strength of PhyCor's strategy of leveraging economies of intellect at the physician frontlines to deliver higher-quality care.[15] It also shows how the detailed operational measures must cascade down through the organization to deliver the top-level strategy.

Measures deployed throughout the accountability cycle also enable a firm to tap a reservoir of improvement ideas outside the company. While most managers worry about losing valuable secrets and know-how through external reporting—loose lips sink ships, as they say—such concerns beg the question: Where will the twenty-first-century company's biggest information advantage come from? Will it come from the inside? Or from the outside? If from outside, management practices that hamper feedback from outside stakeholders hurt a company competitively. To turn the aphorism on its head, zipped lips can sink ships.

Ideas "not invented here" often work better than the brainchildren of a company's best people. That's the point of benchmarking. Today, some companies—like Analog Devices, Intel, Texas Instruments, and Motorola—even share best practices within their industry on management practices. The time has come to extend the openness of benchmarking to the collection of measures that executives use to run the company. We are not talking about family jewels like trade secrets. We're talking about key measures that management uses to execute strategy and stimulate high performance.

Once again, this is the information that allows stakeholders to see the company through the eyes of management. With that new view, stakeholders can provide much more perceptive feedback, and management must encourage that feedback, which amounts to the electricity that surges through the accountability cycle, driving the wheel of value creation. Shareholders don't buy into the argument that the company acts in their interest by keeping so much information hidden. In surveys, half of all shareholders say they want more disclosure of all kinds of data, including more information in the Management Discussion & Analysis section, *even if it may cause competitive disadvantage.*[16]

No company has more visibly tested the concept of stimulating feedback through broad public disclosure than Skandia Group, the $7.5 billion (revenues) financial-services giant based in Stockholm, Sweden. Since 1994, Skandia has published twice yearly, in Intellectual Capital reports, the Navigators for many of its businesses, including American Skandia (see Table 9-3) and Dial (see Table 4-6). The Navigators give a detailed view of performance and, by inference, a clear overview of strategic priorities.

Skandia's Edvinsson, the earnest champion of openness, admits that, to this day, publication of the Navigators provokes debate at headquarters. Naysayers argue the stupidity of letting competitors dine on the smorgasbord of otherwise proprietary intelligence. Yet the naysayers don't have the ear of CEO Lars-Eric Petersson. Edvinsson reports that in the year 2000, for fiscal year 1999, Skandia hopes to publish audited figures for the Navigator in its annual report—placing nonfinancial measures for the first time fully on par with financial ones.[17]

Why the staunch commitment at Skandia to going public? For one thing, Skandia wants to change the way analysts evaluate the company, using nonfinancial measures to assess its ability to create future value. However, the more important purpose is what Edvinsson calls bench learning. He says simply, "You publish, and you get feedback, and you get a steeper learning curve. This is knowledge management in practice."

To that end, Skandia has placed itself at the confluence of a rich current of feedback from around the world. Few other companies could possibly get as much. When Skandia issued its first report in 1994, hundreds of companies called to inquire how to do the same thing. In 1998, the company actually published 40,000 copies of its Intellectual Capital report, four times the print run of its traditional financial report. After Skandia opened its Futures Center in 1996—aimed at capturing and commercializing intelligence—more than 7,000 people visited just by year-end 1997. Skandia opened itself as a sort of pilgrimage for experts seeking ways to more quickly translate learning into action.

More managers must hang out their measures of performance to attract such expert feedback. A more rapid flow of intelligence, circulating through every part of the accountability cycle, will propel higher performance in the future. Companies that cut themselves off from the treasures of global idea flow may well find their practices falling behind the leaders'.

To Conduct Lean, Decentralized, Empowered Operations

As managers take advantage of the powers of operational measures to leverage feedback, they will find this naturally helps a company run leaner. Knowing the rules, knowing the race they have to run, employees, teams, departments, and entire business units can work together with less guidance to pursue the corporate mission and strategy.

Too many managers lapse into using measures to micromanage results. They assign blame for failures and mete out punishment, holding the command-and-control reins in their hands. This is bad-cop accountability, as we've discussed before. It requires a lot of middle managers to prod the rank and file into line. The measures are cruel standards managers use to skewer people.

The challenge for executives is to deploy measures for good-cop accountability. The measures become, as David Norton says, the gyroscope of corporate action. People keep their eyes on the gyro for guidance on what to do, and they put faith in themselves to figure out how to do it. The result is a lean, empowered workforce and the ability to decentralize management radically. Managers focus on getting high performance out of the system, not beating it out of individuals.

Skandia's Boronow takes full advantage of the power of measures to decentralize authority. He gives his teams measures and lets them respond as they see fit to deliver performance. Every quarter, he compiles a Navigator for each team, which details results for twenty measures—sales per team member, assets under management, turnaround time on new contracts, phone wait times, employee competence levels, customer-service representative knowledge levels, number of process-improvement projects, relationships at the four levels, and so on.

The teams can see where they have to do better. They even get graphs of the data to track trends, and they can compare their prowess at building value with that of their peers on other teams. Sharing data among teams, and comparing them to averages, even stimulates some healthy internal competition. "There's a little horse race going on," admits Boronow, "but we try not to overplay that."[18]

Boronow encourages teams to bootstrap their way to better results by tying measures to pay. In an intriguing move, he highlights the relationship-building strategy by singling that element out in a profit-sharing program called "success share." With the help of some cost accounting, American Skandia has actually calculated the rough value of a new relationship, and the value of pushing a relationship from one level to the next higher one.

For the purpose of the plan, American Skandia values new relationships at $40 each. It values the strengthening of each relationship to the next higher category at $40 as well. The company has cleverly translated nonfinancial strategic goals into a financial unit of measure. If a team can take 1,000 new brokers and turn them into 1,000 regular brokers, it earns $40,000 for its profit-sharing pool. The measure and pay plan create a link directly between Boronow's strategy and people's wallets. The link to pay also highlights dollars-and-cents value creation at the operational level, something that remains obscure in many organizations.

So that internal competition spurs organizationwide performance, the company splits the incentives between team and combined pools. Splitting the pool stimulates both team performance and cross-team collaboration. "It becomes a very powerful motivator when you . . . measure the value that is created by a team," says Boronow. Team members have the sense he describes as, "Our team created this value and we are getting a share of that value."

Other managers hoping to achieve the full benefit of the accountability cycle must follow Boronow's lead. As they deploy the measures in every phase of management control and reporting, they must ensure that they use them to liberate innovation and initiative as far down in the company as the team level. Managers need not lock people into an entirely precast business plan. They can simply describe the destination. Says Boronow, "It's motivational, because now they're the owners."

To Demonstrate Performance and Market Organizational Capabilities

In fighting stiff global competition, companies have to constantly find new ways to stand out from the crowd. By demonstrating their performance with the precision of operational measures, they can aggressively market both their historical record of performance and their ability to deliver in the future. This is the ultimate mark of the accountable organization: a robust internal accountability cycle that enables thorough external disclosure.

Without hard numbers, published in ink, managers' promises simply lack punch. "Numbers speak louder than words," as the saying goes. Executives in the health-care industry, whose stories we recounted in Chapter 6, have leaped ahead of their peers in grasping this new competitive opportunity. Executives in other industries will soon realize that they have the same opportunity before them, if only delayed a few years through slower progress of broad social and economic trends.

The reality is, Loeppke says, "To be able to differentiate themselves based on cost and quality, [health-care] providers have to measure certain outcomes, certain performance indicators, certain measures of quality." That competitive reality has obvious future parallels in all industries. According to Loeppke, health-care organizations simply must become more accountable "to demonstrate value to the purchasers and consumers of care."[19]

In markets from Cleveland to California, groups of big employers like Xerox and GTE have pushed health-care providers into public accountability—often with insurers, consumer groups, and government cheering them on. "With the era of consumerism," says PhyCor's Loeppke, "you have the era of accountability."

Executives across industry will find that they cannot continue to rely on a trust-me approach—trust me that if the lagging indicators of financial performance look good, the leading indicators look the same. Instead, in the tradition of GAAP accounting, they will have to rely on a trust-and-verify approach—trust what I say so long as I verify it with numbers, preferably numbers I hire a third party to corroborate with an audit.

Executives should take a cue from such companies as United HealthCare, Group Health Cooperative of Puget Sound, PhyCor, and Aetna U.S. Healthcare, which have adopted the practice of measurement and reporting, creating cycles of accountability other industries can admire. Aetna U.S. Healthcare runs a whole business unit, U.S. Quality Algorithms, for collecting and mining the value from data—and using it to gain a competitive advantage. Like other firms, U.S. Quality Algorithms publishes HEDIS (Health Plan Employer Data and Information Set) report cards that lay out performance according to the standards of the National Committee for Quality Assurance. U.S. Quality Algorithms pioneered these performance reports not just for health plans but for the quality of care and service provided by physicians, pharmacists, hospitals, and dentists. The die of the trend is cast: Health-care organizations must now and for the future compete based on the quality of their information product.

Few companies outside health care can make the claim of accountability that leading executives in the health-care industry can, but as they build the cycle of accountability, they must position themselves for competition on the same terms. As Nicholas Hanchak, president of U.S. Quality Algorithms, says, "Aetna U.S. Healthcare can show plan sponsors that they're getting good value for their dollar."[20] Isn't that a claim executives in other industries would like to make?

To Trump the Flow of Information in Our Information Society

If you can't beat 'em, join 'em. Executives no longer hold the upper hand in controlling the information stakeholders get to appraise a company. Good or bad, thousands of information providers, multiplying at the speed of Internet websites, compete with companies in interpreting performance. J.D. Power is just one of the most prominent. Scores of other firms, the venerable and the upstart, are jumping into the rating game. Consider *Fortune* magazine's latest entry, based on 20,000 questionnaires filled out by employees at 238 companies: "The 100 Best Companies to Work for in America."[21] People pay attention to these rankings.

The only way for executives to retake the high ground in telling the company story is to deliver better information than the information mongers. Even if competitors do not take the first step to disclose, third parties can blunt a company's ability to tell the corporate story. Managers can respond by going out of their way to meet outsiders' appetite for information. In surveys, nine out of ten analysts want more information on corporate and competitive strategy.[22] Managers can give sharp outline to that strategy by simply disclosing, in the annual report president's letter, a handful of measures that define it.

That's not to say that outside ratings don't have their place, but managers who keep all data stockpiled behind the corporate veil invite others to grade their performance for them. Executives must bear in mind that stakeholders view company-supplied information among the most valuable, provided it is useful, credible, quantitative, regularly disclosed, and audited. It is up to management to take advantage of its unique position as an information supplier and demonstrate performance.

At Dow Chemical, the group working on measures for intellectual capital has begun toying with disclosing even the sensitive information on intellectual property. Dow has even created a twelve-page prototype report. Although Dow has not set a date for releasing the report, the company knows full well the value of disclosure. As Gordon Petrash sees it, "When you're all said and done, people thumb through your indicators and say, 'Well, each one of them individually doesn't tell me a whole lot, but as I look at them together, hey, Dow looks like it's pretty much on track.' "[23]

Companies will have trouble competing with information vendors eager to supply the vital few measures of each corporation's mettle. Better that executives create a plan early for displaying a subset of the mother lode of hard data in the company's management accounts, to preempt some of the third-party commentary. With advances in information technology, aggregating and disaggregating the necessary data, and reporting it broadly, is neither difficult nor costly. It may even give the company a leg up on competitors.

THE PRESS OF OUTSIDERS

While managers contemplate broader use of corporate performance measures, they can rest assured that stakeholders have contemplated much the same thing. The stakeholders' appetite for information has climbed in lockstep with the growth of information availability. On the one hand are the expectations of the regulators— and not just at the SEC. Regulators of all kinds, and at both the state and federal levels, favor more corporate reporting.

Consider the commissioners from a number of the nation's state public service commissions. In 1997, they ordered a study of how utilities can measure and report performance data. In the light of deregulation, which in some states enables consumers to choose their electricity supplier, the commissioners wanted a way to make sure electricity producers justify their marketing claims. The commissioners were especially keen on forcing full disclosure at companies trumpeting the use of clean fuel sources. Eventually, the regulators will require utilities to issue performance measures to justify those claims. As of late 1998, regulators in New York State as well as a number of Rocky Mountain states were poised to adopt sweeping disclosure standards.

The 1997 study followed a 1996 resolution by the National Association of Regulatory Utility Commissioners. The wording served notice that the ages of consumerism and accountability have come to the utility industry to stay: "NARUC supports initiatives leading to minimum, enforceable, uniform standards for the form and content of disclosure and labeling that would allow retail and wholesale consumers easily to compare price, price variability, resource mix, and environmental characteristics of their electricity purchases."[24]

Other stakeholders contribute equally to the pressure on companies to release more performance data. Many of the stakeholders feel forever slighted when it comes to getting a thorough accounting of corporate performance. Although most of them, by themselves, have little direct power to demand disclosure of operational measures, institutional investors are an exception. Up to now, the institutions have not exercised their power to demand an accounting of operational performance. But surveys show they are not happy with the information they get. Institutional money managers in both Europe and the United States routinely complain about poor corporate accountability. According to surveys by Shelley Taylor & Associates of twenty-five big-time managers representing billions of dollars in investments, the main kind of operational information the institutions require relates to quality of management, defined as strategy, track record, ability to set and meet objectives, management experience, and integrity.[25] This study simply confirms, once again, the data in earlier studies.[26]

When will the activist institutions insist on a fuller, nonfinancial accounting? Carolyn Brancato, a Conference Board expert in corporate governance who undertook a multiyear study of performance measures, reports that money managers are in fact taking a hard look at "strategic" (nonfinancial) performance measures, especially those indicative of future success. But money managers as yet are not insisting on the numbers. Instead, she says, "Institutions are pushing for assurance that a process exists and the process is being monitored by the board. . . . They want to know the process is valid and they're not being snowed."[27]

Will the activists' reticence last? Time will tell. They can bring about change rapidly if they throw their weight around as they have in the governance arena. The question again may become moot, however, at least for managers bent on gaining the full benefit of building their business on the accountability cycle. The opportunity to step ahead of arm-twisting activists lies before all companies. Accountable managers have only to grab it.

THE IMPERATIVE OF LINKAGE

For all their power, operational measures will not hold up to the test of time unless, through a performance logic, they drive each other and, in turn, drive the financials. Managers must map how the measures work *together* to create value. Though most executives brainstorm a network of measures from an intuitive sense of their interaction, all firms should try to confirm the relationship among their measures. Executives won't win the long-term support needed from operating managers unless they understand, and the company preferably documents, the links between the softer nonfinancial measures and the hard financial ones.

Of course, a number of general studies show correlations. Research by the Gordon Group kicked off a vigorous debate in 1994. The group studied high-performance workplace practices (training, employees involved in decision making, and compensation linked to performance) and found that companies with poor practices often had low stock valuations.[28] That was enough for Calpers, the California Public Employees Retirement System, to announce that it would begin taking such practices into account in its governance program—in which it targets its worst-performing investments for activism.

Later studies have tried to firm up the relationship, but nearly all come up with correlations that wouldn't win over many financial executives. One provocative study, however, by Ernst & Young, quantified, through surveys with 275 portfolio managers, the hypothetical gains in stock price from perceptions of better nonfinancial performance. Testing investor reaction while first holding financials constant and varying the nonfinancials, and then holding the nonfinancials constant and varying the financials, Ernst & Young found that money managers marked valuations up for improvements in nonfinancial variables. The study found, for example, that a "moderate" improvement in perceptions of customer satisfaction in the computer industry led portfolio managers to give a company a roughly 5-percent share-price premium.[29]

Industry-specific studies also show striking correlations between operational measures and financial ones. In the airline industry, researchers found that measures of customer satisfaction, load factor, market share, and available-ton-miles were predictors of quarterly revenues, expenses, and operating income.[30] Despite such studies, the generalizability of each to a single company remains difficult. To the extent that companies are betting their future on their strategy, they should prove the links between specific nonfinancial measures and financial success. In starting this process, managers can look to models like the service profit chain for guidance: internal service quality leads to employee satisfaction and in turn to employee retention, which then leads to external service quality, customer satisfaction, customer retention, and, finally, profit.[31]

That's just what Sears, Roebuck did. Stung by a $3.9 billion loss in 1992, the giant retailer refocused on building customer satisfaction and, more specifically, on the chain of causation from employee attitudes to customer satisfaction to profits.[32] Sears's research in linking one measure to the next sets an example for other companies to follow.

Sears's dedication to nonfinancial performance came after more than a year of executive soul-searching. In 1993 and 1994, the company's top 150 managers crystallized the company's new direction in what they called the three C's: to make Sears a compelling place to work, a compelling place to shop, and a compelling place to invest. They then began to correlate all three. Their finding? They could not only quantify the factors that drive each kind of performance, they could also quantify how much an improvement in each link of the employee-customer-profit chain stemmed from improvements in a previous link.

Sears then transformed how managers gauge success. By 1996, it developed a corporatewide, statistically rigorous means to manage the factors that really matter. It can now actually calculate that a five-point gain in employee attitudes will translate into a 1.3-unit increase in customer impressions. That better customer reading will then boost revenue growth by 0.5 percent. The model even predicts the lag time between one improvement and the next. So strongly does Sears take the value of its measures, that it audits them yearly in the same way as it does financials.

Though many companies rely on a commonsense approach to linkage, Sears relies on data. Company managers found, to their surprise, that two measures originally proposed for the employee-customer-profit chain—personal growth and development, and empowered teams—failed to relate statistically to any customer data. They do matter to managers, but they don't lie on the causal pathway from employee satisfaction to profits. Meanwhile, managers found that ten of seventy questions in the company's employee survey do relate well to customer data, in particular to those in just two categories: peoples' attitude about their jobs and attitude about the company. So Sears uses those ten questions in its employee-customer-profit chain.

Sears's research gives its managers uncanny insight on how to manage the contributors of company value. This is precisely the kind of approach that gives managers confidence in delivering high performance through the accountability cycle.

In the best of all worlds, managers would reduce all measures to a common unit of measurement, namely dollars, as discussed in Chapter 7. Then people could easily aggregate and disaggregate them. They could compare them among teams, departments, business units, and with competitors. They wouldn't have so much trouble trading off increases in one measure with decreases in another, unsure of which creates more value. Although this simply isn't always possible, accountants and managers should devote some ingenuity to this possibility—as did American Skandia with measures of the value of relationships.

The next best thing is to create ratios that fit logically with the family of financial metrics. One example is working capital productivity (revenues divided by average working capital). As Boston Consulting Group found, this figure often makes a good proxy for process efficiency. If a company is working on improving material handling, or on streamlining billing and collection, working capital can stand in as an indicator of progress in process improvements.[33] In any case, the point is not to reflexively invent new measures based on unfamiliar units of measurement, but to first innovate with familiar data.

As executives create nonfinancial measures they will find that their concept of management takes on a brand new look. As Skandia's Leif Edvinsson says, the tradition of executives has been to base management on a sort of weather record, relying on data as simple as temperature, precipitation, and wind speed. In the future, they must manage with a computerized weather map, a real-time mosaic that shows the trend of the vital few parameters of future performance. (In fact, Skandia is actually prototyping such an application.) Only then will they be able to realize the benefits of the fully accountable organization.

Devising the nonfinancial measures of performance poses perhaps the greatest challenge to managers of would-be accountable organizations. These measures require a look into the guts of the business. They demand an understanding of the interactions that create value. Executives must come up with the variables most appropriate for both internal and external decision making, at each point along the accountability cycle. This becomes a particularly tough job in the complex business environment of today, in which the financial and operational measures won't suffice to create maximum value. The social ones, as we will see in the next chapter, must become part of the family of measures as well.

10

A Social
Accounting

Northern Telecom (Nortel Networks) hires 25 percent of all computer science and logic-engineering graduates produced by Canadian universities each year. You could take that as the ultimate sign that the company dominates its market. Its prowess in attracting so many bright workers—whose high-school grade point averages average over ninety percent—is a triumph.

Or is it? Nortel Networks Chief Executive John Roth thinks not. He's pondering instead the long-term health of his company, which employs 80,000. He's also thinking about the welfare of his country. "When one corporation consumes 25 percent of a nation's output of this kind of talent, either Northern is too big or the Canadian school system is too small."[1]

That Roth is concerned about university education illustrates how corporate management has become too complex to divide neatly into just two managerial categories—financial and operational. Competitive issues and societal pressures require executives to add a third category, social. (See Figure 10-1.) Only then can they make day-to-day and long-term decisions with their eyes fully open to all risks and opportunities. Only then can they close performance gaps with complete information about performance drivers. And

Figure 10-1
The Third Element of Performance Measurement: The Socials

only then can they achieve full accountability for delivering long-term value creation for the enterprise as a whole.

In practice, the three threads of accountable management—financial, operational, and social—intertwine like the three strands of a rope. Managers cannot easily separate them—and understandably so because they must ultimately integrate them in one taut management system. We distinguish between them to ensure that managers take a thorough look at all three throughout the accountability cycle.

Executives like Roth are certainly taking a thorough look, and they have come up with a prescient view of the future: Social causes once fawned over as pet projects, from managing diversity to reducing environmental pollution, have become prime corporate concerns. Managers must factor them into strategic and day-to-day management to make the company strong for the long term.

That belief brought Roth to worrying about education. His current focus is on boosting the output of the university system. Although he will take his initiative global, he is kicking off the effort in Canada, where Nortel Networks is headquartered. "From our perspective and from the perspective of our children, the capacity of the university system in this field of endeavor is too small," he says. It is too competitive, too. "There are lots of kids that are perfectly qualified with grade averages in the mid-eighties that would do a superb job," he says. "But we're saying, 'No, we don't have a seat for you'—at least not in the Canadian school system."

Turning away crowds of qualified candidates pains him, as his firm hungers for qualified people to design and build the hardware and software that run global telephone and data networks. "That's a tremendous loss," he says. An engineer by training, he concedes that even his high-school grade point average wouldn't pass muster for a software engineering slot today. "I had other things to do with my time than study the books that hard." So he has drafted a blueprint for change, and he is leading a coalition of companies to work with lawmakers to revamp the Canadian system—for the future of education, the future of young workers, and the future of Nortel Networks.

How will Roth know if he wins with his education platform? In Canada, he will measure Nortel Networks' take of computer science and logic-engineering graduates. He has set a target of hiring just 15 percent of them—which means roughly doubling the number of high-tech slots in Canadian universities—over five years. The goal is ambitious and Roth proposes to back it up by spending the bulk of his company's social moneys on education.

In putting social performance high on his agenda, Roth wants Nortel Networks managers and executives to spring nimbly from accountability for financial and operational numbers to accountability for social ones. He doesn't view this as a handout to society. "The quality of the people is absolutely essential if we're to continue to be a world-leading company," he says. "We have a high self-interest. It's going to return something to Nortel."

However, societal benefit matters to him, too. "If we pull this thing off, we'll increase the pool for Canadian corporations in general," he says. "We'll hire only 15 percent of those kids that graduate; the rest of Canada will get the benefit of the other 85."

The question of which social measures to blend into the mix of measures in the accountability cycle is a tough one, and it is often contentious. Nobody can draw a crisp line around measures that should go squarely on the agenda and those that should get crossed off. To make these decisions, executives should return to their plans for executing company strategy. Which stakeholder relationships ensure the firm's success in winning strategically? Which stakeholders will benefit or lose out in the process? How must executives manage the impacts of corporate decisions?

That's not to say that a company cannot play a pure charitable role in society. Companies can certainly play some philanthropic role, the degree to which we won't argue. However, executives should decide the balance of self-interest and philanthropy only after first understanding strategy and stakeholder relationships. Roth has made an explicit decision on where Nortel Networks' and society's needs intersect and how Nortel will participate to benefit both. He knows well that as his $18 billion firm competes with the likes of Lucent Technologies, the way he manages the world around Nortel Networks has a huge impact on the world inside.

No matter whether the corporate activity is strategic, philanthropic, or some of both, executives must use measures to articulate objectives, monitor results, report performance inside and outside the firm, and respond to failings. This is the message of the accountability cycle, taking a holistic view, making tradeoffs explicit, and striving for feedback to make adjustments that maximize long-term value.

Invoking Milton Friedman, who thirty years ago argued that "the social responsibility of business is to increase profits,"[2] many managers object to an approach that factors social measures into corporate decisions. They see disaster in looking after anything but the bottom line. As discussed in Chapters 1 and 7, a debate rages as to whether companies *should* be in the business of pleasing any stakeholder other than shareholders. However, the practice of separating society and business into discrete units, as if a manager could operate on one while not the other,[3] ceases to make sense (if it ever did). A manager can't separate business from society. Companies, government, communities, civic groups, and other institutions operate in a single system in which all help the company create value.

With this thought in mind, once managers have distinguished among financial, operational, and social issues in the planning stages, they must meld them into one mental model of sustainable value creation. They then put themselves in a position to enjoy the capabilities described in this chapter of leveraging the accountability cycle with social measures to compete in new and revitalized ways.

COUNTING DOWN THE SOCIALS

When it comes to social measures, many people roll their eyes. They prepare themselves for a meandering argument about every possible kind of measure. What they will find instead is an argument for some mainstream measures, evaluating the business in terms that have become increasingly familiar. The bleeding-heart issues of yesterday, like cleaning up polluted rivers, have become the board-level issues of today. The issues once considered solely the province of government, like high-school education, have suddenly become integral to the competitive success of companies from Boeing to Shell Oil.[4]

Whatever a manager's values, his or her decisions must take into account the drivers of business success, social or otherwise. This is not an argument for social activism. It is an argument for business realism. Brainstorming social measures means coming up with long-term drivers of value. The process can become complicated because the scope of social issues can extend so broadly, the connections to the firm become so nebulous, and the obligations and opportunities seem so uncertain. Managers have to use their best judgment, however, to consider the measures that competitive and societal pressures dictate.

The best way to make this judgment is to think through the issues in the same way as for financial and operational measures—stakeholder by stakeholder. Table 10-1 lists a sample of the kinds of measures that a firm might come up with. Note how many of these, perhaps once tangential to the profit-making work of the corporation, now fall well within the conventional array of competitive issues.

Top managers must decide which measures to include in the final list. Most leading companies today address issues such as the following: environmental performance, equal employment opportunity, equal credit opportunity, human rights, international labor standards, ethical business conduct, and corporate giving, including

TABLE 10-1

SAMPLE SOCIAL MEASURES, BY STAKEHOLDER

STAKEHOLDER	MEASURE
Shareholders	Reputation (by survey)
	Ethical practices (by survey)
	Toxic emissions
Customers	Observance of international labor standards
	Environmental impact of products
	Customer satisfaction
	Product safety
	Percentage of recycled and recyclable materials
Employees	Diversity in employment
	Diversity in management
	Daycare utilization and satisfaction
	Family-friendly work environment
	Employee satisfaction
	Environmental quality of facilities
Community	Public health: complaints, legal actions
	Hours of volunteer community service
	Community satisfaction
	Consumption of natural resources
	Index of environmental impact
	Hazardous waste disposal
	Packaging volume
	Job creation

political soft-money contributions. The pertinent issues vary with the company, the industry, and the strategy.[5]

As an indication of the variety of social issues that at least some stakeholders consider important, the Portfolio$creener software developed by the Investor Responsibility Research Center, a leading source of social research for investors, includes most of the categories included in Table 10-1, along with a long list of others. Those categories include alcoholic-beverage production, animal testing, contraceptive production, defense contracting and weapons production, labor relations, maquiladora operations, equal employment opportunity in Northern Ireland, nuclear power, and tobacco production.

Although managers may question the validity of this list, they should be prepared to manage the constituencies that take it seriously.

Many of these issues won't cross a manager's desk, but managers don't want to be in the dark if they do. Too often, the only issues managers look at are the ones, as a variation of the old joke goes, under the financial lamppost, because that's where the light is. The issues in the shadows, left unmeasured and thus unmanaged, are the ones that may well knock the company for a loop. Creating an accountable organization that includes social measurement makes visible and clear what managers should be managing. Even if executives choose not to manage certain social issues, they should informally gauge the winnings and losses of their stakeholders to at least understand the impacts.

The importance of taking a broad view was illustrated by Texaco, which sent the public into an uproar over its alleged culture of discrimination in late 1996. In the heat of early press coverage, observers bashed Texaco's image and consumers boycotted its stations. In the aftermath, Texaco agreed to a $176 million settlement of a racial-discrimination lawsuit filed earlier by six employees. The company's experience showed how quickly a social issue could become a financial one.

Despite the settlement, or perhaps because of it, socially responsible investors applied continuing pressure on Texaco. They filed a shareholder resolution to demand an updated diversity report, as well as summary results of its employee survey and new diversity assessment survey.[6] Investors later withdrew the resolution when Texaco agreed to comply. But United States Trust Company of Boston official Scott Klinger still lobbied hard for information to gauge the long-term impact on Texaco. At the 1997 annual meeting, Klinger asked, "How many more multimillion-dollar settlements will need to hit the evening news and how many more shareholder suits will have to be filed before Texaco discloses to its shareholders the risks they face from past acts of discrimination?"[7]

In mid-1997, Texaco issued a diversity report that detailed not just policies, programs, and equal employment opportunity data but also its legal record, including pending legal matters and cost of settling lawsuits. The Texaco affair shows how critical social accountability can become. To shareholders who fret corporate earnings are endangered by hidden corporate liabilities, measuring equal employment opportunity performance has become a business imperative.[8]

GETTING THE POWER

Managers must not shy from using social measures in the same way as financial and operational ones, to gain value at every point in the accountability cycle. They must renounce the bunker mentality to social issues, in which they withdraw from forthright handling of environmental, equal employment opportunity, overseas labor, or other social issues. They must manage these critical issues in the open. By developing social measures, they can exercise a range of new capabilities that move them into the lead among competitors.

To Improve Decision Making

Social measures supply the information necessary for making better decisions. Any number of companies, like Texaco, can cite stories of getting caught not having used social measures to better inform their decision making. For example, as late as 1997, skittish social investors still knocked Bristol-Myers Squibb for its spill and compliance record, based on four misdemeanor criminal violations of the Clean Water Act in 1992, for which the company paid a $3.5 million settlement. Bristol-Myers Squibb was cited at the time for irregularities in discharge permits and effluent pH levels at its Syracuse, New York, plant. What's notable is that the incident blemished the health and beauty company's reputation for five years even though investigators reported that the public was never at risk.[9]

It was partly in response to this incident that Bristol-Myers Squibb integrated a full set of environmental measures into its cycle of accountability. Its corporatewide software system, installed in 1992, enables each plant to track and report environmental, health, and safety progress based on the 16 Codes of Practice mentioned in Chapter 6. Sites transmit assessment data to headquarters each December. These data, consolidated, are published in the company's biennial environmental report and updated annually on the company's website.

"The Codes of Practice operationalize the corporate environment, health, and safety policy and integrate EHS into our day-to-day business management systems," says Thomas M. Hellman, vice president, environment, health, and safety.

Along with tracking and reporting its progress in improving each element of environment, health, and safety management, the company also tracks and reports items like toxic releases, hazardous waste disposal, carbon dioxide emissions (greenhouse gases), and the use of ozone-depleting substances. In a step that fully integrates environmental concerns into decision making, it created Product Life Cycle (PLC) reviews, a process that encourages employees to gauge impacts of each product from R&D to marketing, manufacturing, packaging, sales and distribution, customer use, and final disposition. PLC reviews help the company factor into decisions early on every manner of environmental impact.

In 1995, the company launched a PLC review of the Matrix Essentials line of hair-care products.[10] The PLC team analyzed impacts at each stage of the life cycle, finding thirty-seven ways to improve—promising $200,000 in yearly savings. For example, facility personnel used to landfill damaged or off-specification shampoo and conditioner bottles because third-party recycling facilities would not accept bottles containing liquids. The PLC team advised management to purchase special equipment to shred the plastic bottles to make the waste plastic more acceptable to recyclers. The capital cost of the shredder was quickly paid for in reduced landfill costs.

The net result was that by developing measures at the highest level of the company to gauge environmental performance, Bristol-Myers Squibb enlightened decision making at each level of the hierarchy. Companywide, the firm estimates savings of $3.5 million just from product life cycle reviews like those at Matrix Essentials.[11] Full accountability for environmental performance was the driver and motivator. Charles Heimbold, chief executive, maintains that excellence in environment, health, and safety helps the firm achieve its three strategic goals: a dynamic operating environment, productivity, and growth.[12]

To Clarify and Communicate Strategy

In the same way as with financial and operational measures, executives must use social measures to communicate strategy. As people throughout the company engage outside stakeholders, the measures give clear guidance on how to handle environmental, ethical, community, and other issues those stakeholders care about.

Executives must not leave these issues undefined, in the shadow, lest their work force go astray.

Columbia/HCA Healthcare, the nationwide hospital chain, seemed to have stumbled from such ambiguity. The company is especially well-known for the culture of measurement built by its former chief executive. "People who are successful with me are people who like measurement and who like change," said Richard Scott, before he resigned in 1997. "You will like or dislike working here as much as you like or dislike measurement."[13]

In 1997, however, an army of federal investigators descended on Columbia, alleging illegal billing practices and other irregularities. Scott's statement about measures begs the question: Did he have adequate measures for, say, ethical dealings with his biggest customer— the government? Scott resigned as Columbia/HCA came under a cloud of controversy. Maybe he should have cast his measurement net a little wider. Maybe the Columbia/HCA board should have cast the net wider.

Ethics remains one of the most ill-defined elements of corporate performance, but make no mistake, accountable executives must act to clarify their companies' ethical standards. No company can afford to let develop a pattern of ethical lapses for lack of clarity by top management. Executives have to worry about both the short-term direct financial cost of ethical lapses and the long-term costs that come from a spoiled reputation.

As Nortel Networks' Roth took over the top job in late 1997, he set out to give people a crisper picture of their ethical responsibilities. What he had in mind was more than exhorting people to do better. He set in motion a plan to measure ethical performance quantitatively. His emphasis on ethics stems from the view widely held in Nortel Networks that ethics can differentiate the company in global markets, especially as the company migrates from selling stand-alone products to packages of products and services.

"We're moving to a more relational approach: thinking in terms of the whole 'package' or value proposition that we bring to a customer relationship," says Margaret Kerr, senior vice president, human resources and environment. "Trust that both sides will act ethically is an important underpinning of this relationship. Customers need to know that we will deliver on our commitments . . . that they are getting value for their money."[14]

In a 1994 investigation of employee opinions, comprising forty focus groups and sixty executive interviews, Nortel Networks found employees unclear on their ethical commitments. Many feared coming forward with ethical concerns, sensing a "shoot the messenger" mentality among management.[15] Nortel Networks therefore rewrote its code of business conduct. The new code defined ethical conduct as fulfilling commitments to five stakeholders (customers, employees, shareholders, suppliers, and the community).

Nortel Networks' ethical standards are not unusual—"Nortel is fair in its choice of suppliers and honest in all business interactions with them." What is unusual is that the company started measuring compliance with the standards. In early 1998, it circulated a 150-question survey to 2,500 employees specifically to gauge ethical behavior. Employees rated from one to five agreement with such statements as the following: I can live at work with the same values as at home. People are willing to report to managers ethics problems. I prefer this company because of its ethics. Decision making is better because of ethics and compliance programs. As an example of results, employees rated the first a 4.15 (5 is best) and the last 3.1.

Nortel Networks will eventually correlate survey data with each element of the company code, allowing an assessment of whether the company is living up to the code. It will also benchmark its performance with its competitors, quantitatively, a capability the board of directors' audit committee has been requesting. The benchmarking, which began in 1998, involves a dozen companies participating in the Ethics Officers Association consortium. A half dozen of the same questions will appear on each of the companies' surveys. After pooling the data, the companies will have the data to embark on continuous improvement programs, targeted specifically at ethical behavior, that will signal the companies' ethical priorities with a clarity unknown in most of industry.

Another firm advancing the frontier of using social measures to deliver a crisp message to employees is Diageo, the merged company of Grand Metropolitan and Guinness, now parent to Pillsbury, Burger King, Guinness, and United Distillers & Vintners. Grand Met's 1997 *Report on Corporate Citizenship* (see Chapter 6) enabled top executives to communicate a clear agenda, performance expectations, and a method for measuring company impacts on communities around the world.

"Our prime target was our own people," says Geoffrey Bush, the worldwide director of corporate citizenship for the merged $24 billion company.[16]

The report, the forerunner of a similar Diageo document, clarifies Grand Met's four company commitments: to pure charity, to social investment, to commercial initiatives, and to basic socially responsible business practices. For 1996, charity included $40,000 for adult literacy in South Africa, social investment included $4 million for surplus food donations by Pillsbury in the United States, commercial initiatives included $45,000 for the Malibu (rum) Surfers Against Sewage program, and business basics included ongoing programs like environmental and social management audits. Diageo expects managers to make good in all four performance categories, and the report delivers that message not just with anecdote but with as much quantification as the firm can so far muster. Bush notes that the report has had the intended impact. For instance, it spurred the company's Irish unit to review its operation, meet with outside groups for comments, and assemble a nationwide corporate citizenship strategy.

To Accelerate Feedback and Learning

Combining social measures with financial and operational ones, managers can also stimulate fast feedback for corporate learning and improvement. Experience shows time and again that companies without healthy, visible feedback—in environmental affairs, equal employment opportunity, and community reinvestment—get caught engaging in sloppy practices. These lapses in social performance end up costing a bundle, if not in fines, in lost revenue. Yet executives who use social measures to pinpoint failings can clean up their corporate act quickly.

Many companies facing environmental problems—including Nortel Networks, Bristol-Myers Squibb,[17] and Baxter International—have set an example of how to use measurement-driven feedback to their advantage. Baxter stimulates feedback by translating environmental performance measures as much as possible into financial ones. In other words, Baxter's environmental staff tries to speak the language of business, says William Blackburn, vice president and chief counsel, corporate environmental, health and safety. In a one-of-a-kind environmental financial statement, Baxter tallies environmental costs and savings, in dollars, in a format that mimics a traditional financial statement.

On the cost side, the company lists everything from auditors' and attorneys' fees ($500,000 in 1997) to pollution controls ($3.6 million). On the savings side, it lists everything from packaging reduction ($1.3 million) to recycling income ($4.6 million). Total savings in 1997 were $13.8 million, 108 percent of the cost of Baxter's basic environmental program. Dollars, the common unit of measurement for all environmental concerns, stimulate dialogue like never before. "You've got EHS people talking finance and the financial people talking EHS," says Blackburn.

At Baxter's Irish manufacturing operation, managers have fashioned their own environmental financial statement. The statement helps the 900 employees, who make renal dialysis and intravenous analysis products, get quick feedback on where they burn up dollars and where they could save. In packaging alone, the unit documented savings in 1996 of $83,000. The savings came from reducing the thickness and size of cardboard and plastic packaging, and in figuring out how to put more product in each container. The unit saved another $181,000 in reducing nonhazardous waste by retrieving pallets from customers, by repairing damaged pallets, and by creating a returnable "just-in-time" container to replace nonreturnable ones.[18]

This can seem pretty basic, but Baxter has used its dollar-based measures to merge the environmental and financial managers' agendas. Few firms have accomplished this feat. With the common language—and comparable units of measure, across time, divisions, and among competing companies—employees at every level within Baxter can more readily feed the company a valuable stream of insight on how to operate better.[19] The dollar-based approach works so well that Blackburn is pressing division managers to attach financial targets to every annual goal for environment, health, and safety.

Baxter has already set corporate-level targets in dollar terms. Having collected financial data for a number of years, it is one of the few companies that can confidently forecast future financial gains from environmental improvements. For 2005, it has set a target of $110 million in savings. Among the itemized goals (and savings): slashing toxic emissions by 80 percent ($4 million), boosting energy efficiency by 10 percent ($13 million), reducing hazardous waste by 35 percent ($3 million), and cutting packaging materials by 20 percent ($35 million).

The beauty of the Baxter system is that Blackburn has linked the environment with the most looked-at feedback system in the company: the budget. "If you didn't have that financial link, you wouldn't have such obvious and enthusiastic cooperation," says Blackburn. "You need this financial piece as a driver."[20]

Even without the financial link, though, accountable managers can use social measurements to increase feedback throughout the accountability cycle. One measure attracting growing interest is corporate reputation. Indeed, many executives believe their ability to generate value depends on their company continuing to look good in the public's eyes. Little surprise that executives keep close track of *Fortune* magazine's annual most-admired survey. It gives them a reading of how much "social capital" they have to spend.

British Telecom executives have even declared, as one of their key objectives, to "continually improve British Telecom's corporate reputation."[21] To incorporate reputation into the company's cycle of accountability, they have created a sophisticated way to measure it. On their corporate scorecard, they actually include a category for impact on society, in keeping with European Foundation for Quality Management guidelines. British Telecom's overarching measure of satisfying the expectations of its local, national, and international communities is the "key corporate attitude score." British Telecom calculates the score from a monthly random survey of 9,000 members of the general public. The feedback gives a clear idea of whether the company is building or losing social capital.

British Telecom gains further feedback by tracking perceptions that contribute to the overall attitude score. It tracks five categories of perceptions: help for U.K. business (for example, training), support for charities, support for the community (for example, education, employment, charities, and the arts), nonprofitable services (for example, emergency phone service), and environmental impact (for example, air emissions). In assessing perceptions, British Telecom asks people in its survey to rate their agreement with four statements: British Telecom services help U.K. businesses do better; British Telecom provides essential services even when not profitable; British Telecom is environmentally responsible; and British Telecom supports charities and other worthy causes.

What British Telecom ends up with are measures of two kinds. The first is a sort of social satisfaction score. Since 1993, roughly three out of four people agreed with all of the statements. More than four out of five agreed with the first two. The second is a score of progress. Using measures of jobs and training places created, funds raised for charity, and employee involvement, recycled fiber in telephone directories, volatile organic compound emissions from British Telecom's vehicle fleet, and so on, managers learn how well the company has performed in multiple programs to improve social performance. All of these measures help British Telecom fulfill its mission statement: "To make a fitting contribution to the community in which we conduct our business."

To be sure, most measures capture an incomplete picture of all social impacts. But even if incomplete and even if the measures don't translate into dollars and cents, they create the feedback loop that, particularly when coming from the outside, feeds the company with invaluable insight. This kind of feedback must not simply be a PR exercise, a matter of feigned listening to outsiders. It must take the form proposed by Royal Dutch/Shell Group, where executives have singled out "engagement"—actively stimulating dialogue with all stakeholders—as an integral part of future management systems.

To maximize feedback, Shell envisions eventually creating alliances with key stakeholder organizations. The firm wants to understand and act on outside expectations—before confronting the uproar from incidents like the deep-sea disposal of the Brent Spar off-shore storage buoy.[22] This is ultimately a prime goal of managing through the accountability cycle: integrating feedback into management decision making early on, which enables managers to craft a solid strategy in the first place, and then constantly improve operations, refine long-term strategy, and produce greater value in the future.

To Inspire Loyalty Among Stakeholders

Executives must not stop there, however. They must leverage social measures to develop loyalty among constituencies that support the company. Of course, gaining enduring loyalty of all stakeholders would call on managers to consider a dizzying variety of concerns. Managers can't address every splinter group's pet notion of corporate responsibilities. But companies can often assuage the most common concerns by publishing social performance measures. In the best of cases, they can even endear customers, employees, shareholders, and other stakeholders to the company with a level of loyalty that beats the competition.

Exxon, which lost face with the public when the Exxon Valdez fouled Alaskan waters with crude oil, has learned this lesson in the years since. In 1998, the New York-based watchdog group Council on Economic Priorities actually named Exxon one of the top three petroleum refiners in its Campaign for Cleaner Corporations.[23] The Council on Economic Priorities' ranking will no doubt help reverse flagging loyalties of many Exxon customers—and it comes on the heels of improved disclosure by Exxon of environmental performance.

Many companies understandably limit their social disclosure to measures of environmental performance, one of the key social issues of recent decades. However, managers must consider the same kind of forthright reporting in other social areas. Ben & Jerry's and The Body Shop have taken a lead in social reporting, but many others are following, including General Motors, Diageo, British Telecom, and Royal Dutch/Shell. These firms have come to understand that their business depends on social responsibility. Customers, suppliers, employees, even shareholders increasingly look to a social record, if only at the margin of decision making, before deciding where to place their loyalties. Companies will increasingly have to show with measures that they are the most appealing place to invest, work, and shop.

Vancouver City Savings Credit Union, the largest credit union in Canada, has taken that approach. Its board of directors has long favored a strong socially responsible bent. In 1989, VanCity launched a socially responsible real-estate development subsidiary to provide affordable housing. It also founded the VanCity Community Foundation, a charitable organization that contributes to programs like a six-month apprenticeship course for auto repair. VanCity, with 250,000 credit-union members and $5 billion in assets, has come to rely on its record of heavy community involvement to attract its customers.[24]

VanCity managers thought they were doing a good job of broadcasting their message of social responsibility in the early 1990s, but, in 1992, an independent survey showed the organization fell short of the board of directors' expectations. A Society of Management Accountants (Canada) (SMAC) study ranked the firm forty-seventh among 750 Canadian companies in social reporting. The Royal Bank of Canada, a big-bank competitor, rated far higher. The board, surprised and disappointed, responded immediately.

For fiscal year 1992, VanCity issued an improved annual report that helped it streak to eighth place in the SMAC's social reporting rankings. Since then, for both competitive and philosophical reasons, VanCity has continuously upgraded the annual report to include a vast array of social information. An added impetus to the effort was a 1993 study: VanCity found that 38 percent of members and 17 percent of nonmembers considered the social accounting section "extremely important." So, by 1996, VanCity dedicated eight of the forty-eight pages in its annual report to social reporting. Among the topics were energy conservation, paper consumption, waste reduction, employee turnover and diversity, community donations, and community economic-development grants.

Even while producing the expanded annual report, however, VanCity managers came to conclude that the report was still deficient. They believed it weak because of a lack of external validation, too little quantification of social performance, and too little dialogue with stakeholders to determine which measures VanCity should use to gauge its performance. So the company launched a complete social audit that it released in 1998. The new report addresses the deficiencies head-on. It opens with a statement from an external auditor, which lists areas for improvement—for example, adding suppliers to the next audit. It breaks its stakeholders into ten groups and details the interviews, focus groups, and surveys conducted to gather comments from each. And it publishes a range of quantitative indicators of company social performance—percentage of totally satisfied members, percentage of staff that would recommend VanCity as a place to work, percentage of pretax earnings donated to charity. Finally, it discloses all relationships with suppliers and joint ventures, committing VanCity to require all subsidiaries to participate in future audit cycles or to develop their own audit processes meeting minimum standards of social performance acceptable to the parent company.[25]

Managers at other companies may view VanCity's approach as irrelevant. They may believe their market does not demand it. They may disagree with VanCity's sense of corporate social responsibility. However, they should note the interesting lesson about competition that VanCity managers have been rapidly learning: The competitive playing field can change suddenly to make social issues much more critical. Giant bank mergers and intense competition from nonbank firms like GE Capital have started to give VanCity managers a run for their business.

VanCity now makes a point to differentiate itself with its social-minded approach. Transparent disclosure has evolved beyond the day when it was optional. It has become a management tool for responding to market requirements and improving internal management decisions. It has become a competitive tool to build reputation and brand equity. The disclosure is not a veneer that VanCity has painted over its operations, either. In line with the notion of the accountability cycle, it has now integrated social issues into the company's annual planning cycle. VanCity has merged financial, operational, and social measures into a model of the fully accountable organization.

How far should other companies go in following the VanCity approach? That is hard to say. What we can say is that VanCity's experience is not an anomaly; it gives clues to a trend that managers at other companies must watch—and must respond to faster than their competitors. Every company can leverage social measures throughout the accountability cycle to its advantage. The opportunity awaits. Sustainable profits depend on it. More managers must take advantage.

PRESSURES FROM THE OUTSIDE

Most managers will want to back away from the unfamiliar territory of social measures and reporting. After all, it seems far afield from the press of day-to-day operations. However, they will find forces crowding all around pressing them onto this new turf. These are the forces of stakeholders who have an inexhaustible thirst for information—a thirst not so different from managers' own thirst in getting the data they need to run the business internally. Many constituencies believe they have a right to know much of the information gathered on the inside—in the same way shareholders believe they have a right to know about basic financial measures. Therefore, executives may find that stakeholders oblige them to disclose much more, lest the corporation suffer a black eye.

Regulators at agencies like the Equal Employment Opportunity Commission, Occupational Safety and Health Administration, and Environmental Protection Agency continually crank up the heat for disclosure. Viewed over the span of a decade or more, this trend is particularly obvious. In 1987, the Environmental Protection Agency demanded data on more than 300 chemicals to fulfill toxic release inventory reporting. Since then, it has added 286 more chemicals, mandated that by June 1999 tens of thousands of facilities issue "worst-case" disaster scenarios, and, in early 1998, even began posting plant-by-plant pollution and compliance data on the Internet for over 600 company facilities.[26]

The same disclosure-hungry approach pops up at the Equal Employment Opportunity Commission. In 1995, the twenty-one-member, bipartisan Glass Ceiling Commission, created following the Civil Rights Act of 1991, voted unanimously for making diversity data public. The commission's recommendation: "Public disclosure of diversity data—specifically, data on the most senior positions—is an effective incentive to develop and maintain innovative, effective programs to break glass ceiling barriers. The commission recommends that both the public and private sectors work toward increased public disclosure of diversity data."[27] The commission even suggested a place for the disclosures: form 10-K filed with the SEC.

The regulators aren't acting on just their own penchant for writing disclosure rules. Congress and the executive branch are abetting their zeal for transparency. In his first annual message to Congress in 1901, Teddy Roosevelt declared, "Great corporations exist only because they are created and safeguarded by our institutions; and it is our right and our duty to see that they work in harmony with these institutions. . . . The first requisite is knowledge, full and complete; knowledge which may be made public to the world."[28]

This kind of thinking hasn't changed a bit. In the spirit of such words, Congress created the SEC in 1934. More recently, SEC chairman Arthur Levitt declared disclosure the "dominating innovation" distinguishing the wild days of Wall Street before 1933 and the more sober ones after.[29] It was also in the spirit of those words that Democratic Representative Lane Evans recently sponsored a bill to require U.S. multinationals to report annually on treatment of foreign workers.

Company managers weighing whether to factor social measures into their accountability cycles should take their cue accordingly. They should bear in mind that, if they operate globally, the drift in legislative, regulatory, and social thinking has already gone further elsewhere in the world than in the United States. A number of countries have even toyed with the idea of legislating the disclosure of environmental costs. Denmark has required, since 1996, that over 3,000 companies produce a set of "green accounts."[30] In the United Kingdom, legislators are considering the same. In France, companies have, by law, produced social reports since 1977.

Regulators, of course, simply respond to changing views in other parts of society. They are very much in step with customers, suppliers, communities, and advocacy groups that coax or coerce companies to publish more about their social performance. In just one example, the Council on Economic Priorities announced in 1997 that it was creating a labor auditing process, with its own performance metrics.[31] Avon Products' Suffern, New York, plant was the first factory certified as meeting the Council's social accountability standards—known as SA8000—which relate to such issues as child labor, forced labor, health and safety, freedom of association, and discrimination. Avon will also adopt the standards at its eighteen other plants. Toys "R" Us will ask its 5,000 suppliers to adopt the standards.[32]

Assisted by the press, the Council is likely to gain tremendous leverage to press companies to audit and report working conditions in overseas factories.[33] It was unwittingly assisted last year by the SEC. In May 1998, the SEC reversed the so-called Cracker Barrel decision, which had enabled executives to exclude proxy resolutions relating to personnel issues that the executives deemed "ordinary business." With the new SEC ruling, shareholders can once again submit resolutions that would, for example, require disclosure of overseas labor conditions.

Armed with the clout of the proxy, institutional investors can now weigh in with perhaps even more pressure than regulators, customers, suppliers, and communities. These investors, particularly socially minded ones, manage a mountain of assets, and they want more social reporting of all kinds. As recently as 1995, the Social Investment Forum estimated that 182 institutions with $639 billion in investments—nearly one of every ten dollars under management in the United States—were involved in either shareholder advocacy or social screening of stock portfolios.[34] By 1997, that number had soared 85 percent to $1.2 trillion. At the same time, the number of mutual funds using social or environmental criteria in their investment policy tripled between 1995 and 1997, from 55 to 144.[35]

One of the institutions managing socially responsive portfolios is United States Trust Company of Boston, a manager of over $700 million screened for corporate social responsibility. United States Trust Company wields the clout of its shareholding both in public and behind the scenes. It targets companies persistently and persuasively to become more socially accountable.

In one instance, United States Trust Company applied the pressure of its shareholders at Albertson's Inc., the giant supermarket chain. A holder for a decade of a million shares of Albertson's, USTC expressed disappointment in meetings with company executives in the firm's progress from 1989 to 1994 in promoting women and minorities into management. It then filed a shareholder proposal in 1995 to force Albertson's to provide annual equal employment opportunity statistics. USTC withdrew the resolution before a shareholder vote when Albertson's executives agreed to start publishing a report showing trends in woman and minority employment.[36] United States Trust Company believes the reporting has spurred improvement. Albertson's 1997 report shows female officials and managers jumping from 26.4 percent to 33.4 percent of the workforce from 1995 to 1997. Minorities rose from 13.3 percent to 16.6.

Another prominent player in pushing the social agenda through its stock holdings is the ICCR, the association that represents $75 billion in assets for organizations like the Presbyterian Church and the Rabbinical Pension Board (see Chapter 2). Over the years, the ICCR has stirred action in U.S. corporations across a broad set of issues. Since 1996, it has sponsored over 500 shareholder resolutions at hundreds of companies challenging executives on issues relating to tobacco production; business in Burma and China; equal employment opportunity; board diversity; equal credit opportunity;

urban, rural, and international lending; environmental reporting; maquiladoras; the McBride Principles on Northern Ireland; sweat-shop labor; and military production. ICCR, often allied with other investors, relentlessly presses for reporting of diversity, environmental, and fair-lending data.

Adding to the pressure for data, though not vociferously, are the many mutual funds popping up that require social data for their analysts. One of the best established is the socially minded Calvert Group, which manages $5 billion in assets. However, a number of mainstream fund families have launched new socially responsible funds in recent years to capture do-gooder dollars. In 1998, even Merrill Lynch did so. It created the Principled Values Portfolio. The message for executives is this: You can follow the strengthening of social issues by following the flow of money into mutual funds.

The money invested in socially minded funds comes not just from a marginal group of investors willing to sacrifice profits for social good. A flow of data from advisory firms like Kinder, Lydenberg, and Domini, based in Cambridge, Massachusetts, shows the funds can attract money from people demanding a competitive return. In 1990, Kinder, Lydenberg, and Domini developed the Domini Social Index of 400 socially responsible corporations. From 1990 through 1997, it yielded total annual returns of 19.90 percent, beating the Standard & Poor's 500 return of 18.23 percent.

With such data in hand, even mainstream money managers have begun to roll social criteria into stock picking. Financial-services giant Swiss Bank Corporation, since merged with UBS, has devised a four-stage methodology for assessing the environmental performance of potential stock picks. Analysts first dig for data in a company's report. They also pluck facts and figures from company answers to a bank questionnaire. They then create an aggregated final ranking of overall financial and environmental performance.[37]

As investment managers press their case for more reporting of social performance measures, pension funds may not be far behind. Until now, pension-fund managers have mainly wielded their clout to strengthen the accountability of corporate boards. But they could easily apply their muscle to getting companies to improve social measurement and reporting. Already, hints of their willingness to act have cropped up. Florida's pension fund voted in May 1997 to sell its $825 million in tobacco stocks. Washington voted in June 1997 to sell its $250 million.[38]

Social issues have moved up the pension-fund managers' agendas. How high they will go, nobody knows, but the lesson is that even when socially responsible business practices don't make clear financial sense, the public and state legislators can press fiduciaries into action. As the fiduciaries feel the pressure, companies will, too.

Whatever the merits of the forces gathering to push companies into social accountability, executives have no choice but to pay more attention. Socially conscious investors are more sophisticated, affluent and focused than ever. Consider that, in 1997, the pension funds allied with the International Brotherhood of Teamsters filed a shareholder resolution calling on H.J. Heinz to disclose the amount and recipients of soft-dollar political contributions. Under pressure, Heinz agreed to the disclosure.[39]

These external forces prescribe a bad-cop form of accountability, of course. Better that business self-prescribe good-cop accountability. Managers should take the measure of their stakeholders and preempt the possibility of getting put on the stand, under bright lights, in a court of public opinion. No public firm can afford to lose stakeholder loyalty through deficient or impenetrable social reporting. They must manage with social metrics throughout the accountability cycle, internally and externally. With appropriate social performance measurement and reporting, they can preserve profits as well as boost societal standing.

THE IMPERATIVE OF LINKAGE

Many social investors don't care about quantifying the link between social action and financial gain. They are happy to go with what their gut tells them—good behavior is good business. However, executives who want to develop a durable, credible set of measures should put a pencil to paper figuring out the linkage. Otherwise, they risk seeing social measures tossed aside and ignored in the same way as were operational measures, as discussed in the last chapter. Creating sustainable value for the enterprise requires creating value for both shareholders and society at the same time.

Margaret Kerr, at Northern Telecom, argues for a practical approach. "The reality is that programs put in place only because it's the 'right thing to do'—or because governments require them—are vulnerable," she says. "They're subject to the whim of legislators, swaying public priorities, and financial cycles."[40] Kerr urges managers to quantify how one variable drives another until the link to profit stands clear.

Research investigating the link between social and financial performance has yielded conclusions pro and con.[41] The partisans of socially responsible business point to studies that show, for example, that the stock prices of the twenty-eight companies that won the U.S. Department of Labor's award for exemplary affirmative action jumped 1 percent on the day of and day after the award's announcement. They add that companies that lost discrimination suits saw their stocks slip 0.5 percent.[42] The most that can be concluded from such studies, however, is that investors *do* pay attention to disclosure of social performance information.

A study reported in 1997 illustrates the overall contradictory nature of the social-financial link.[43] Researchers Jennifer Griffin and John Mahon looked at the relationship between four measures of social performance and five measures of financial performance in just the chemical industry. The four social measures are *Fortune* magazine's most-admired company scores; the Kinder, Lydenberg, Domini index of social performance, which scores firms in eight social categories; the Toxics Release Inventory reported to the Environmental Protection Agency; and the "generosity index" of corporate philanthropy devised by the publishers of *Corporate 500 Directory of Corporate Philanthropy*. The five financial measures are return on equity, return on assets, total assets, asset age, and five-year return on sales.

Griffin and Mahon found that the *Fortune* and Kinder, Lydenberg, and Domini measures do, to some extent, correlate with financial performance, whereas the Toxics Release Inventory and generosity index do not. Dow Chemical and Monsanto, for example, ranked high in the *Fortune* and social scores as well as the financial ones. Their Toxics Release Inventory and philanthropy scores did not correlate with financial results at all.

The lesson, as with operational measures, is that each company must examine the links in its own chain of causation to isolate the factors that drive the creation of value. Gut feel and generalized data won't do. Nortel Networks statisticians, working with the

Ethics Officers Consortium, are now seeking to quantify the link between ethical performance and employee satisfaction. The company has already quantified the link among employee satisfaction, customer satisfaction, and profits, much as at Sears (see Chapter 9). It now seeks to complete the chain of causation from ethical behavior to profits. (Nortel believes that high ethics also lead to a great reputation, but the company has as yet found no way to quantify the link between reputation and profits.[44])

Other firms should follow Nortel Networks' lead. They need to show how the dominoes of social performance—and which dominoes—fall forward to knock down the targets of financial performance. In the best of all worlds, executives should convert social targets directly into financial ones—like Baxter International does with environmental management. Many already do when it comes to the easy targets, like reducing landfill costs. But companies have to extend that thinking across each social performance area executives target for action.

Yale researchers recently showed how the poor translation of performance measures into graspable terms bars their incorporation into mainstream decision making. In a survey of selected *Fortune 500* CFOs, respondents noted four obstacles to the use of environmental indicators to measure corporate performance: too few data sources, lack of quantified data, lack of tools for quantifying environmental data, and unreliable data. The researchers conclude that "the absence of available data linking environmental and financial performance, not a belief that environmental issues are irrelevant, is preventing a broader consideration of environmental factors."[45]

The challenge is to create the links that will help social measures pass the CFOs' sniff test for useful management information. This will require a proven link to critical financial measures like cash flow and earnings growth. While this is not always readily possible, the effort spent to clarify the connections, even if ultimately qualitative, will pay back in managers' better understanding the variables in the stakeholder-shareholder equation.

Of course, managers should not rule out a measure simply because of difficulty in quantifying its link to financial measures. Many measures offer useful decision-making information. They allow managers to trade off costs and benefits, even if not reported in the same unit of measure. Managers may also decide to go ahead with programs that contribute to social goals with no apparent financial benefit. But the investigation of the causal links among all measures gives managers much more insight to run daily operations and execute corporate strategy.

THE SOCIAL AUDIT

In many people's minds, the way to handle social measurement and disclosure is with a social audit. Since the 1970s, various researchers and companies have pioneered methods of "social auditing," an ambiguous term that has come to mean various combinations of accounting for, reporting on, and auditing social impacts.[46] Few companies adopted the early models, and those that did dropped them with other fads of the 1970s. Social auditing became no more than a sterile accounting exercise. Companies never adopted it as a tool for articulating strategy, improving performance, or delivering value. To operating managers, it was a public-relations gimmick.

Among the early developers of social auditing were Raymond Bauer and Daniel Fenn, who developed an audit of specific programs, like minority hiring and pollution control. They then compared costs and benefits to both company and community.[47] At about the same time, David Linowes proposed a socioeconomic operating statement that showed improvements and detriments to people, the environment, and consumers.[48] Ralph Estes proposed a cost-benefit statement that produced a bottom-line net social surplus or cost to society.[49] Abt Associates, a consulting firm based in Cambridge, Massachusetts, produced a social balance sheet and income statement in 1973. The statements from Abt, where one of the authors, Marc Epstein, was director of Social Measurement Services, divided benefits and costs, in dollars, by stakeholders. Abt then computed net social income. In the early 1970s, Abt even published its own social accounting in its annual report.[50]

These and a number of other efforts brought the social audit to methodological maturity, but they eventually slipped into the annals of academia. Only in recent years have companies like The Body Shop and Ben & Jerry's revived the social audit. They have begun to make social-performance measures part of the core of company operations. As a result, the audits, in some form, are likely to endure.

The audits by various companies today each take a different form. We believe, however, that companies need not adopt a pre-defined format for measuring and reporting social performance. Instead, they should take the same approach as with financial and operational measures: Reconsider strategy. Articulate objectives. Pinpoint critical success factors. Devise measures that gauge success among appropriate stakeholders. Evaluate impacts on company stakeholders. Work the measures into the remaining steps of the accountability cycle to drive high performance.

If not integrated into the workings of the accountable corporation in this fashion, social-performance measurement will become as irrelevant as much of today's financial accounting. It will become an after-the-fact exercise that follows fixed rules that have little relation to the strategy or business of the company. It must be a proactive exercise that drives continuous and breakthrough improvement.

As for reporting on social performance, managers again should not choose predefined categories. They should choose to disclose the most pertinent of the measures selected for managing the business internally. The choice of measures must reflect the long term, must encompass all stakeholders, and must get at the drivers of value. Executives must report them in a package along with financial and operational performance—even if the company issues a separate social report for the benefit of target audiences.

Executives have no choice but to make this happen. As society's other institutions flounder, corporations must fill the void to ensure their own success. That means executives must sort out which arenas of social performance they must participate in, even if only for the sake of fulfilling society's notion of appropriate corporate social responsibility and philanthropy. They must not let the ambiguity of the task become an excuse for failing to act. Only by creating the fully accountable organization—financially, operationally, and socially—can executives create wealth and well-being for themselves, for the company, and for society.

PART FOUR

OPPORTUNITY
BEYOND CRISIS

11

The
Accountable Manager

W e all admire accountable managers. They stand tall at the podium and declare ambitious goals. They boldly launch initiatives to meet each goal. They stand tall once again to report on success. No brag, just fact.

Accountable managers are heroic figures. They act with candor, optimism, and tenacity. They wield, as a precision tool, an accounting of financial, operational, and social performance, to change behavior and motivate excellence—in themselves and in others. As John Browne, chief executive of British Petroleum, has said, "We have an aspiration to lead through performance—on a sustained basis over time—on a range of different parameters."[1]

Accountable managers are rarer than they should be. Why? Because most managers fail to grasp the opportunity before them. They interpret accountability as a tool from the dark side of management, as a noose of obligations. Too few comprehend accountability as a tool to empower the organization, as a lever for unparalleled performance.

Managing the accountable organization today has become a challenge on many fronts. Fast disappearing are the days when delivering just the budget made a manager a hero. To be sure, the financials remain all-important. As Browne has said, "Our responsibility is to deliver a highly competitive return to our shareholders—each quarter. If we fail to do that and if our performance is weak, we're letting down the people who have trusted us with their money."[2]

Nonfinancial performance, however, has risen in importance to rival financial. At British Petroleum, Browne has called on all employees to embrace the principle of "mutual advantage," engaging in business that benefits British Petroleum as well as local communities and other stakeholders. In 1998, British Petroleum even came out with a social-performance report, in which Browne committed to detailed measurement of social impacts and contributions in future reports.[3] "Now there is a wider agenda," he says, "including the environment, employment and labour standards, distribution of income . . . as well as business ethics."[4]

Business historian Alfred D. Chandler, Jr., noted the broadening scope of management more than twenty-five years ago: "In the past, businessmen have devoted their energies to economic affairs, giving far less attention to cultural, social, or even political matters. Precisely because they have created an enormously productive economy and the most affluent society in the world, the non-economic challenges are now becoming more critical than the economic ones."[5]

If they have not already done so, business people need to redefine the scope of the business challenge. They cannot deliver long-term results if they view their jobs as simply maximizing short-term results for shareholders. Nor can they view their jobs as solely maximizing value for customers, or employees, or any other single group. In the words of Peter Drucker, they must "maximize the wealth-producing capacity of the enterprise."[6]

That is the job of the accountable manager, to create new value through the collaborative efforts of all stakeholders. As detailed earlier in this book, meeting the challenge of accountability requires an active, independent board of directors. It requires a family of measures for performance in all dimensions—financial, operational, and social. It requires the management control systems—planning, budgeting, feedback, pay—that operate in a cycle of accountability that delivers continuous learning and improvement. It also requires candid reporting, inside and outside the company, to establish the complete commitment of all stakeholders to create a winning performance.

Perhaps the most critical element of all are measures, which are the currency of the accountable organization. Without them, accountable relationships cease. People have no clear way of articulating the details of strategy. They have no credible way of setting targets, assessing value, and appraising performance. They have no useful medium of exchanging comparative information for fact-based improvement. Numbers are a hard currency. Yet, without them, managers can buy and sell the notion of "accountability" too cheaply. Only the genuine article will yield the sought-after benefits.

Broad reporting, internally and externally, is perhaps the second-most critical element of accountability. Without it, a company cannot completely mature into a fully accountable organization. By setting targets behind closed doors, executives can cut people off from the gravity—and motivating power—of making commitments. By circumscribing reporting, they can dry up the rejuvenating stream of feedback, from both employees and an enlightened public, that spurs competitive advances. Accountability without the transparency of broad disclosure can break into bud, but it cannot bloom.

What measures should a company report? Many measures should properly remain proprietary, like those that grade individual performance or those that would telegraph trade secrets to competitors. That leaves a host of data that top managers can safely put on stage. As a general rule, managers should provide the high-level figures that they use to guide strategic and day-to-day decision making. These are the figures from the matrix first introduced in Chapter 7. Table 11-1 completes this matrix with a sampling of measures from Chapters 8 through 10.

LEADING THE ACCOUNTABLE ORGANIZATION

The task of creating the accountable organization doesn't begin, or end, with installing the systems of accountability. It starts and finishes with acts of leadership. The systems for governance, measurement, control, and reporting require untold discipline to

TABLE 11-1

THE CORPORATE FAMILY OF MEASURES, BY STAKEHOLDER

STAKEHOLDER	MEASURES (FINANCIAL, OPERATIONAL, SOCIAL)
Shareholders	Earnings-per-share growth Cash flow per share Economic profit Total factor productivity Percentage of new-product sales
Customers	Customer satisfaction Product quality index Repair incidence Customer loyalty
Employees	Employee satisfaction Employee turnover Productivity Diversity in management Training time per year
Community	Index of environmental impacts Safety record Community satisfaction Charitable and community contributions

Note: The choice of stakeholder groups depends entirely on strategy. It generally would include four or five groups.

implement. But the success of accountable management also depends on soft managerial skills.

One of the first tasks of leadership is communication. Top managers must communicate the values of the accountable organization, the goals of the organization, the behaviors they expect, and the results ultimately achieved, blemishes and all. Consistent, frequent reinforcement signals to employees that accountability counts.

When Michael Walsh took over as chief executive of Tenneco in the early 1990s, he gathered people in Houston and asked a question: How many people felt that he could guarantee them their jobs in one year? About 80 percent said no. About 20 percent said yes. Walsh told the 80 percent they were right. Only they, working together as a team, could turn the company around and guarantee themselves a job. He made his point: people had to be accountable, together, to make the company prosper.[7]

Walsh and later chief executive Mead reinforced this sort of message at every opportunity. When they observed a tradition of executives excusing negative variances—often blaming weather or economic factors—they insisted the executives replace that tradition with a new one, handling negative variances with a group discussion on how to reverse them. As Mead used to joke, "You only get one weather excuse a year, and then that's it."[8]

A second task of leaders of accountable organizations is demonstrating accountable behavior. They must set an example of evaluating performance with numbers, of eliciting feedback, and of coaching and consulting. Day in and day out, they must use the objective measures of accountability to further continuous improvement, in the spirit of slaying the dragon of organizational mediocrity, not in slaying the careers of competent people.

Accountable managers guard against playing the role of dictator and prosecutor. They know that instilling fear will knock the benefits of accountability from their grasp. In the beginning, employees often interpret measures as tools to affix blame for failures, as the noose dangled about their necks. They then knuckle under, complying narrowly with the dictates of their jobs, unless shown otherwise.

The leaders of accountable organizations walk a fine line. On the negative side, they can create a culture of compliance. On the positive side, they can cultivate a culture of commitment. Staying on the positive side is the nub of the leadership. As Allstate's former CEO Jerry Choate once said, "We have to create an environment that makes it easy for people to commit to excellence, and commit to winning in the marketplace. I can commit for me; I cannot commit for anybody else."[9]

Allstate spells out the behaviors necessary for commitment in "The Allstate Partnership." The Partnership first lists what Allstate expects of employees: "Perform at levels that significantly increase our ability to outperform the competition. . . . Take on assignments critical to meeting business objectives. . . . Demonstrate a high level of commitment to achieving company goals." It then lists what employees can expect of Allstate: "Offer work that is meaningful. . . . Advise you on your performance through regular feedback. . . . Create learning opportunities through education and job assignments."[10]

When Choate was CEO, he showed how serious he was about developing appropriate behavior when, in 1994, he launched the Quarterly Leadership Measurement System, which measures the perceptions of employees twice each year. Among other questions, employees answer eight that relate to leadership. For example, to gauge empowerment: "How often do you have the responsibility and authority you need to assure you can deliver quality service to your customers?" To gauge trust and open communications: "How confident are you that our company gives you the straight story on company issues?" From the answers, Allstate compiles a "Leadership Index" for senior managers. In 1996, Allstate began to pay a portion of senior managers' incentive pay according to the index.[11]

When Choate went to the field, he asked employees to make sure they challenged local management and him to live up to the Allstate Partnership. "Leadership really controls the work environment, the atmosphere," says Choate.

A third task of leaders of accountable organizations is inspiring, insisting on, and implementing action plans for boosting performance, often radically. From the start, top executives have to challenge the organization to achieve or surpass goals that will guarantee rapid competitive advances.

In 1993, Northern Telecom faced a quality crisis. It shipped large telephone switching systems that customers later had to update with thousands of "patches," or software fixes. By 1995, its central office switches required 2,800 patches. Every time customers installed a patch, they worked on a live switch, always risking, at least to a small extent, severing phone service to sometimes thousands of callers. "We were asking our customers to go through this, what I call, 'exciting' experience 2,800 times in the course of this one software release," recalls John Roth, Nortel Networks chief executive.[12]

How did Nortel Networks reverse course so that, today, its software quality ranks among the best? "We set unreasonable targets," says Roth, then head of North American operations. Customers, he believed, needed an order of magnitude improvement, so, in the face of engineers' objections, he set a target of cutting patches to 20 percent of the current number. Engineers beat that goal, and a recent release had just one hundred patches. "It was an act of will," says Roth.

An act of will. Accountable leaders must take many of them if they hope to create the accountable organization.

One of the more ticklish tasks of leadership is making sure that pay systems reward accountability. Too often, incentive plans succumb to the failings outlined in General Electric Vice President Steven Kerr's classic article "On the Folly of Rewarding A, While Hoping for B." As Kerr notes, management wants long-term growth but rewards quarterly earnings; or management wants teamwork yet rewards individual effort; or management wants candor but rewards only the bearers of good news.[13]

Though no formula works for all companies, management should bear in mind several things: Supporting accountability requires pay only for long-term financial performance, like the rewards at Briggs & Stratton, which pay off only if the company earns more than the cost of capital for years to come. It requires pay for managerial practices and process results that lead to better long-term financial performance, like the rewards at Nortel Networks that pay for customer-satisfaction scores. It requires pay for the behaviors that support accountability, like the quarterly indexes of leadership and diversity performance at Allstate. Incentive pay that promotes behavior at odds with accountability can make a charade of the whole notion.

The ultimate act of leadership is sticking with the principles and practices of accountability long enough to institutionalize the concept. Accountability is not just an add-on program. It is a way of life. The goal is to integrate it into the foundation of the business. Like the principles of quality management and cross-functional teamwork, accountability must become a component of the basic skill set of managers in the competitive enterprise of the future. People then more readily do what managers expect, rather than just what they inspect. When everyone understands his or her marching orders, the leaders of the organization can ease their emphasis on systems that manage individual behavior.

At Tenneco, Mead first stressed new systems to instill accountability. Managers regularly submitted to quality reviews; operations reviews; capital reviews; executive personnel reviews; strategy reviews; and environment, health, and safety reviews—all linked with planning, budgeting, measurement, performance management, and compensation systems. In recent years, however, as the discipline of an accountable culture has taken hold, Mead has begun to look at paring the systems.[14] His belief is that the will of leadership, exercised over and over, eventually supersedes at least some of the systems of accountability.

Senior executives who exercise such leadership, and install the systems of the accountable organization, stand to reap the rewards we've detailed throughout this book. They will also remain one step ahead of outsiders—regulators, the public, the press, lawmakers, and key stakeholders—that are pressing them for greater accountability. They will position themselves to win—in the markets for capital, for labor, for customers, for suppliers, and for community support.

THE SOCIAL DIVIDEND

Senior executives will also position themselves to win in society. Whatever stand managers take over the role of business in society, they will find that practicing accountability for long-term, sustainable success places them squarely in line of doing well by doing good. This does not mean that leaders will achieve excellence by instructing their people to wake up every morning and prepare to work for society. If only because such a goal is so vague, such a directive would, for most companies, be an operational mistake.

As Eastman Chemical's Earnest Deavenport says, "You can get into a lot of trouble if you're talking to a big shareholder and saying, 'Well, as CEO, I think my accountability is to the greater society.' And he'd say, 'The heck you say, your accountability is to me; I own a million shares of your stock!'"

Framing the debate as one of sorting out who should work for whom gets managers and employees pondering the wrong challenge. By placing the interest of business above society, or the interest of society above business, managers lock themselves in a no-win squabble over how they should *divide* value. That debate, though a serious one, shifts with social and economic winds, often driven by special-interest groups, economic cycles, and politics. Instead, the argument should turn around the question of how to craft strategies to *create* value.

Recall that Eastman's mission is to create "superior value" for customers, employees, investors, suppliers, and publics (communities, government agencies) *at the same time.*

To be sure, managers struggling to produce value for a community of stakeholders must make tradeoffs. For starters, they have to deliver at least the opportunity cost of capital to shareholders or they will lose access to the money supporting the business. They also have to deliver value to other stakeholders, however. How much value? Something roughly commensurate to each constituency's contribution to company prosperity. If they don't deliver that value, they risk losing talented workers, customers, and even community favor. That's why Briggs & Stratton's John Shiely says, "We create no value at all unless we effectively integrate our employees, customers, suppliers and the community into the process of value creation."[15]

Experience shows that few people agree on how companies should slice the economic pie. That's why accountable managers should not focus on slicing at all. They should focus on enlarging. "In the United States today, we spend far too much energy on value allocation and far too little on value creation," says Shiely.[16]

The notion to which accountable managers should aspire is that of value creator. It may sound like a heroic ideal today; yet, it should not remain so for the future. Competitive forces require that more firms deliver more value than ever before. They must deliver that value through astute management of the collective efforts of people inside and outside the company. The principles of accountable management provide a mindset, model, and set of tools for achieving this value.

How to get started? Most managers would do well to begin their journey toward realizing the potential of the accountable organization with the same courageous move of Ed Woolard: A public commitment to measuring and accounting for value never before thought possible.

NOTES

Chapter One: The Accountability Advantage

1. Bill Birchard, "Going Green," *Enterprise*, January 1993, 13.
2. DuPont Safety, Health and the Environment 1997 Progress Report. Includes data as of year-end 1997. The reductions in air emissions and carcinogens are since 1997. The reductions in hazardous waste are since 1991. To view these figures on-line, see http://www.dupont.com/corp/environment
3. Transcript of author interview with Ed Woolard for Birchard, "Going Green," 10–14.
4. The DuPont Commitment, Safety, Health, and Environment, undated, page 1.
5. Charles Handy, *The Age of Paradox* (Boston: Harvard Business School Press, 1994), 230.
6. Robert Denham and Michael Porter, "Lifting All Boats: Increasing the Payoff from Private Investment in the U.S. Economy (Report of the Capital Allocation Subcouncil to the Competitiveness Policy Council)" (Washington, D.C.: Competitiveness Policy Council, 1995), xv, 76.
7. Ira M. Millstein, "Director Professionalism (Report of the National Association of Corporate Directors Blue Ribbon Commission)" (Washington, D.C.: National Association of Corporate Directors, 1996), Appendix A1.
8. General Motors Board of Directors Corporate Governance Guidelines, revised August 1995, as cited in Millstein, "Director Professionalism," 25.
9. Peter F. Drucker, "We Need to Measure, Not Count," *Wall Street Journal*, 13 April 1993.
10. Steven Hronec, Partner, Arthur Andersen. Personal communication, October 1998.
11. Many authors have made this point. See, for example, Robert S. Kaplan and David P. Norton, *The Balanced Scorecard* (Boston: Harvard Business School Press, 1996); Geary A. Rummler and Alan P. Brache, *Improving Performance: How to Manage the White Space on the Organization Chart* (San Francisco:

Jossey-Bass Publishers, 1995); and Steven M. Hronec, *Vital Signs: Using Quality, Time, and Cost Performance Measurements to Chart Your Company's Future* (New York: American Management Association, 1993).

12. James L. Heskett, W. Earl Sasser, Jr., and Leonard A. Schlesinger, *The Service Profit Chain: How Leading Companies Link Profit and Growth to Loyalty, Satisfaction, and Value* (New York: The Free Press, 1997), 210.

13. Renaissance Solutions and *CFO* magazine, "Building a Management System to Implement Your Strategy: Survey Findings on the Effectiveness of Strategic Management and Implementation" (Lincoln, MA: Renaissance Solutions, Inc. [Renaissance Worldwide, Inc.], 1996), 2, 5.

14. Bill Birchard, "Closing the Strategy Gap," *CFO*, October 1996, 29.

15. See, for example, John Case, "Opening the Books," *Harvard Business Review* 75, no. 2 (1997): 118–127.

16. Sonja Gallhofer, and Jim Haslam, "Approaching Corporate Accountability: Fragments of the Past," *Accounting and Business Research* 23 (1993): 320, 321.

17. Pamela Sebastian, "Business Bulletin: Corporate Giving Would Face Scrutiny Under Two Proposed Bills," *Wall Street Journal*, 18 Dec. 1997, A1. As of mid-1998, the bill was in committee stage, pending a report by the SEC. See also Anonymous, "The View from Main Street," *The Economist*, 30 May 1998, 20.

18. Louis D. Brandeis, *Other People's Money* (New York: Frederick A. Stokes Company, 1914; Canadian edition, 1932).

19. Tom Copeland, personal communication, September 1998. For further detail on this subject, see Tom Copeland, Tim Koller, and Jack Murrin, *Valuation: Measuring and Managing the Value of Companies*. 2nd ed. (New York: John Wiley & Sons, 1994).

20. Birchard, "How Many Masters," 50, 51. See also John P. Kotter and James L. Heskett, *Corporate Culture and Performance* (New York: The Free Press/Macmillan, 1992), 46–57.

21. Marc J. Epstein, "The Annual Report Report Card," *Business and Society Review* Spring, no. 81 (1992): 83, see table.

22. Author interview with Francis Corby, April 1998. Comment first appeared in Birchard, "How Many Masters," 54.

23. See also Marc J. Epstein, *Measuring Corporate Environmental Performance* (Chicago: Irwin Professional Publishing, 1996).

24. Barbara Rosewicz, "The Checkoff," *Wall Street Journal*, 21 May 1996, A1.

25. William J. Holstein, "Drink Coke, and Be Nice," *U.S. News & World Report*, 9 June 1997, 50–51.

26. H. Thomas Johnson and Robert S. Kaplan, *Relevance Lost: The Rise and Fall of Management Accounting* (Boston: Harvard Business School Press, 1987; paperback edition, 1991).

27. Robert S. Kaplan and Robin Cooper, *Cost & Effect: Using Integrated Cost Systems to Drive Profitability and Performance* (Boston: Harvard Business School Press, 1998).

Chapter Two: Facing the Crisis

1. The Tenneco story in this chapter is based on author interviews with multiple Tenneco executives, in October 1997. Included were Chief Executive Dana

Mead, Chief Financial Officer Bob Blakely, Senior Vice President Barry Schuman, and Executive Vice President Richard Wambold.

2. Joel Kurtzman, "Is Your Company Off Course? Now You Can Find Out Why," *Fortune* 17 February 1997, 128–130.

3. Once again, this argument derives from H. Thomas Johnson and Robert S. Kaplan, *Relevance Lost: The Rise and Fall of Management Accounting* (Boston: Harvard Business School Press, 1987; paperback edition, 1991).

4. For an excellent discussion of how managers make operational decisions, based on extensive research, see Sharon M. McKinnon and William J. Bruns, Jr., *The Information Mosaic* (Boston: Harvard Business School Press, 1992).

5. Some of the history of Tenneco is based on interviews with former controller Ed Milan in July 1994.

6. Arthur Levitt, "The 'Numbers Game.'" (Speech given at the New York University Center for Law and Business, New York, New York: U.S. Securities and Exchange Commission, September 28, 1998). See also Arthur Levitt, "A Financial Partnership" (Speech given at the Financial Executives Institute, New York, New York: U.S. Securities and Exchange Commission, November 16, 1998).

7. Kenneth Rosenzweig and Marilyn Fischer, "Is Managing Earnings Ethically Acceptable?" *Management Accounting* 75, no. 9 (March 1994): 32.

8. Stephen Barr, "Misreporting Results," *CFO*, December 1998, 40.

9. Johnson and Kaplan, *Relevance Lost*, (1987; paperback edition, 1991), 1.

10. Bill Birchard, "The New Finance," *Enterprise*, October 1992, 24.

11. Activity-based costing has spread rapidly across industry, of course. See Robert S. Kaplan and Robin Cooper, *Cost & Effect: Using Integrated Cost Systems to Drive Profitability and Performance* (Boston: Harvard Business School Press, 1997). Some of the earlier cases that have driven progress include: R. S. Kaplan, "Kanthal (A)," Harvard Business School Case #9-190-002, Boston, 1989; R. Cooper and K. H. Wruck, "Siemens Electric Motor Works (A)," Harvard Business School Case #9-191-006, Boston, 1988; S. Datar and R. S. Kaplan, "The Co-operative Bank," Harvard Business School Case #9-195-196, Boston, 1995. The Kanthal and Co-operative Bank cases address customer profitability. The Siemens case addresses product profitability.

12. Birchard, "New Finance," 24.

13. Robert Stasey, "What We've Learned About Using Scorecards" (Internal document, Analog Devices Inc., 1997), 8–9.

14. Deloitte & Touche Management Consulting, "Performance Measurement Survey" (New York: Deloitte & Touche LLP, 1995). In a June 1998 phone conversation, Deloitte & Touche's John Powers confirmed that the dismal results of the 1995 survey persist largely unchanged.

15. Overhead slides and author interview with Robert Stasey, director of quality improvement, September 1997.

16. See John Case, *Open-Book Management* (New York: HarperBusiness, 1995). See also John F. Case, *The Open-Book Experience: Lessons from over 100 Companies Who Successfully Transformed Themselves* (Reading, MA: Addison-Wesley, 1998).

17. Bill Birchard, "Finding Their Smiles," *CFO*, December 1994, 42. A more detailed story about AES appeared in Bill Birchard, "Power to the People," *CFO*, March 1995, 38–43.

18. Author interview with Gerry Isom, July 1996. Material updated in authors' interviews with Tom Valerio, senior vice president and transformation officer, September and November 1997.

19. Francis J. Gouillart and James N. Kelly, *Transforming the Organization* (New York: McGraw-Hill, 1995): 29.

20. Marc J. Epstein and Moses L. Pava, "The Shareholder's Use of Corporate Annual Reports: A Summary of Findings" (Paper presented at the Annual Congress of the European Accounting Association, Turku, Finland, April 1993), 18, 21, 22. See also Marc J. Epstein and Moses L. Pava, *The Shareholder's Use of Corporate Annual Reports* (Greenwich, CT: JAI Press, 1993).

21. Pat McConnell, Janet Pegg, and David Zion, "Employee Stock Option Expense Pro Forma Impact on EPS and Operating Margins" (New York: Bear Stearns & Co. Inc., 1 May 1998).

22. Daniel Murray, Andrew Smithers, and John Emerson, "USA: The Impact of Employee Stock Options" (London: Smithers & Co. Ltd., 1998). On the subject of options accounting, see also Elizabeth MacDonald, "Options' Effect on Earnings Sparks Debate," *Wall Street Journal*, 13 May 1998, C1, C2; and Gretchen Morgenson, "Stock Options Are Not a Free Lunch," *Forbes*, 18 May 1998: 212–217.

23. Marc J. Epstein and Krishna G. Palepu, "Analysts Speak Out on Corporate Communications" (Unpublished manuscript, 1998), 5. Note that the research surveyed only "star analysts" identified annually by *Institutional Investor* and the *Wall Street Journal*.

24. Epstein and Palepu, "Analysts Speak," 5, 6.

25. Ibid., 7.

26. Shelley Taylor, "Full Disclosure 1998" (Palo Alto: Shelley Taylor & Associates, 1998).

27. Joann S. Lublin, "Minimal Disclosure Sparks Holder Suits," *Wall Street Journal*, 17 June 1998).

28. Ernst & Young, "Measures That Matter" (Boston: Ernst & Young LLP, 1997), 8–9. For other recent research that shows that analysts increasingly value non-financial information, see Gaetan Breton and Richard J. Taffler, "What Drives Sell-Side Analyst Stock Recommendation Decisions: A Content Analysis Approach," *Working Paper* (1998).

29. Arthur Levitt, "Investor Education: Disclosure for the 1990s" (Speech given at McIntire School of Commerce, Charlottesville, Virginia: Securities and Exchange Commission, 1995).

30. Steven M. H. Wallman, "The Future of Accounting and Financial Reporting Part II: The Colorized Approach," *Accounting Horizons* 10, no. 2 (July 1996): 138.

31. American Institute of Certified Public Accountants, "Improving Business Reporting—A Customer Focus (Executive Summary report)" (New York: American Institute of Certified Public Accountants, 1994), 9.

32. C. Richard Aldridge and Janet L. Colbert, "We Need Better Financial Reporting," *Management Accounting* 79, no. 1 (July 1997): 36.

33. American Institute of Certified Public Accountants, "Improving Business Reporting—A Customer Focus (Executive Summary report)" (New York: American Institute of Certified Public Accountants, 1994), 3.

34. For a detailed description of Cleveland's health-care measurement system, see Gary E. Rosenthal and Dwain L. Harper, "Cleveland Health Quality

Choice: A Model for Collaborative Community-Based Outcomes Assessment," *Journal on Quality Improvement (Joint Commission on Accreditation of Healthcare Organizations)* 20, no. 8 (1994): 425–442.

35. Raquel Santiago, "MetLife Scalpel to Lop HMO's Hospitals, Doctors," *Crain's Cleveland Business* (18 July 1994): 1, 27.

36. Raquel Santiago, "Aetna to Open Care Sites," *Crain's Cleveland Business* (11 April 1994): 1, 23.

37. For the complete story of the 1994 changes in the structure of the health-care industry in Cleveland, see Anonymous, "The Battle for Cleveland," *Integrated Healthcare Report* 3, no. 3 (September 1994): 1–8.

38. Pamela Sebastian "Clothing Labels," *Wall Street Journal,* 22 August 1996, A1.

39. See, for example, www.jcaho.org/perfmeas/oryx/op_oncol.htm

40. Joint Commission on Accreditation of Healthcare Organizations, "Joint Commission Announces ORYX; The Next Evolution in Accreditation" (Oakbrook Terrace, IL: Joint Commission on Accreditation of Healthcare Organizations, 1997).

41. See also Joint Commission on Accreditation of Healthcare Organizations, "ORYX: The Next Evolution in Accreditation—Questions and Answers about the Joint Commission's Planned Integration of Performance Measures into the Accreditation Process" (Oakbrook Terrace, IL: Joint Commission on Accreditation of Healthcare Organizations, 1998).

42. Author interview with Alan Fisher, executive director of California Reinvestment Committee, October 1997.

43. Coalition for Environmentally Responsible Economies, "CERES Report Standard Form" (Boston, MA: Coalition for Environmentally Responsible Economies, 1998).

44. Author interview with Philip Hillman, September 1997.

45. Author interview with Gary Brouse, ICCR director of equality programs, September 1997.

46. Interfaith Center on Corporate Responsibility, *The Proxy Resolutions Book* (New York: Interfaith Center on Corporate Responsibility, 1998). See also Interfaith Center on Corporate Responsibility, "1996–1997 Annual Report of the Interfaith Center on Corporate Responsibility," *The Corporate Examiner,* 17 October 1997, 9.

47. Andrew J. Hoffman, "A Strategic Response to Investor Activism," *Sloan Management Review* 37, no. 2 (1996): 51(14).

48. Sue Shellenbarger, "If You Want a Firm That's Family Friendly, the List Is Very Short, " *Wall Street Journal,* 6 September 1995, B1. See also Sue Shellenbarger, "Those Lists Ranking Best Places to Work Are Rising in Influence," *Wall Street Journal,* 26 August 1998, B1.

49. Keith H. Hammonds, Roy Furchgott, Steve Hamm, and Paul C. Judge, "Work and Family," *Business Week,* 15 September 1997, 96–99.

50. Carl Quintanilla, "AMR's American Wins Top Honors in Study of Airlines," *Wall Street Journal,* 25 April 1995.

51. Alex Markels, "Customer Satisfaction Falls Broadly, Paced by Complaints About Insurers," *Wall Street Journal,* 7 November 1995, A4. See also Lindley H. Clark, "Consumers, in New Satisfaction Index, Rate U.S.-Made Goods Over Services," *Wall Street Journal,* 26 October 1994.

52. Leon E. Wynter, "Report Cards, Not Placards for NAACP (Business & Race Column)," *Wall Street Journal,* 3 September 1997, B1.

53. Roy S. Johnson, "The 50 Best Companies for Asians, Blacks & Hispanics," *Fortune*, 3 August 1998, 94–122.

Chapter Three: Calling for Governance

1. The story of Tyco International in this chapter is based on author interviews with Dennis Kozlowski, October 1997, and Philip Hampton, September 1997.
2. For more information on the role of boards of directors, see the extensive research of Jay Lorsch. For example, Jay W. Lorsch, "Empowering the Board," *Harvard Business Review* 73, no. 1 (January/February 1995): 107–117. See also Jay W. Lorsch and Elizabeth MacIver, *Pawns or Potentates* (Boston: Harvard Business School Press, 1989).
3. Adolf A. Berle and Gardiner C. Means, *The Modern Corporation and Private Property* (New York: Macmillan, 1932).
4. Marc J. Epstein and Krishna G. Palepu, "Analysts Speak Out on Corporate Communications" (Unpublished manuscript, 1998).
5. 1997 Campbell Soup proxy statement, 9.
6. 1998 Campbell Soup proxy statement, 13–15.
7. As cited in John A. Byrne, "Putting More Stock in Good Governance, " *Business Week*, 15 September 1997, 116. For a current description of Calpers's policy, see California Public Employees Retirement System, "U.S. Corporate Governance Core Principles and Guidelines" (Sacramento: California Public Employees Retirement System, 1998).
8. See, for example, Anonymous, "Not Awakening the Dead," *The Economist*, 10 August 1996, 51.
9. Robert F. Felton, Alec Hudnut, and Jennifer van Heeckeren, "Putting Value on Corporate Governance," *The McKinsey Quarterly* 4 (1996): 170.
10. Jennifer H. van Heeckeren, "Why Investors Push for Strong Corporate Boards," *Wall Street Journal*, 30 June 1997, A14.
11. Current Trends: Board Independence Continues to Grow. Institutional Shareholder Services, www.cda.com/iss
12. National Association of Corporate Directors, "1997 Corporate Governance Survey" (Washington, D.C.: National Association of Corporate Directors, 1997), 20.
13. Rosemary Lally, "CEO Succession at Campbell Soup," *Corporate Governance Bulletin (Investor Responsibility Research Center)*, July 1997, 3. See also John A. Byrne and Jennifer Reingold, "Wanted: A Few Good CEOs," *Business Week*, 11 August 1997, 64–70.
14. Korn/Ferry International, "Twenty-fifth Annual Board of Directors Study" (New York: Korn/Ferry International, 1998), 28.
15. Author interview with John Nash, October 1997.
16. 1998 Campbell Soup proxy statement, 13.
17. Two independent studies yielded roughly the same results. See National Association of Corporate Directors, "1997 Corporate," 18, 19, and Korn/Ferry International, "Twenty-fifth Annual," 34.
18. Ira M. Millstein, "Director Professionalism (Report of the National Association of Corporate Directors Blue Ribbon Commission)" (Washington, D.C.: National Association of Corporate Directors, 1996).
19. The Business Roundtable, "Statement on Corporate Governance" (Washington, D.C.: The Business Roundtable, 1997).

20. Council of Institutional Investors, "Core Policies, Policies, & Positions" (Washington, D.C.: Council of Institutional Investors, 1998).

21. For an institutional investor's view of enlightened governance practices, see Calpers, "U.S. Corporate."

22. National Association of Corporate Directors, "1997 Corporate." The American Society of Corporate Secretaries published a study of the most common board practices adopted between 1995 and 1997. The results of that study mirror those of the study by the National Association of Corporate Directors. See *Current Board Practices: Second Study*, published February 1998, available from the American Society of Corporate Secretaries, New York. For a synopsis of the study, see American Society of Corporate Secretaries, "New Society Study Notes Emerging Governance Trends," *ASCS Newsletter*, April 1998. The synopsis is also available on the Society's website: www.ascs.org. For added detail on how chief executives and directors of just *Fortune* 500 firms see governance changing in the future, see Korn/Ferry International, "Twenty-fifth Annual."

23. See Hermes Investment Management Limited, "Statement on Corporate Governance and Voting Policy" (London: Hermes Investment Management Limited, 1998).

24. Robert Monks, "Sears, Roebuck & Co. Annual Meeting of Shareholders: Robert A. G. Monks Remarks," delivered in Atlanta, Georgia, 1992.

25. Author interview with Robert Monks, October 1997.

26. S. L. Mintz, "True Lies: How GAAP Conceals the Real Story at Stone & Webster," *CFO*, September 1994, 49–56.

27. Robert Monks recounts the Stone & Webster story in his recent book. See Robert A. G. Monks, *The Emperor's Nightingale: Restoring the Integrity of the Corporation in the Age of Shareholder Activism* (Reading, MA: Addison-Wesley, 1998). See also www.lens-inc.com (www.lens-inc.com/sw/sw.html)

28. 1997 Stone & Webster proxy statement.

29. Robert A. G. Monks and Nell Minow, *Power and Accountability* (New York: HarperBusiness, 1991).

30. Author interview with Robert Monks, October 1997.

31. Carolyn Kay Brancato, "Turnover, Investment Strategies, and Ownership Patterns," *Institutional Investment Report* 2, no. 2 (1998): 21.

32. Ibid., 25, 29.

33. National Association of Corporate Directors, "1997 Corporate," 26.

34. Epstein and Palepu, "Analysts Speak Out."

35. Leland Montgomery, "The Three Faces of Rand," *Financial World* 26 (20 July 1993): 20.

36. Dana Wechsler Linden and Nancy Rotenier, "Good-bye to Berle & Means," *Forbes*, 3 January 1994, 100–103.

37. Carolyn Kay Brancato, "Turnover, Investment Strategies, and Ownership Patterns," *Institutional Investment Report* 2, no. 1 (1998): 46.

38. Willard T. Carleton, James M. Nelson, and Michael S. Weisbach, "The Influence of Institutions on Corporate Governance Through Private Negotiations: Evidence from TIAA-CREF," *Journal of Finance*, in press (1998).

39. International Brotherhood of Teamsters, "America's Least Valuable Directors: A Study of Corporate Board Directors" (Washington, D.C.: International Brotherhood of Teamsters, 1998). See also International Brotherhood of Teamsters, "America's Least Valuable Directors: A Study of Corporate Board

Directors" (Washington, D.C.: The International Brotherhood of Teamsters, Office of Corporate Affairs, 1997).

40. See www.ciicentral.com

41. California Public Employees' Retirement System, "Company Responses to Request for Board Governance Self-Evaluation" (Sacramento: California Public Employees' Retirement System, 1995).

42. John Byrne, Leslie Brown, and Joyce Barnathan, "The Best and Worst Boards," *Business Week,* 8 December 1997, 90–98. See also John A. Byrne and Richard A. Melcher, "The Best and Worst Boards," *Business Week,* 25 November 1996, 62–68.

43. AFL-CIO, "Too Close for Comfort: How Corporate Boardrooms Are Rigged to Overpay CEOs" (Washington, D.C.: American Federation of Labor and Congress of Industrial Organizations, 1998).

44. Kenneth A. Bertsch and Virginia Rosenbaum, "Shareholders Increase Support for Resolutions on Board Independence, Annual Election of Directors," *Corporate Governance Bulletin (Investor Responsibility Research Center)* 15, no. 2 (1998): 4.

45. Kenneth A. Bertsch and Virginia Rosenbaum, "Shareholders Increase Support for Resolutions on Board Independence, Annual Election of Directors," *Corporate Governance Bulletin (Investor Responsibility Research Center)* 15, no. 2 (1998): 3.

46. California Public Employees' Retirement System, "CalPERS Shareholder Proposal to De-Stagger Reebok Board of Directors Passes" (Sacramento: Calpers, 1997).

47. Ken Bertsch, "1998 Shareholder Resolutions: A Proxy Season Overview," *Corporate Governance Highlights (Investor Responsibility Research Center),* 13 February 1998, 2.

48. Kenneth A. Bertsch, Stephen R. Tobey, Robert Newbury, Eric Ovsiew, and Virginia Rosenbaum, "Shareholders, Companies at Odds on Takeover Defenses, But Find Agreement on Board Issues (Proxy Season Wrap-Up)," *Corporate Governance Bulletin (Investor Responsibility Research Center)* 14, no. 2 (1997): 5 sidebar.

49. 1997 Walt Disney Company proxy statement, 14, 16.

50. For the full story, see, for example, Bruce Orwall and Joann S. Lublin, "Investors Take Aim at Disney Board Again," *Wall Street Journal,* 20 February 1998, C1. See also Mark Albright, "After Debate, Disney Shareholders Approve Eisner Pay Package," *Knight-Ridder/Tribune Business News* (Originated from *St. Petersburg Times,* Florida), 26 February 1997, 226B1152.

51. Bruce Orwall, "Disney Holders Use Annual Meeting to Protest Lack of Independent Board," *Wall Street Journal,* 25 February 1998, B8.

52. 1997 Walt Disney Company proxy statement.

53. 1998 Walt Disney Company proxy statement, 25.

54. For full information on the lawsuit, see the website of the New York State Comptroller's Office: www.osc.state.ny.us/divisions/press_office/columb2.htm

55. California Public Employees' Retirement System, "CalPERS Joins Lawsuit Against Columbia/HCA" (Sacramento: Calpers, 1997).

56. Author interview with B. Kenneth West, senior consultant for Corporate Governance, November 1997. For background, see John A. Biggs, "Corporate Governance Assessment: A TIAA-CREF Initiative," *Director's Monthly* 20,

no. 10 (1996): 1–8. See also Teachers Insurance and Annuity Association–College Retirement Equities Fund, "TIAA-CREF Policy Statement on Corporate Governance" (New York: Teachers Insurance and Annuity Association–College Retirement Equities Fund 1997), 20.

57. Sarah A. B. Teslik, "Letter to Jonathan G. Katz, Secretary of the U.S. Securities and Exchange Commission" (Washington, D.C.: Council of Institutional Investors, 1997).

58. AFL-CIO, "Investing in Our Future" (Washington, D.C.: American Federation of Labor and Congress of Industrial Organizations, 1997).

59. As of 1998, the Office of Investment of the AFL-CIO estimated that multi-employer funds held $329 billion. Single-employer funds held $551 billion. For comparison, all pension funds hold $5.2 trillion, or nearly 26 percent of all corporate stock.

60. Author interview with Bill Patterson, October 1997. The AFL-CIO has since released a report that shows that professional managers have a mixed record in voting according to union wishes. See AFL-CIO, "10 Key Votes Survey" (Washington, D.C.: American Federation of Labor and Congress of Industrial Organizations, 1998).

61. Other international organizations addressing governance standards include the European Corporate Governance Network (ECGN), the Asia-Pacific Economic Cooperation (APEC), and the International Corporate Governance Network (ICGN). See Jason Stuart, "Recent Initiatives in Global Corporate Standards," *Corporate Governance Bulletin (Investor Responsibility Research Center)* 15, no. 2 (1998): 20–21.

62. Wirthlin Worldwide, "Furthering the Global Dialogue on Corporate Governance: 1998 International Survey of Institutional Investors" (New York: Russell Reynolds Associates, 1998).

63. D. Jeanne Patterson, "The Link Between Corporate Governance and Performance" (New York: The Conference Board, 1998).

64. Stephen L. Nesbitt, "Do CalPERS Corporate Governance Activities Work?" (Presentation to the California Public Employees' Retirement System board of administration, 1998). See also Stephen L. Nesbitt, "The 'Calpers Effect': A Corporate Governance Update" (Santa Monica, CA: Wilshire Associates Incorporated, 1995), 4, and Stephen L. Nesbitt, "Long-Term Rewards from Shareholder Activism: A Study of the 'Calpers Effect'," *Journal of Applied Corporate Finance* 6, no. 4 (Winter 1994): 75–80.

65. Tim C. Opler and Jonathan Sokobin, "Does Coordinated Institutional Shareholder Activism Work? An Analysis of the Activities of the Council of Institutional Investors" (See www.ciicentral.com 1997), 1 and Table VI.

66. Author interview with Carolyn Brancato, October 1997. For much more insight on this subject, see Carolyn Kay Brancato, *Institutional Investors and Corporate Governance: Best Practices for Increasing Corporate Value* (Chicago: Irwin Professional Publishing/McGraw-Hill, 1997).

Chapter Four: Inventing New Measures

1. The Allstate story in this chapter is based on interviews with Allstate executives Jerry Choate in December 1997 and Chief Financial Officer Tom Wilson and Loren Hall in 1995.

2. Alfred Rappaport, *Creating Shareholder Value: The New Standard for Business Performance* (New York: The Free Press, 1986). See also the revised edition, Alfred Rappaport, *Creating Shareholder Value: A Guide for Managers and Investors*, rev. ed. (New York: The Free Press, 1997).

3. See, for example, Tom Copeland, Tim Koller, and Jack Murrin, *Valuation: Measuring and Managing the Value of Companies* (New York: John Wiley & Sons, 1991). See also James M. McTaggart, Peter W. Kontes, and Michael C. Mankins, *The Value Imperative: Managing for Superior Shareholder Returns* (New York: The Free Press, 1994) and G. Bennett Stewart III, *The Quest for Value* (New York: HarperBusiness, 1991).

4. Baruch Lev, "The Boundaries of Financial Reporting and How to Extend Them" (Unpublished paper, 1996): 5. See also James Chang, "The Decline in Value Relevance of Earnings and Book Values" (Working paper, 1998).

5. Baruch Lev, " The Old Rules No Longer Apply," *Forbes ASAP,* 7 April 1997, 35–36. Although most research shows a decrease in the value relevance of earnings and book value over the past forty years, there is some contrary evidence. See Daniel W. Collins, Edward L. Maydew, and Ira S. Weiss, "Changes in the Value-Relevance of Earnings and Book Values Over the Past Forty Years," *Journal of Accounting & Economics* 24 (1997): 39–67.

6. Stewart, *Quest for Value.*

7. Gary C. Biddle, Robert M. Bowen, and James S. Wallace, "Evidence on the Relative and Incremental Information Content of EVA, Residual Income, Earnings and Operating Cash Flow" (Working paper, 1996): 25+.

8. Both empirical studies and surveys support this notion. Using economic profit to measure and pay for performance prompts people to better utilize assets. See James S. Wallace, "EVA Financial Systems: Management Perspectives," *Advances in Management Accounting* 6 (1998): 1–15.

9. We will come back to this subject in Chapter 8. See also Jacques Bughin and Thomas E. Copeland, "The Virtuous Cycle of Shareholder Value," *The McKinsey Quarterly,* no. 2 (1997): 156–167.

10. The Valmont story is based on interviews in March 1998 and in 1995 with CFO Terry McClain. Some of this story appeared in Bill Birchard, " 'Do It Yourself': How Valmont Industries Implemented EVA," *CFO,* March 1996, 34–40.

11. Stewart, *Quest for Value.*

12. The Harnischfeger story relies heavily on the interview published in William L. Simon, *Beyond the Numbers* (New York: Van Nostrand Reinhold, 1997), 29–41. It also relies on an author interview with CFO Francis Corby in April 1998.

13. Renaissance Solutions and *CFO* magazine, "Building a Management System to Implement Your Strategy: Survey Findings on the Effectiveness of Strategic Management and Implementation" (Lincoln, MA: Renaissance Solutions, Inc. [Renaissance Worldwide, Inc.], 1996).

14. Bonnie P. Stivers, Teresa Joyce Covin, Nancy Green Hall, and Steven W. Smalt, "How Nonfinancial Performance Measures Are Used," *Management Accounting* 79, no. 8 (February 1998): 46.

15. Marc J. Epstein and Jean-François Manzoni, "Implementing Corporate Strategy: From Tableaux de Bord to Balanced Scorecard," *European Management Journal* 16, no. 2 (April 1998): 190–203.

16. For a history on Analog, see Robert S. Kaplan, "Analog Devices: The Half-Life System (Case #190-161)" (Boston: Harvard Business School Press, 1990).

17. The information on Analog Devices comes from overhead slides and author interview with Robert Stasey, director of quality improvement, in November 1997 and October 1998.

18. This section is based on an author interview with Ralph Hake in March 1998. Some of this material appeared earlier in Bill Birchard, "The Call for Full Disclosure" *CFO*, December 1994, 30–42.

19. Birchard, "Call for Full Disclosure," 30–42.

20. Anonymous, "1997 Balanced Scorecard Results," *Vision (Published for the People of Whirlpool)* (March 1998): 4.

21. The CIGNA Property & Casualty story came to light in a Harvard Business School case: Richard L. Nolan and Donna B. Stoddard, "CIGNA Property and Casualty Reengineering (A) (Case #9-196-059)" 25 (Boston: Harvard Business School, 1995). The story was expanded in Francis J. Gouillart and James N. Kelly, *Transforming the Organization* (New York: McGraw-Hill, 1995). The story here is based on interviews with Gerry Isom, president, and Tom Valerio, senior vice president and transformation officer, in November 1997 and in 1996. Some of this material also appeared in Bill Birchard, "Closing the Strategy Gap" *CFO*, October 1996, 26–36.

22. Kaplan and Norton introduced their balanced scorecard concept first in 1992. See Robert S. Kaplan and David P. Norton, "The Balanced Scorecard—Measures that Drive Performance," *Harvard Business Review* 70, no. 1 (January–February 1992): 71–79. Over the course of four years, and in many additional articles, they expanded the scorecard concept to demonstrate how it had evolved from a tool for measuring performance to a system for articulating, communicating, executing, and revising strategy. For a complete understanding of the scorecard, see Robert S. Kaplan and David P. Norton, *The Balanced Scorecard* (Boston: Harvard Business School Press, 1996).

23. This section is based on Robert S. Kaplan, "Mobil USM&R (A): Linking the Balanced Scorecard (Case #9-197-025)" (Boston: Harvard Business School, 1996), 1, 3. See also Robert S. Kaplan, "Mobil USM&R (B): New England Sales and Distribution (Case #9-197-026)" (Boston: Harvard Business School, 1996).

24. Personal communication with Edward Lewis, Mobil Supervisor of Strategic Planning, U.S. Marketing & Refining Division, September 1998.

25. Kaplan, "Mobil USM&R (A)," 2, 10.

26. The material on the Bank of Montreal comes mainly from author interviews with CFO Robert Wells in January 1998 and 1994. Some of this material appeared in Bill Birchard, "Making It Count," *CFO*, October 1995, 42–51.

27. Leif Edvinsson and Michael S. Malone, *Intellectual Capital: Realizing Your Company's True Value by Finding Its Hidden Roots* (New York: HarperCollins, 1997). This section is based on Chapter 3, and page 41.

28. Skandia Group, "Visualizing Intellectual Capital at Skandia" (Stockholm: Skandia Group, 1994), 5.

29. Note that other authors have also made a substantial contribution to the understanding of how to measure and manage intellectual capital to a firm's advantage. See, for example, Thomas A. Stewart, *Intellectual Capital: The New Wealth of Organizations* (New York: Doubleday, 1997).

30. Author interview with Leif Edvinsson, December 1997. For his pioneering work in intellectual capital, Edvinsson was awarded The Brain of the Year 1998 by the Brain Trust Foundation U.K.

31. Price Waterhouse Change Integration Team, *Better Change: Best Practices for Transforming Your Organization* (Burr Ridge, IL: Irwin Professional Publishing, 1995), 174.

32. Geary A. Rummler and Alan P. Brache, *Improving Performance: How to Manage the White Space on the Organization Chart* (San Francisco: Jossey-Bass Publishers, 1995). This section supplemented by author interview with Alan Brache in May 1996.

33. Deloitte & Touche Management Consulting, "Performance Measurement Survey" (New York: Deloitte & Touche LLP, 1995).

34. James L. Heskett, W. Earl Sasser, Jr., and Leonard A. Schlesinger, *The Service Profit Chain: How Leading Companies Link Profit and Growth to Loyalty, Satisfaction, and Value.* (New York: The Free Press, 1997), 32–34.

35. Mary E. Barth, Michael Clement, George Foster, and Ron Kasznik, "Brand Values and Capital Market Valuation," forthcoming, *Reviews of Accounting Studies,* 1998.

36. Author interview with Dana Mead, October 1997.

Chapter Five: Managing the System

1. The story of Eastman Chemical in this chapter is based on multiple interviews with Earnest Deavenport; Virgil Stephens, former CFO; and Jimmy Tackett, former vice president, corporate development and strategy, in 1996 and 1997.

2. Robert Simons, *Levers of Control: How Managers Use Innovative Control Systems to Drive Strategic Renewal* (Boston: Harvard Business School Press, 1995), ix, 4. The systems we refer to in this chapter are what Robert Simons calls "diagnostic" control systems. For a summary discussion of other systems, and how they work together in the modern corporation (including belief systems, boundary systems, and interactive control systems), see Robert Simons, "Control in an Age of Empowerment," *Harvard Business Review* 73, no. 2 (1995): 81–88.

3. For another discussion of management control, see Anthony A. Atkinson, Rajiv D. Banker, Robert S. Kaplan, and S. Mark Young, *Management Accounting,* 2nd ed. (Upper Saddle River, NJ: Prentice-Hall, 1997), Chapter 11.

4. Author interview with Steven Hronec, July 1996.

5. Many books discuss this concept. See, for example, Geary A. Rummler and Alan P. Brache, *Improving Performance: How to Manage the White Space on the Organization Chart* (San Francisco: Jossey-Bass Publishers, 1995). See also Kenneth A. Merchant, *Modern Management Control Systems: Text and Cases* (Upper Saddle River, NJ: Prentice-Hall, 1998).

6. Internal Eastman strategic planning and quality-process documents.

7. Ibid.

8. The Tenneco story in this chapter is based on interviews with Dana Mead, Robert Blakely, Barry Schuman, and Richard Wambold in October 1997.

9. 1996 Tenneco Annual Report, tables on pages 8–10.

10. Robert S. Kaplan, "Mobil USM&R (A): Linking the Balanced Scorecard (Case #N9-197-025)" (Boston: Harvard Business School, 1996), 9.

11. Author interview with Loren Hall, July 1995.

12. Virgil Stephens, "Benchmarking CFO Effectiveness" (Paper presented at the *Business Week* Conference, March 20, 1997), 6.

13. See, for example, Peter M. Senge, *The Fifth Discipline: The Art and Practice of the Learning Organization* (New York: Currency Doubleday, 1990). See also D. A. Garvin, "Building a Learning Organization," *Harvard Business Review* 71, no. 4 (July–August 1993): 79–91.

14. For more on the folly of single-loop learning, see, for example, Chris Argyris, "Good Communication That Blocks Learning," *Harvard Business Review* 72, no. 4 (1994): 77–85.

15. Author interview with Christopher Meyer, June 1995.

16. Author interview with David Norton, August 1996.

17. The section on CIGNA Property & Casualty in this chapter is based on author interviews with Tom Valerio, senior vice president and transformation officer, November 1997.

18. For more on the importance of making accounting information easy to interpret by foreign investors, see Takashi Yaekura, "The Interpretation of Accounting Information by Foreign Investors: Do We Really Need International Accounting Harmonization?" (Working paper, 1998).

Chapter Six: Lifting the Veil

1. The story of United HealthCare in this chapter comes from an author interview with CEO William McGuire, M.D., in December 1997 and from company annual reports from 1991 through 1997.

2. The format of United HealthCare's report cards has recently changed to conform to HEDIS standards. These figures represent the format of the earlier report cards.

3. Edmund L. Jenkins, "Nonfinancial Measures of Business Performance" (Washington D.C.: Competitiveness Policy Council, Subcouncil on Corporate Governance and Financial Markets, 1992).

4. 1992 United HealthCare annual report, 15.

5. American Institute of Certified Public Accountants, "Improving Business Reporting—A Customer Focus (Executive Summary report)" (New York: American Institute of Certified Public Accountants, 1994), 2.

6. Marc J. Epstein and Krishna G. Palepu, "Analysts Speak Out on Corporate Communications" (Unpublished manuscript, 1998).

7. The case on IP is based on Mary E. Barth and Charles A. Nichols III, "International Paper (A) (Case #193-160)" (Boston: Harvard Business School, 1992). See also Mary E. Barth and Charles A. Nichols III, "International Paper (B) (Case #193-061)" (Boston: Harvard Business School, 1992).

8. Baruch Lev, "Information Disclosure Strategy," *California Management Review* 34, no. 4 (1992): 12.

9. Mark H. Lang, and Russell J. Lundholm, "Corporate Disclosure Policy and Analyst Behavior," *Accounting Review* 71, no. 4 (1996): 469, 490.

10. Marc J. Epstein and Moses L. Pava, *The Shareholder's Use of Corporate Annual Reports* (Greenwich, CT: JAI Press, 1993), 153–156. Note that this study was duplicated by Epstein and Ray Anderson for Australia and New Zealand in 1995. The results were similar. For a summary, see Ray Anderson and Marc J. Epstein, "The Usefulness of Annual Reports," *Australian Accountant* (1995): 25–28. For a full account, see Ray H. Anderson and Marc J. Epstein,

The Usefulness of Corporate Annual Reports to Shareholders in Australia, New Zealand, and the United States: An International Comparison (Greenwich, CT: JAI Press Inc., 1996).

11. 1996 Rouse Company form 10-K, 24, 31.

12. Author interview with David Tripp, Rouse vice president and director of investor relations, August 1998.

13. Cambrex information from 1997 SEC form 10-K and author interviews and personal communication with Frederick Larcombe, April 1996 and September 1998. Some of this material appeared earlier in Marc J. Epstein, *Measuring Corporate Environmental Performance* (Chicago: Irwin Professional Publishing, 1996), 112. See also Bill Birchard, "Hidden Sites, Hidden Costs," *Tomorrow*, November 1996, 30–31.

14. Microsoft 1997 form 10-K and form 10-Q. This story appeared in Roger Lowenstein, "Microsoft and Its Two Constituencies," *Wall Street Journal*, 4 December, 1997, C1.

15. Epstein and Palepu, "Analysts Speak." Some of this work appeared in Marc J. Epstein and Krishna G. Palepu, "What Analysts Really Want," *CFO*, October 1997, 47.

16. Author interview with Nancy Ford, assistant manager of investor relations, Coca-Cola, April 1996.

17. Al Jackson, worldwide head of equity research at First Boston, is one such analyst. He and value-based analysis expert Michael Mauboussin further believe that the act of disclosing EVA raises analysts' and investors' expectations as to the extent to which managers will focus on shareholder value, especially through better capital allocation. Nearly all of First Boston analysts use EVA as an analytical tool. The sources for this information were author interviews with Al Jackson, March 1996, and Michael Mauboussin, July 1998.

18. Lev, "Information Disclosure," 21.

19. *Wall Street Journal*, 26 March, 1996, p. A10.

20. Elaine Zablocki, "Employer Report Cards," *HMO*, March 1994, 29.

21. Sheila Leatherman and Deborah Chase, "Using Report Cards to Grade Health Plan Quality," *Journal of American Health Policy* (January 1994): 34.

22. For ratings information, see www.ncqa.org

23. HealthPartners, "Prescriptions for Health Improvement (Report on the Partners for Better Health Program)" (Minneapolis: HealthPartners, 1998), 5.

24. Maggie Mahar, "How's Your HMO?" *Barron's*, 4 March, 1996, 35.

25. Susan Williams, "Equal Employment and Disclosure: A Report on U.S. Corporate Practices" (Washington, D.C.: Investor Responsibility Research Center, 1996), 1.

26. Author interview with Jerry Choate, December 1997.

27. Allstate Insurance Company, "Workplace Diversity at Allstate Insurance Company" (Northbrook, IL: Allstate Insurance Company, 1997), 1.

28. This section is based on author interviews with Don Mullane, executive vice president, Bank of America, December 1997 and August 1998.

29. Author interview and personal communication with Geoffrey Bush, director of Corporate Citizenship, Diageo, February 1998 and August 1998.

30. Shell International Ltd., "Profits and Principles—Does There Have to be a Choice?" (London: Royal Dutch/Shell Group, 1998), 48–51.

31. Bill Birchard, "Going Green," *Enterprise*, January 1993, 13.

32. Comments by MacAllister Booth, October 1995, at the Society of Environmental Journalists Conference, Cambridge, Massachusetts.

33. Polaroid Report on the Environment, 1995 (p. 24) and 1996 (p. 45).

34. See John Elkington, Niklas Kreander, and Shelly Fennel, "Targeting the Non-Reporters." *Tomorrow* (September 1998): 58. Note that by counting the more than 2,000 sites registered under Europe's Eco-Management and Audit Scheme, the number would be far greater. EMAS requires the production of an audited, publicly available, environmental report.

35. For a thorough understanding of the ISO 14000 standard, see Marc J. Epstein and Marie-Josée Roy, "Understanding and Implementing ISO 14000" (Hamilton, Ontario: The Society of Management Accountants of Canada, 1998).

36. Allen L. White and Diana M. Zinkl, "Raising Standardization," *The Environmental Forum* 15, no. 1 (January/February 1998): 28–37.

37. World Business Council for Sustainable Development, "Finding the Numbers That Show How Well Companies Are Performing," *Tomorrow* (May 1998): 42.

38. Carolyn Mathiasen, Meg Voorhes, and Heidi Welsh, "1998 Proxy Season Proves More Contentious," *Corporate Social Issues Reporter (Investor Responsibility Research Center)*, July 1998, 8.

39. Author interview with Thomas H. Hellman, Ph.D., vice president, environment, health, and safety, Bristol-Myers Squibb, December 1996.

40. Lise Kingo and Marianne Gamstrup, "Environment & Bioethics Report 1997" (Bagsværd, Denmark: Novo Nordisk A/S, 1998).

41. The E.B. Eddy Group, "A Question of Balance: Third Status Report on Sustainable Development" (Espanola, Ontario: The E.B. Eddy Group, 1996).

42. Author interview with Bob Banks, Sun Company vice president of health, environment, and safety, March 1996.

43. Marc J. Epstein, *Measuring Corporate Environmental Performance* (Chicago: Irwin Professional Publishing, 1996), 124.

44. Shell International Ltd., "Profits and Principles."

45. *Aeneid,* act. XI, line 283.

Chapter Seven: The Accountability Cycle

1. They evolve in the same way as described by earlier authors. See Robert S. Kaplan and David P. Norton, *The Balanced Scorecard* (Boston: Harvard Business School Press, 1996), 197. See also the work originally published in 1990, Geary A. Rummler and Alan P. Brache, *Improving Performance: How to Manage the White Space on the Organization Chart* (San Francisco: Jossey-Bass Publishers, 1995), Chapter 7.

2. A special committee of the U.K.'s Royal Society of Arts came to a similar conclusion. See Mark Goyder and Neil Hartley, "Tomorrow's Company" (London: The Royal Society for the Encouragement of Arts, Manufactures and Commerce, 1995).

3. John P. Kotter and James L. Heskett, *Corporate Culture and Performance* (New York: The Free Press/Macmillan, 1992), 11.

4. Author interview with Robert Wells, January 1998.

5. Bill Birchard, "How Many Masters Can You Serve?" *CFO,* July 1995, 49.

6. 1996 Annual Report, 11.

7. Marc J. Epstein and S. David Young, "Improving Corporate Environmental Performance Through Economic Value Added," *Environmental Quality Management* (Summer 1998): 1–7.

8. Author interview with Jimmy Tackett, former vice president, corporate development and strategy, and former CFO Virgil Stephens, July 1996.

9. Author interview with Robert Stasey, director of quality improvement, November 1997.

10. Robert A. Howell, *Developing Comprehensive Performance Indicators,* vol. 31 (Hamilton, Ontario: The Society of Management Accountants of Canada, 1994), 4–6.

11. Marc J. Epstein and Jean-François Manzoni, "Implementing Corporate Strategy: From Tableaux de Bord to Balanced Scorecard," *European Management Journal* 16, no. 2 (April 1998): 190–203, see sidebar, "The Basic Performance Measurement Problem."

12. Author interview with Steven Hronec, July 1996. See also Steven M. Hronec, *Vital Signs: Using Quality, Time, and Cost Performance Measurements to Chart Your Company's Future* (New York: American Management Association, 1993).

13. Information supplied by Eastman Chemical communications staff, August 1996.

14. Marshall W. Meyer and Vipin Gupta, "The Performance Paradox," *Research in Organizational Behavior* 16 (1994): 309–369. An interesting side note: Meyer and Gupta point to research showing that the same "running down" happened over many decades with batting averages in baseball. Since 1876, the averages have come to cluster in a very narrow range, making them far less useful than previously as a gauge of batting prowess; see page 331.

15. Bill Birchard, "The Paragon and the Paradox," *CFO,* December 1994, 33.

16. Birchard, "Paragon and the Paradox," 33.

17. Sue Shellenbarger, "Accounting Firms Battle to Be Known as Best Workplaces," *Wall Street Journal,* 21 January 1998, C1.

18. Marc J. Epstein and Krishna G. Palepu, "Analysts Speak Out on Corporate Communications" (Unpublished manuscript, 1998), 7.

19. Thomas A. Lee, "To Become a Better Manager, Shed Those Old Inhibitions," *Accounting Today,* 25 July 1994, 12. See also Thomas A. Lee, "Financial Reporting Key to Increasing Corporate Credibility," *Accounting Today,* 11 July 1994, 12–13.

20. Robert G. Eccles and Sarah C. Mavrinac, "Improving the Corporate Disclosure Process" (Boston: Graduate School of Business Administration, Harvard University, 1994).

21. Author interviews with Baruch Lev, December 1997 and October 1998.

22. For a discussion of management communications, see Krishna G. Palepu, Victor L. Bernard, and Paul M. Healy, *Business Analysis & Valuation: Using Financial Statements* (Cincinnati: South-Western Publishing, 1996).

23. As suggested by others, especially in American Institute of Certified Public Accountants, "Improving Business Reporting—A Customer Focus (Comprehensive Report of the Special Committee on Financial Reporting)" (New York: American Institute of Certified Public Accountants, 1994), 132.

24. This section on Bank of Montreal is based on an author interview with Robert Wells, January 1998.

25. Marc J. Epstein and Albert D. Spalding, Jr., *The Accountant's Guide to Legal Liability and Ethics* (Homewood, IL: Business One Irwin, 1993).

26. Yankelovich Partners, "A Study of Corporate Annual Reports" (Cloquet, Minn.: Potlach Corporation, 1995).

27. See, especially, pages 133–134 of American Institute of Certified Public Accountants, "Improving Business Reporting—A Customer Focus (Comprehensive Report of the Special Committee on Financial Reporting)" (New York: American Institute of Certified Public Accountants, 1994).

28. See, for example, Ralph W. Estes, *Tyranny of the Bottom Line: Why Corporations Make Good People Do Bad Things* (San Francisco: Berrett-Koehler Publishers, 1996). See also Ralph Estes, "The Sunshine Standards for Corporate Reporting to Stakeholders," *Business Ethics* Special Report #1 (1996).

29. A good example of an expanded reporting format has been produced by Price Waterhouse. See Philip D. Wright and Daniel P. Keegan, "Pursuing Value: The Emerging Art of Reporting on the Future," *PW Papers: Insights for Decision Makers* (1997), 14.

30. We even feel that the critical elements of performance can be included in a summary annual report. The point is to communicate the key factors by which report users can judge performance of all kinds.

31. Marc J. Epstein and Moses L. Pava, "Profile of an Annual Report," *Financial Executive* 10, no. 1 (January/February 1994): 41.

32. Warren Burger, in *United States of America v. Arthur Young & Co.* (52 U.S.L.W. 4355, March 1984).

33. Author interview with Robert Kaplan, July 1995. For a longer explanation of this idea, see Kaplan and Norton, *Balanced Scorecard,* 310, note 2.

34. Marc J. Epstein and Moses L. Pava, *The Shareholder's Use of Corporate Annual Reports* (Greenwich, CT: JAI Press, 1993), 157.

35. For a broad view of the strategic systems audit, see Timothy Bell, Frank Marrs, Ira Solomon, and Howard Thomas, *Auditing Organizations Through a Strategic Systems Lens* (KPMG Peat Marwick, 1997).

36. Arthur Levitt, "Investor Education: Disclosure for the 1990s" (Speech given at McIntire School of Commerce, Charlottesville, VA: Securities and Exchange Commission, 1995).

Chapter Eight: Financials Revisited

1. The Monsanto story in this chapter is based on author interviews with Robert Hoffman, vice chairman and CFO, who retired in early 1999, Steve Stetz, corporate vice president, Mergers and Acquisitions and Licensing; and Tom Hartley, assistant controller, in March 1998.

2. James J. Glasser, "How EVA Works Against GATX," *Chief Executive (US),* January 1996, 42.

3. Jacques Bughin and Thomas E. Copeland, "The Virtuous Cycle of Shareholder Value," *The McKinsey Quarterly* 1997, no. 2 (1997): 159.

4. Kenneth Lehn and Anil K. Makhija, "EVA & MVA as Performance Measures and Signals for Strategic Change," *Strategy & Leadership* 24, no. 3 (1996): 34 (5).

5. Alfred Rappaport, "Three Ways Stock-Market Investors Can Stack the Odds in Their Favor," *Wall Street Journal,* 26 February, 1998, R6.

6. Remarks by Frederick P. Stratton, Jr., accepting the 1994 Baird Award for Management Excellence. Reprinted in the 1994 Briggs & Stratton annual report, 5.

7. The section on Briggs & Stratton is based on internal documents and author interview with John Shiely in February 1998. A wealth of added information comes from John Goff, "Lawnmower Men," _EVAngelist_ 1, no. 4 (1997): 9–18.

8. John Shiely, "Managing for Value Creation at Briggs & Stratton" (Unpublished manuscript, 1994): 30.

9. For a lengthy discussion of this issue, see Marc J. Epstein, "Accounting for Product Take Back," _Management Accounting_ (August 1996).

10. This section based on author interviews with Robert Hoffman, Steve Stetz, and Tom Hartley. See note 1.

11. For a fuller explanation of choosing financial measures, see Robert S. Kaplan and David P. Norton, _The Balanced Scorecard_ (Boston: Harvard Business School Press, 1996), 48. For a good review of company experience, see Randy Myers, "Measure for Measure," _CFO_, November 1997, 44–56.

12. Kaplan and Norton, _Balanced Scorecard_, 62.

13. From Eastman Chemical internal documents.

14. Bill Birchard, "Closing the Strategy Gap," _CFO_, October 1996, 36.

15. This section based on Goff, "Lawnmower Men," 13–15.

16. John S. Shiely, "Is Value Management the Answer?" _Chief Executive_, December 1996, 55–57. Added information from Briggs & Stratton proxy statement.

17. Author interview with Don Macleod, February 1998.

18. Pat McConnell and Janet Pegg, "Comprehending Comprehensive Income," in _Accounting Issues: Pat McConnell_, vol. 14 (New York: Bear Stearns & Co. Inc., 1997). See also Elizabeth MacDonald, "FASB Requires New Profit Data from Businesses," _Wall Street Journal_, 30 September, 1997, C1.

19. Frances L. Ayres, "What Managers Need to Know," _Management Accounting_, (March 1994): 27–29.

20. Mary E. Barth and Greg Clinch, "Revalued Financial, Tangible, and Intangible Assets: Associations with Share Prices and Non Market-Based Value Estimates" forthcoming, _Journal of Accounting Research_, supplement 1998. See also David Aboody, M. E. Barth, and Ron Kasznik, "Revaluations of Fixed Assets and Future Firm Performance from the U.K." forthcoming, _Journal of Accounting and Economics_, 1998.

21. Victor L. Bernard, Robert C. Merton, and Krishna G. Palepu, "Mark-to-Market Accounting for Banks and Thrifts: Lessons from the Danish Experience," _Journal of Accounting Research_ 33, no. 1 (Spring 1995): 1–32.

22. Paul Healy, Amy Hutton, and Krishna Palepu, "Stock Performance and Intermediation Changes Surrounding Sustained Increases in Disclosure" (Working paper, 1998), 49.

23. Author interview with Mary Barth, February 1998.

24. Marc J. Epstein and Moses L. Pava, _The Shareholder's Use of Corporate Annual Reports_ (Greenwich, CT: JAI Press, 1993), 151.

25. Marc J. Epstein and Krishna G. Palepu, "Analysts Speak Out on Corporate Communications" (Unpublished manuscript, 1998).

26. Campbell Soup 1993 annual report. Additional information from Bill Saporito, "Campbell Soup Gets Piping Hot," _Fortune_, 9 September 1991, 142–148.

27. 1995 Campbell Soup annual report, 3.
28. Author interview with John Shiely, February 1998.
29. Mary E. Barth and Christine M. Murphy, "Required Financial Statement Disclosures: Purposes, Subject, Number, and Trends," *Accounting Horizons* 8, no. 4 (1995): 1–22.
30. Anonymous, "SEC Orders Disclosures of Year 2000 Exposure," *Wall Street Journal*, 23 October 1997, A2.
31. James Lyons, "Crusade for Candor," *Forbes*, 25 May 1992, 74.
32. American Institute of Certified Public Accountants, "Improving Business Reporting—A Customer Focus (Comprehensive Report of the Special Committee on Financial Reporting)" (New York: American Institute of Certified Public Accountants, 1994).
33. Epstein and Pava, *Shareholder's Use*, 156.
34. For more detail on this concept, see Marc J. Epstein and Moses L. Pava, "Shareholders' Perceptions on the Usefulness of MD&As," *Managerial Finance* 21, no. 3 (1995): 68–83. For related discussion, see also Moses L. Pava and Marc J. Epstein, "How Good is MD&A as an Investment Tool?" *Journal of Accountancy* 175, no. 3 (March 1993): 51–53.
35. Joann S. Lublin, "Calpers List Targets EDS, Louisiana-Pacific for Performance," *Wall Street Journal*, 24 February 1998, A4.
36. John Dorfman, "Shareholder Scoreboard: How Well Do America's Top Corporations Treat Their Shareholders? Here's a Ranking of 1,000 Companies, for the Past One, Three and Five Years," *Wall Street Journal*, 29 February 1996, R1–R8.
37. Paul Healy, Amy Hutton, and Krishna Palepu, "Stock Performance and Intermediation Changes Surrounding Sustained Increases in Disclosure" (Working paper, 1998), 49.
38. Author interview with Krishna Palepu, February 1998.
39. Richard Frankel, Maureen McNichols, and G. Peter Wilson, "Discretionary Disclosure and External Financing," *Accounting Review* 70, no. 1 (1995): 135(16).

Chapter Nine: Beyond Financials

1. The American Skandia story in this chapter is based on interviews with Gordon Boronow, president, and Jan Hoffmeister, vice president, in December 1997.
2. Skandia Insurance Company, "Intelligent Enterprising: Intellectual Capital Supplement to Skandia's 6-Month Interim Report 1997" (Stockholm: Skandia Insurance Company Ltd., 1997), 14.
3. Internal American Skandia memorandum, October 1997.
4. Author interview with Mark Green, Pitney Bowes Mailing Systems director of Strategic Marketing, Finance, December 1997. See also Mark D. Green, "Executive Information Systems at Pitney Bowes Mailing Systems," in *New Management Accounting: How Leading-Edge Companies Use Management Accounting to Improve Performance*, edited by William F. Christopher (Menlo Park, CA: Crisp Publications, 1998), 71–84.
5. Comments by Leif Edvinsson in this chapter come from an author interview in December 1997.

6. The Dow Chemical story in this chapter is based on an author interview with Gordon Petrash, January 1998. Petrash has since become a partner at PricewaterhouseCoopers.

7. See note 1.

8. Internal American Skandia memorandum, October 1997.

9. Robert Simons, *Levers of Control: How Managers Use Innovative Control Systems to Drive Strategic Renewal* (Boston: Harvard Business School Press, 1995), 133–145.

10. Author interview with Gerry Isom, July 1996.

11. Author interview with Dana Mead, October 1997.

12. Author interview with Richard Wambold, October 1997.

13. For more on the subject of organizational learning, see Peter M. Senge, *The Fifth Discipline: The Art and Practice of the Learning Organization* (New York: Currency Doubleday, 1990); D. A. Garvin, "Building a Learning Organization," *Harvard Business Review* 71, no. 4 (July–August 1993): 79–91; Dorothy Leonard-Barton, *Wellsprings of Knowledge: Building and Sustaining the Sources of Innovation* (Boston: Harvard Business School Press, 1995); and Chris Argyris and D. A. Schoen, *Organizational Learning II: Theory, Method, and Practice* (Reading, MA: Addison-Wesley, 1996).

14. The section on PhyCor in this chapter is based on author interviews with Ronald Loeppke, M.D., vice president and chief medical officer; Jerry Howell, director of the PhyCor Institute for Health Care Management; and Marlene Giesecke, R.N., Manager of Care Management, in January 1998.

15. Data from selection of internal slides supplied by Marlene Giesecke, R.N., Manager of Care Management.

16. Marc J. Epstein and Moses L. Pava, *The Shareholder's Use of Corporate Annual Reports* (Greenwich, CT: JAI Press, 1993), 126, 155.

17. Information on Skandia Group in this section from author interview with Leif Edvinsson, December 1997.

18. See note 1.

19. Author interview with Ron Loeppke, M.D., January 1998.

20. Nicholas A. Hanchak, M.D., "From the Editor," *USQA Quality Monitor* 4, no. 1 (July 1997): i.

21. Anne Fisher, "The 100 Best Companies to Work For in America," *Fortune*, 12 January 1998, 68–70.

22. Marc J. Epstein and Krishna G. Palepu, "Analysts Speak Out on Corporate Communications" (Unpublished manuscript, 1998). Some of this work also appeared in Marc J. Epstein and Krishna G. Palepu, "What Analysts Really Want," *CFO*, October 1997, 47.

23. Author interview with Gordon Petrash, January 1998.

24. Tom Austin, David Moskovitz, and Cheryl Harrington, "Uniform Consumer Disclosure Standards for New England" (Gardner, ME: Regulatory Assistance Project, 1997), 1. For more information on the trend in utility disclosure standards, see the Regulatory Assistance Project's website: www.rapmaine.org

25. Epstein and Pava, *The Shareholder's Use of Corporate Annual Reports.*

26. Shelley Taylor, "Full Disclosure 1996 Highlights" (Palo Alto: Shelley Taylor & Associates, 1996), 1–5.

27. Author interview with Carolyn Brancato, October 1997. See also Carolyn Kay Brancato, "Communicating Corporate Performance: A Delicate Balance"

(New York: The Conference Board, 1997), Chapter 6; and Carolyn Kay Brancato, *Institutional Investors and Corporate Governance: Best Practices for Increasing Corporate Value* (Chicago: Irwin Professional Publishing/ McGraw-Hill, 1997).

28. Lilli A. Gordon, John Pound, and Todd Porter, "High-Performance Workplaces: Implications for Investment Research and Active Investing Strategies" (Waban, MA: Gordon Group, Inc., 1994), 2.

29. Ernst & Young, "Measures That Matter" (Boston: Ernst & Young LLP, 1997), 10–12.

30. Bruce K. Behn and Richard A. Riley, Jr., "Using Non-Financial Information to Predict Financial Performance: The Case of the U.S. Airline Industry" (Working paper, 1998).

31. James L. Heskett, W. Earl Sasser, Jr., and Leonard A. Schlesinger, *The Service Profit Chain: How Leading Companies Link Profit and Growth to Loyalty, Satisfaction, and Value* (New York: The Free Press, 1997).

32. This entire section is based on Anthony J. Rucci, Steven P. Kirn, and Richard T. Quinn, "The Employee-Customer-Profit Chain," *Harvard Business Review* 76, no. 1 (January/February 1998): 84–91.

33. Tom Richman, "Briefings from the Editors: Performance Measurement: Working Capital Productivity," *Harvard Business Review* 73, no. 4 (1995): 10–11.

Chapter Ten: A Social Accounting

1. Much of the story of Northern Telecom is based on an author interview with John Roth, January 1998.

2. Milton Friedman, "The Social Responsibility of Business Is to Increase Its Profits," *New York Times Magazine,* 13 September 1970, 32.

3. As argued by Max B. E. Clarkson, "A Stakeholder Framework for Analyzing and Evaluating Corporate Social Performance," *Academy of Management Review* 20, no. 1 (1995): 102–103.

4. See, for example, Brandon Copple and Louise Lee, "Formative Years: Labor Squeeze Forces Corporate America Back to High School," *Wall Street Journal,* 22 July 1998, A1, A9.

5. Note that many academics and a handful of companies have experimented with social measures for several decades. We provide here a practical approach for managers wishing to incorporate social measurements into their routine of management. Some of the early work includes that by one of the authors: Marc J. Epstein, Joanne B. Epstein, and Earl Jay Weiss, *Introduction to Social Accounting* (Los Angeles: Western Consulting Group, Inc., 1977). See also Marc J. Epstein, E. Flamholtz, and J. J. McDonough, "Corporate Social Accounting in the United States of America: State of the Art and Future Prospects," *Accounting, Organizations, and Society* 1, no. 1 (1976): 23–42.

6. Interfaith Center on Corporate Responsibility, *The Proxy Resolutions Book* (New York: Interfaith Center on Corporate Responsibility, 1997), 57.

7. Heidi Soumerai, "Affirmative Activism: Season Round-Up," *Values,* July 1997, 3.

8. The Texaco case provides a rare public look inside a large company whose managers are now championing equal employment opportunity as an objective

equal to or greater than profits. For detail, refer to one of the reports that stems from the settlement of *Roberts et al.* v. *Texaco*. For example, see *Report of the Equality and Fairness Task Force (for year ending June 30, 1998)*, available from Texaco.

9. This material originally appeared in Bill Birchard, "If You Measure, It Will Come," *Tomorrow*, March 1997, 34–35.

10. This case is based on Srikant Datar, Marc Epstein, and Karen White, "Bristol-Myers Squibb: Accounting for Product Life Cycle Costs at Matrix Essentials (Case #S-F-214)" (Stanford: Stanford University, Graduate School of Business, 1996), 5, 9, 15.

11. Bristol-Myers Squibb, "Report on Environmental Health and Safety Progress" (New York: Bristol-Myers Squibb, 1997), 5.

12. For more on Bristol-Myers Squibb, see Marc J. Epstein, *Measuring Corporate Environmental Performance* (Chicago: Irwin Professional Publishing, 1996).

13. Anita Sharpe and Greg Jaffe, "Cutting Edge: Columbia/HCA Plans for More Big Changes in Health-Care World," *Wall Street Journal*, 28 May 1997, A8.

14. Margaret Kerr, "Evolving the Business Ethics Function: From Compliance to Customer Value" (Presentation to the Ethics Officer Association Annual Conference: Northern Telecom Ltd., 1995), 8.

15. This passage is based on author interviews with Megan Barry, Northern Telecom Director of Business Ethics, February 1998 and July 1998.

16. Author interview with Geoffrey Bush, February 1998.

17. One unique Nortel innovation is the environmental-performance index devised jointly with consultants Arthur D. Little, Inc. The index aggregates and weights twenty-five variables of environmental performance—from energy consumption to hazardous waste cleanup—to come up with a single number for environmental performance. For 1997, Nortel reported an index score of 158 (out of an optimal 175), up from a baseline 100 in 1993. Nortel is just one of the companies worldwide that has experimented with measures that consolidate environmental performance into one figure.

18. Martin Bennett and Peter James, "The Preparation of an Environmental Financial Statement at Baxter International's Irish Manufacturing Operations Facility" (Unpublished paper, 1997).

19. For more on translating environmental decisions into financial terms, specifically economic profit, see Marc J. Epstein and S. David Young, "Improving Corporate Environmental Performance Through Economic Value Added," *Environmental Quality Management* (Summer 1998): 1–7.

20. Author interview with William Blackburn, February 1998.

21. British Telecom, "Impact on Society: A Quality Model for Continuous Improvement and Benchmarking of Community Programmes" (London: British Telecom, 1997).

22. Shell International Ltd., "Profits and Principles—Does There Have to Be a Choice?" (London: Royal Dutch/Shell Group, 1998), 51.

23. Ronald Alsop, "Business Bulletin: Sun Co. Shines in a Report Card on Oil Companies' Environmental Performance," *Wall Street Journal*, 12 February 1998, A1.

24. Current information on VanCity Savings comes from an author interview with Mark Lee, co-leader of the social audit. Background also comes from Cathy

Brisebois, "Ranking Disclosure: VanCity Savings & Credit Union, Canada," in *Building Corporate Accountability: Emerging Practices in Social and Ethical Accounting, Auditing and Reporting,* ed. Simon Zadek, Peter Pruzan, and Richard Evans (London: Earthscan Publications Ltd., 1997).

25. Vancouver City Savings Credit Union, Social Report 1997 (Vancouver: Vancouver City Savings Credit Union, 1998).

26. See http://es.epa.gov/oeca/sfi/ and, for background, see also John J. Fialka, "EPA Pollution-Grading Plan Provokes Opposition of Companies, State Officials," *Wall Street Journal,* 17 February 1998, B8.

27. As quoted in Susan Williams, "Equal Employment and Disclosure: A Report on U.S. Corporate Practices" (Washington, D.C.: Investor Responsibility Research Center, 1996), 22.

28. As quoted in Ralph Estes, "The Sunshine Standards for Corporate Reporting to Stakeholders," *Business Ethics Special Report #1* (1996), 6.

29. Arthur Levitt, "Investor Education: Disclosure for the 1990s" (Speech given at McIntire School of Commerce, Charlottesville, Virginia: Securities and Exchange Commission, 1995).

30. KPMG, "The KPMG Survey of Environmental Reporting" (London: KPMG, 1997), 4, 23.

31. Deborah Leipziger, "Social Accountability 8000: CEP Accreditation Agency Launches Standard on Workplace Issues" (New York: Council on Economic Priorities, 1998).

32. Pamela Sebastian, "A Workplace Code Gains Ground Among Multinational Companies," *Wall Street Journal,* 16 July 1998, A1. See also Anonymous, "CEP's Labor Auditing Takes Off," *Business Ethics,* July 1998, 8.

33. Aaron Bernstein, "Sweatshop Police: Business Backs an Initiative on Global Working Conditions," *Business Week,* 20 October 1997, 39.

34. Social Investment Forum, "After South Africa" (Washington, D.C.: Social Investment Forum, 1995).

35. Steve Schueth and Alisa Gravitz, "1997 Report on Responsible Investing Trends in the United States" (Washington, D.C.: Social Investment Forum, 1998).

36. Ann Taylor, "USTC's Push Sends Albertson's Flying," *Values (United States Trust Company of Boston),* April 1995, 7.

37. Jerald Blumberg, Georges Blum, and Åge Korsvold, "Environmental Performance and Shareholder Value" (Geneva: World Business Council for Sustainable Development, 1997), 62. Another unique method for ranking stocks according to environmental criteria has been developed by Norwegian insurer Storebrand and U.S. mutual fund operator Scudder Kemper Investments. Managers of the Storebrand Scudder Environmental Value fund rank stocks according to a "sustainability index," the weighted average of eight indicators, relating to everything from global warming and material efficiency to toxic releases and environmental reporting. See Amy Brown and Espen Dietrichs, "The Top Diggers," *Tomorrow,* July 1998, 22–23.

38. Desiree J. Hanford, "States Face Pressure to Invest Morally: Pension Funds Unload Tobacco, Entertainment Stocks," *Wall Street Journal,* 9 June 1997, B7A.

39. International Brotherhood of Teamsters, "1996–1997 Proxy Season Overview" (Washington, D.C.: International Brotherhood of Teamsters, Office of Corporate Affairs, 1997), 2.

40. Margaret Kerr, "Evolving the Business Ethics Function: From Compliance to Customer Value" (Presentation to the Ethics Officer Association Annual Conference: Northern Telecom Ltd., 1995), 3.

41. The results of these studies are generally inconclusive or show moderately positive results. Research correlates social and financial performance, but it has not clarified satisfactorily whether social performance causes or results from financial performance. An example of a recent study is Sandra A. Waddock and Samuel B. Graves, "The Corporate Social Performance-Financial Performance Link," *Strategic Management Journal* 18, no. 4 (1998): 303–320.

42. As cited in Williams, "Equal Employment," 27.

43. Jennifer J. Griffin and John F. Mahon, "The Corporate Social Performance and Corporate Financial Performance Debate: Twenty-Five Years of Incomparable Research," *Business and Society* 36, no. 1 (1997): 5 (27).

44. Author interview with Megan Barry, Nortel ethics chief, February 1998.

45. Bradford S. Gentry and Lisa O. Fernandez, "Valuing the Environment: How *Fortune 500* CFOs & Analysts Measure Corporate Performance" (Geneva: United Nations Development Program, Office of Development Studies, 1997), 11.

46. For a brief summary of the methods of social accounting, see Appendix B of Epstein, *Measuring Corporate.* See also Chapter 9 of Lee D. Parker, Kenneth R. Ferris, and David T. Otley, *Accounting for the Human Factor* (New York: Prentice Hall, 1989).

47. R. A. Bauer and D. Fenn, Jr., *The Corporate Social Audit* (New York: Russell Sage Foundation, 1972). See also R. A. Bauer and D. Fenn, Jr., "What Is a Corporate Social Audit?" *Harvard Business Review* 51, no. 1 (January/February 1973).

48. David F. Linowes, "Measuring Social Programs in Business: A Social Audit Proposal for Immediate Implementation" (Paper presented at the American Accounting Association, Louisiana State University, Baton Rouge, Louisiana, April 28, 1972).

49. Ralph W. Estes, *Corporate Social Accounting* (New York: John Wiley & Sons, Inc., 1976).

50. Abt Associates Annual Report & Social Audit, 1973.

Chapter Eleven: The Accountable Manager

1. John Browne, "Leading a Global Company: The Case of BP" (Speech delivered to Yale School of Management, September 18, 1998. London: British Petroleum, 1998).

2. John Browne, "Corporate Responsibility in an International Context (Speech to Council on Foreign Relations)" (London: British Petroleum, 1997), 5.

3. British Petroleum Company, *BP Social Report 1997* (London: British Petroleum Company, April 1998), 1.

4. Browne, "Corporate Responsibility," 3.

5. Alfred D. Chandler, Jr., "The Role of Business in the United States: A Historical Survey," *Daedalus* 98, no. 1 (1969): 40.

6. Peter F. Drucker, "Reckoning with the Pension Fund Revolution," *Harvard Business Review* 69, no. 2 (March/April 1991): 112.

7. Author interview with Bob Blakely, Tenneco CFO, October 1997.

8. Author interview with Dana Mead, Tenneco CEO, October, 1997.

9. Author interview with Jerry Choate, Allstate CEO, December 1997.

10. "The Allstate Partnership: Meeting Mutual Expectations for Success" (Internal document, undated).

11. Author interview with Jerry Choate in December 1997, and Allstate internal documents.

12. Author interview with John Roth, Northern Telecom CEO, January 1998.

13. Steven Kerr, "On the Folly of Rewarding A, While Hoping for B," *Academy of Management Executive* 9, no. 1 (February 1995): Table 1. Originally published in 1975.

14. Author interview with Dana Mead, Tenneco CEO, October 1997.

15. John Shiely, "Managing for Value Creation at Briggs & Stratton" (Unpublished manuscript, 1994), 22.

16. Shiely, "Managing for Value," 35.

SELECTED
BIBLIOGRAPHY

ABOODY, DAVID, and BARUCH LEV. "Politics and Substance of Standard-Setting: The Case of Software Capitalization." *Working Paper*, New York University, 1997.

AFL-CIO. "10 Key Votes Survey." Washington, D.C.: American Federation of Labor and Congress of Industrial Organizations, 1998.

AFL-CIO. "Investing in Our Future." Washington, D.C.: American Federation of Labor and Congress of Industrial Organizations, 1997.

AFL-CIO. "Too Close for Comfort: How Corporate Boardrooms Are Rigged to Overpay CEOs." Washington, D.C.: American Federation of Labor and Congress of Industrial Organizations, 1998.

ALDRIDGE, C. RICHARD, and JANET L. COLBERT. "We Need Better Financial Reporting." *Management Accounting* 79, no. 1 (July 1997): 32–36.

AMERICAN INSTITUTE OF CERTIFIED PUBLIC ACCOUNTANTS. "Improving Business Reporting—A Customer Focus (Comprehensive Report of the Special Committee on Financial Reporting)." New York: American Institute of Certified Public Accountants, 1994.

AMIR, ELI, and BARUCH LEV. "Value-Relevance of Nonfinancial Information: The Wireless Communications Industry." *Journal of Accounting and Economics* 22, no. 1 (August 1996): 3–30.

ANDERSON, RAY, and MARC EPSTEIN. "The Usefulness of Annual Reports." *Australian Accountant* (1995): 25–28.

ANDERSON, RAY H., and MARC J. EPSTEIN. *The Usefulness of Corporate Annual Reports to Shareholders in Australia, New Zealand, and the United States: An International Comparison.* Greenwich, Conn.: JAI Press Inc., 1996.

ANONYMOUS. "1997 Balanced Scorecard Results." *Vision (Published for the People of Whirlpool),* March 1998, 4.

ANONYMOUS. "The Battle for Cleveland." *Integrated Healthcare Report* 3, no. 3 (September 1994): 1–8.

ANONYMOUS. "Does Quality Data Equal Market Power?" *American Medical News* 36, no. 19 (1993): 3(2).

ANONYMOUS. "The New CEP Overseas Labor Auditing Process." *Business Ethics,* July 1997, 6.

ARGYRIS, CHRIS. "Good Communication That Blocks Learning." *Harvard Business Review* 72, no. 4 (1994): 77–85.

ARGYRIS, CHRIS, and ROBERT S. KAPLAN. "Implementing New Knowledge: The Case of Activity-Based Costing." *Accounting Horizons* 18, no. 3 (1994): 83–105.

ARGYRIS, CHRIS, and D. A. SCHOEN. *Organizational Learning II: Theory, Method, and Practice.* Reading, Mass.: Addison-Wesley, 1996.

ATKINSON, ANTHONY A., RAJIV D. BANKER, ROBERT S. KAPLAN, and S. MARK YOUNG. *Management Accounting.* 2d ed. Upper Saddle River, N.J.: Prentice-Hall, 1997.

ATKINSON, ANTHONY A., JOHN H. WATERHOUSE, and ROBERT B. WELLS. "A Stakeholder Approach to Strategic Performance Measurement." *Sloan Management Review* 38, no. 3 (1997): 25(13).

AUSTIN, TOM, DAVID MOSKOVITZ, and CHERYL HARRINGTON. "Uniform Consumer Disclosure Standards for New England." Gardner, Maine: Regulatory Assistance Project, 1997.

AYRES, FRANCES L. "What Managers Need to Know." *Management Accounting,* March (1994): 27–29.

BARR, STEPHEN. "Misreporting Results." *CFO,* December 1998, 36–48.

BARTH, MARY E., MICHAEL CLEMENT, GEORGE FOSTER, and RON KASZNIK. "Brand Values and Capital Market Valuation." Stanford, Calif.: Stanford Business School, May 1998.

BARTH, MARY E., and GREG CLINCH. "Revalued Financial, Tangible, and Intangible Assets: Associations with Share Prices and Non Market-Based Value Estimates." *Working Paper,* 1997.

BARTH, MARY E., MAUREEN F. MCNICHOLS, and G. PETER WILSON. "Factors Influencing Firms' Disclosures about Environmental Liabilities." *Review of Accounting Studies,* no. 2 (1997): 35–64.

BARTH, MARY E., and CHRISTINE M. MURPHY. "Required Financial Statement Disclosures: Purposes, Subject, Number, and Trends." *Accounting Horizons* 8, no. 4 (1995): 1–22.

BARTH, MARY E., and CHARLES A. NICHOLS III. "International Paper (A) (Case #193-160)." Boston: Harvard Business School, 1992.

BARTH, MARY E., and CHARLES A. NICHOLS III. "International Paper (B) (Case #193-061)." Boston: Harvard Business School, 1992.

BARTH, MARY E., and AMY P. SWEENEY. "Differential Information Environments and the Relation Between Accounting Amounts and Share Prices: Cost of Capital and Recognition versus Disclosure." *Working Paper,* Stanford University, 1995.

BAUER, R. A., and D. FENN, JR. *The Corporate Social Audit:* New York: Russell Sage Foundation, 1972.

BAUER, R. A., and D. FENN, JR. "What Is a Corporate Social Audit?" *Harvard Business Review* 51, no. 1 (January/February 1973).

BEHN, BRUCE K., and RICHARD A. RILEY, JR. "Using Non-Financial Information to Predict Financial Performance: The Case of the U.S. Airline Industry." *Working Paper,* 1998.

BELL, TIMOTHY, FRANK MARRS, IRA SOLOMON, and HOWARD THOMAS. *Auditing Organizations Through a Strategic Systems Lens.* Montvale, N.J.: KPMG Peat Marwick, 1997.

BENNETT, MARTIN, and PETER JAMES. "The Preparation of an Environmental Financial Statement at Baxter International's Irish Manufacturing Operations Facility." *Unpublished Paper,* University of Wolverhampton Business School, U.K., 1997.

BERLE, ADOLF A., and GARDINER C. MEANS. *The Modern Corporation and Private Property.* New York: Macmillan, 1932.

BERNARD, VICTOR L., ROBERT C. MERTON, and KRISHNA G. PALEPU. "Mark-to-Market Accounting for Banks and Thrifts: Lessons from the Danish Experience." *Journal of Accounting Research* 33, no. 1 (Spring 1995): 1–32.

BERTSCH, KEN. "1998 Shareholder Resolutions: A Proxy Season Overview." *Corporate Governance Highlights (Investor Responsibility Research Center),* 13 February 1998, 2–6.

BERTSCH, KENNETH A. "Voting on Major U.S. Governance Issues." *Corporate Governance Bulletin (Investor Responsibility Research Center)* 1997, 10.

BERTSCH, KENNETH A., and VIRGINIA ROSENBAUM. "Shareholders Increase Support for Resolutions on Board Independence, Annual Election of Directors." *Corporate Governance Bulletin (Investor Responsibility Research Center)* 15, no. 2 (1998): 1, 3–10.

BERTSCH, KENNETH A., STEPHEN R. TOBEY, ROBERT NEWBURY, ERIC OVSIEW, and VIRGINIA ROSENBAUM. "Shareholders, Companies at Odds on Takeover Defenses, But Find Agreement on Board Issues (Proxy Season Wrap-Up)." *Corporate Governance Bulletin (Investor Responsibility Research Center)* 14, no. 2 (1997): 1–12.

BIDDLE, GARY C., ROBERT M. BOWEN, and JAMES S. WALLACE. "Evidence on the Relative and Incremental Information Content of EVA, Residual Income, Earnings and Operating Cash Flow." *Working Paper,* University of Washington, Seattle, 1996, 25+.

BIGGS, JOHN A. "Corporate Governance Assessment: A TIAA-CREF Initiative." *Director's Monthly* 20, no. 10 (1996): 1–8.

BINNERSLEY, MARK. "Do You Measure Up? The Role of Management Accountants in Performance Measurement." *Management Accounting (British),* 1 November 1996, 32–35.

BIRCHARD, BILL. "Adding Nonfinancial Measures to the Mix." *CFO,* October 1994, 37.

BIRCHARD, BILL. "By the Numbers." *Tomorrow,* January 1995, 52–53.

BIRCHARD, BILL. "The Call for Full Disclosure." *CFO,* December 1994, 30–42.

BIRCHARD, BILL. "CFOs on Review." *CFO,* September 1997, 46–51.

BIRCHARD, BILL. "Closing the Strategy Gap." *CFO,* October 1996, 26–36.

BIRCHARD, BILL. "'Do It Yourself': How Valmont Industries Implemented EVA." *CFO,* March 1996, 34–40.

BIRCHARD, BILL. "Does Anyone Read This Stuff? Many Financial Analysts Are Still Indifferent or Worse to Environmental Reports . . . " *Tomorrow,* November 1996, 54–55.

BIRCHARD, BILL. "DuPont Integrates Worldwide." *Enterprise,* January 1993, 16–17.

BIRCHARD, BILL. "Finding Their Smiles." *CFO,* December 1994, 42.

BIRCHARD, BILL. "Going Green." *Enterprise,* January 1993, 10–14.

BIRCHARD, BILL. "Green Management." *Enterprise,* January 1993, 14–19.

BIRCHARD, BILL. "Hidden Sites, Hidden Costs." *Tomorrow,* November 1996, 30–31.

BIRCHARD, BILL. "How Many Masters Can You Serve?" *CFO,* July 1995, 48–54.

BIRCHARD, BILL. "If You Measure, It Will Come." *Tomorrow,* March 1997, 34–35.

BIRCHARD, BILL. "The Latest and Greatest Environmental Measures." *Tomorrow* 6, no. 3 (1996): 33–34.

BIRCHARD, BILL. "Make Environmental Reports Relevant." *CFO,* June 1997, 79–80.

BIRCHARD, BILL. "Making It Count." *CFO,* October 1995, 42–51.

BIRCHARD, BILL. "Mastering the New Metrics." *CFO,* October 1994, 30–38.

BIRCHARD, BILL. "The Measure of Good Business: Delivering Superior Value to the Stakeholders: That's All There Is to It." *Tomorrow,* January 1997, 50–53.

BIRCHARD, BILL. "Measurement: It's Time to Admit Stakeholders." *CFO,* November 1995, 51.

BIRCHARD, BILL. "The New Finance." *Enterprise,* October 1992, 20–25.

BIRCHARD, BILL. "The Paragon and the Paradox." *CFO,* December 1994, 33.

BIRCHARD, BILL. "Power to the People." *CFO,* March 1995, 38–43.

BIRCHARD, BILL. "The Right to Know." *CFO,* November 1993, 28–38.

BIRCHARD, BILL. "Scaling Up for the 90s (Interview with Dr. Joseph Juran)." *Enterprise,* July 1992, 36–39.

BIRCHARD, BILL. "Shareholders' Demands." *CFO,* November 1993, 38.

BIRCHARD, BILL. "Where Performance Measures Fail." *CFO,* October 1996, 36.

BLUMBERG, JERALD, GEORGES BLUM, and ÅGE KORSVOLD. "Environmental Performance and Shareholder Value." Geneva: World Business Council for Sustainable Development, 1997.

BRANCATO, CAROLYN KAY. "Communicating Corporate Performance: A Delicate Balance." New York: The Conference Board, 1997.

BRANCATO, CAROLYN KAY. *Institutional Investors and Corporate Governance: Best Practices for Increasing Corporate Value.* Chicago: Irwin Professional Publishing (McGraw-Hill), 1997.

BRANCATO, CAROLYN KAY. "New Corporate Performance Measures." New York: The Conference Board, 1995.

BRANCATO, CAROLYN KAY. "Turnover, Investment Strategies, and Ownership Patterns." *Institutional Investment Report* 2, no. 2 (1998): 5–47.

BRETON, GAETAN, and RICHARD J. TAFFLER. "What Drives Sell-Side Analyst Stock Recommendation Decisions: A Content Analysis Approach." *Working Paper,* University of Quebec at Montreal, 1998.

BRISEBOIS, CATHY. "Ranking Disclosure: VanCity Savings & Credit Union, Canada." In *Building Corporate Accountability: Emerging Practices in Social and Ethical Accounting, Auditing and Reporting,* edited by Simon Zadek, Peter Pruzan, and Richard Evans. London: Earthscan Publications Ltd, 1997.

BRITISH TELECOM. "Impact on Society: A Quality Model for Continuous Improvement and Benchmarking of Community Programmes." London: British Telecom, 1997.

BROOK, ROBERT H., ELIZABETH A. MCGLYNN, and PAUL D. CLEARY. "Quality of Health Care, Part 2: Measuring Quality of Care." *New England Journal of Medicine* 335, no. 13 (1996): 966–969.

BROWNE, JOHN. "Corporate Responsibility in an International Context (Speech to Council on Foreign Relations)." London: British Petroleum, 1997.

BUGHIN, JACQUES, and THOMAS E. COPELAND. "The Virtuous Cycle of Shareholder Value." *The McKinsey Quarterly* 1997, no. 2 (1997): 156–167.

BUKOWITZ, WENDI R., and GORDON P. PETRASH. "Visualizing, Measuring and Managing Knowledge." *Research & Technology Management* 40, no. 4 (July/August 1997): 24–31.

BYRNE, JOHN, LESLIE BROWN, and JOYCE BARNATHAN. "The Best and Worst Boards." *Business Week,* 8 December 1997, 90–98.

BYRNE, JOHN A. "The CEO and the Board." *Business Week,* 15 September 1997, 107–116.

BYRNE, JOHN A. "Governance: CEOs Catch Up with Shareholder Activist." *Business Week,* 22 September 1997, 36.

BYRNE, JOHN A. "Putting More Stock in Good Governance." *Business Week,* 15 September 1997, 116.

BYRNE, JOHN A., and RICHARD A. MELCHER. "The Best and Worst Boards." *Business Week,* 25 November 1996, 62–68.

BYRNE, JOHN A., and JENNIFER REINGOLD. "Wanted: A Few Good CEOs." *Business Week,* 11 August 1997, 64–70.

CALIFORNIA PUBLIC EMPLOYEES RETIREMENT SYSTEM. "U.S. Corporate Governance Core Principles and Guidelines." Sacramento: California Public Employees Retirement System, 1998.

CALIFORNIA PUBLIC EMPLOYEES RETIREMENT SYSTEM. "Company Responses to Request for Board Governance Self-Evaluation." Sacramento: California Public Employees Retirement System, 1995.

CARLETON, WILLARD T., JAMES M. NELSON, and MICHAEL S. WEISBACH. "The Influence of Institutions on Corporate Governance Through Private Negotiations: Evidence from TIAA-CREF." *Journal of Finance,* In Press (1998).

CASE, JOHN. *Open-Book Management.* New York: HarperBusiness, 1995.

CASE, JOHN. "Opening the Books." *Harvard Business Review* 75, no. 2 (1997): 118–127.

CASE, JOHN F. *The Open-Book Experience: Lessons from over 100 Companies Who Successfully Transformed Themselves.* Reading, Mass.: Addison-Wesley, 1998.

CHANDLER, ALFRED D., JR. "The Role of Business in the United States: A Historical Survey." *Daedalus* 98, no. 1 (1969): 23–40.

CHANEY, PAUL K., TIMOTHY M. DEVINNEY, and RUSSELL S. WINER. "The Impact of New Product Introductions on the Market Value of Firms." *Journal of Business Finance* 64, no. 4 (October 1991): 573.

CHANG, JAMES. "The Decline in Value Relevance of Earnings and Book Values." *Working Paper,* 1998.

CHRISTOPHER, WILLIAM F., editor. *New Management Accounting: How Leading-Edge Companies Use Management Accounting to Improve Performance.* Menlo Park, Calif.: Crisp Publications, 1998.

CIULLA, JOANNE B. "Why Is Business Talking About Ethics? Reflections on Foreign Conversations." *California Management Review* 34, no. 1 (1991): 67–86.

CLARKSON, MAX B. E. "A Stakeholder Framework for Analyzing and Evaluating Corporate Social Performance." *Academy of Management Review* 20, no. 1 (1995): 92–117.

COLLINS, DANIEL W., EDWARD L. MAYDEW, and IRA S. WEISS. "Changes in the Value-Relevance of Earnings and Book Values over the Past Forty Years." *Journal of Accounting & Economics* 24 (1997): 39–67.

CONDON, BERNARD. "Pick a Number, Any Number." *Forbes*, 23 March 1998, 124–128.

CONGER, JAY A., DAVID FINEGOLD, and EDWARD E. LAWLER III. "Appraising Boardroom Performance." *Harvard Business Review* 76, no. 1 (January–February 1998): 136–148.

COOPER, ROBIN. "You Need a New Cost System When . . ." *Harvard Business Review* 67, no. 1 (January–February 1989): 77–82.

COOPER, ROBIN, and ROBERT S. KAPLAN. "Profit Priorities from Activity-Based Costing." *Harvard Business Review* 69, no. 3 (May–June 1991): 130–135.

COPELAND, TOM, TIM KOLLER, and JACK MURRIN. *Valuation: Measuring and Managing the Value of Companies*. New York: John Wiley & Sons, 2nd edition, 1994.

COUNCIL OF INSTITUTIONAL INVESTORS. "Core Policies, Policies, & Positions." Washington, D.C.: Council of Institutional Investors, 1998.

CRYSTAL, GRAEF S. *In Search of Excess: The Overcompensation of American Executives*. New York: W. W. Norton & Company, 1991.

DATAR, SRIKANT, MARC EPSTEIN, and KAREN WHITE. "Bristol-Myers Squibb: Accounting for Product Life Cycle Costs at Matrix Essentials (Case #S-F-214)." Stanford: Stanford University, Graduate School of Business, 1996.

DELOITTE & TOUCHE LLP. *Summary Annual Reporting: Improving Shareholder Communications*. New York: Deloitte & Touche, 1995.

DELOITTE & TOUCHE MANAGEMENT CONSULTING. "Performance Measurement Survey." New York: Deloitte & Touche LLP, 1995.

DENHAM, ROBERT, and MICHAEL PORTER. "Lifting All Boats: Increasing the Payoff from Private Investment in the US Economy (Report of the Capital Allocation Subcouncil to the Competitiveness Policy Council)." Washington, D.C.: Competitiveness Policy Council, 1995.

DICHAUT, JOHN W., and KEVIN A. MCCABE. "The Behavioral Foundations of Stewardship Accounting and a Proposed Program of Research: What Is Accountability?" *Behavioral Research in Accounting* 9 (1997): 60–87.

DONALDSON, MOLLA S., and KATHLEEN N. LOHR. *Health Data in the Information Age: Use, Disclosure, and Privacy*. Washington, D.C.: National Academy Press (Institute of Medicine), 1994.

DONOVAN, JOHN, RICHARD TULLY, and BRENT WORTMAN. *The Value Enterprise*. New York: McGraw-Hill Ryerson, 1997.

DRUCKER, PETER F. "The Information Executives Truly Need." *Harvard Business Review* 73, no. 1 (1995): 54–62.

DRUCKER, PETER F. "Reckoning with the Pension Fund Revolution." *Harvard Business Review* 69, no. 2 (March/April 1991): 106–114.

DRUCKER, PETER F. "We Need to Measure, Not Count." *Wall Street Journal*, 13 April 1993.

EATON, TIM V., and HAROLD P. ROTH. "Disclosing Managerial Information: The Jenkins Committee Recommendations." *Journal of Cost Management*, 1998 (January/February): 37–41.

ECCLES, ROBERT G. "Boards Need Better Information." *Directors & Boards* 18, no. 4 (Summer 1994): 31–33.

ECCLES, ROBERT G. "The Performance Measurement Manifesto." *Harvard Business Review* 69, no. 1 (January–February 1991): 131–137.

ECCLES, ROBERT G., and SARAH C. MAVRINAC. "Improving the Corporate Disclosure Process." Boston: Graduate School of Business Administration, Harvard University, 1994.

ECCLES, ROBERT G., and NITIN NOHRIA. *Beyond the Hype: Rediscovering the Essence of Management.* Boston: Harvard Business School Press, 1992.

EDVINSSON, LEIF. "Developing Intellectual Capital at Skandia." *Long Range Planning* 30, no. 3 (1997): 366–373.

EDVINSSON, LEIF, and MICHAEL S. MALONE. *Intellectual Capital: Realizing Your Company's True Value by Finding Its Hidden Roots.* New York: Harper-Collins, 1997.

ELKINGTON, JOHN. *Cannibals with Forks: The Triple Bottom Line of 21st Century Business.* London: New Society Publishers, 1998.

ELKINGTON, JOHN, SHELLY FENNELL, and NIKLAS KREANDER. "Engaging Shareholders." *Tomorrow,* July 1998, 54–57.

ELKINGTON, JOHN, NIKLAS KREANDER, and SHELLY FENNEL. "Targeting the Non-Reporters." *Tomorrow,* September 1998, 58–61.

ELKINGTON, JOHN, NIKLAS KREANDER, and HELEN STIBBARD. "The 1997 Benchmark Results: Leading-Edge Companies Are Making Dramatic Progress in Reporting—But Contrarian Sympathizers Lag Behind." *Tomorrow,* January 1998, 56–60.

ELLIOTT, ROBERT K. "The Future of Audits: The Power of Information Technology Is Threatening the Audit Function." *Journal of Accountancy,* 1994 (September): 74–82.

ELLIOTT, ROBERT K. "The Third Wave Breaks on the Shores of Accounting." *Accounting Horizons* 6, no. 2 (June 1992): 61–85.

ELLIOTT, ROBERT K., and PETER D. JACOBSON. "Commentary: Costs and Benefits of Business Information Disclosure." *Accounting Horizons* 8, no. 4 (December 1994): 80–96.

ELLIOTT, ROBERT K., and DON M. PALLAIS. "Are You Ready for New Assurance Services?" *Journal of Accountancy* 183, no. 6 (1997): 47–51.

EPSTEIN, MARC J. "Accounting for Product Take Back." *Management Accounting,* 1996 (August): 29–33.

EPSTEIN, MARC J. "The Annual Report Report Card." *Business and Society Review* 1992, no. 81 (Spring): 81–83.

EPSTEIN, MARC J. "Annual Reports and Shareholders." *The Journal of Corporate Governance* 12, no. 69 (July/August 1991): 10–12.

EPSTEIN, MARC J. "Corporate Governance and the Shareholders' Revolt." *Management Accounting* 74, no. 2 (1992): 32–35.

EPSTEIN, MARC J. "The Expanding Role of Accountants in Society." *Management Accounting* 74, no. 10 (April 1993): 22–26.

EPSTEIN, MARC J. *Measuring Corporate Environmental Performance.* Chicago: Irwin Professional Publishing, 1996.

EPSTEIN, MARC J. "What Shareholders Really Want." *New York Times,* 28 April 1991, F11.

EPSTEIN, MARC J., JOANNE B. EPSTEIN, and EARL JAY WEISS. *Introduction to Social Accounting.* Los Angeles: Western Consulting Group, Inc., 1977.

EPSTEIN, MARC J., E. FLAMHOLTZ, and J. J. McDONOUGH. "Corporate Social Accounting in the United States of America: State of the Art and Future Prospects." *Accounting, Organizations, and Society* 1, no. 1 (1976): 23–42.

EPSTEIN, MARC J., and JEAN-FRANÇOIS MANZONI. "The Balanced Scorecard and Tableau de Bord: Translating Strategy into Action." *Management Accounting* 79, no. 2 (1997): 28–36.

EPSTEIN, MARC J., and JEAN-FRANÇOIS MANZONI. "Implementing Corporate Strategy: From Tableaux de Bord to Balanced Scorecard." *European Management Journal* 16, no. 2 (April 1998): 190–203.

EPSTEIN, MARC J., and KRISHNA G. PALEPU. "Analysts Speak Out on Corporate Communications." *Unpublished manuscript,* Rice University, 1998.

EPSTEIN, MARC J., and KRISHNA G. PALEPU. "What Analysts Really Want." *CFO,* October 1997, 47.

EPSTEIN, MARC J., and MOSES L. PAVA. "How Useful Is the Statement of Cash Flows?" *Management Accounting* 74, no. 1 (July 1992): 52–55.

EPSTEIN, MARC J., and MOSES L. PAVA. "Profile of an Annual Report." *Financial Executive* 10, no. 1 (January/February 1994): 41–43.

EPSTEIN, MARC J., and MOSES L. PAVA. "Shareholders' Perceptions on the Usefulness of MD&As." *Managerial Finance* 21, no. 3 (1995): 68–83.

EPSTEIN, MARC J., and MOSES L. PAVA. "The Shareholder's Use of Corporate Annual Reports: A Summary of Findings." Paper presented at the Annual Congress of the European Accounting Association, Turku, Finland, April 1993.

EPSTEIN, M. J., and M. J. ROY. "Using ISO 14000 for Improved Organizational Learning and Environmental Management." *Environmental Quality Management,* 1997 (Autumn): 21–30.

EPSTEIN, MARC J., and ALBERT D. SPALDING, JR. *The Accountant's Guide to Legal Liability and Ethics.* Homewood, Ill.: Business One Irwin, 1993.

EPSTEIN, MARC J., and S. DAVID YOUNG. "Improving Corporate Environmental Performance Through Economic Value Added." *Environmental Quality Management,* 1998 (Summer): 1–7.

ERNST & YOUNG. "Measures That Matter." Boston: Ernst & Young LLP, 1997.

ESTES, RALPH. "The Sunshine Standards for Corporate Reporting to Stakeholders." *Business Ethics Special Report #1,* 1996.

ESTES, RALPH W. *Corporate Social Accounting.* New York: John Wiley & Sons, Inc., 1976.

ESTES, RALPH W. *Tyranny of the Bottom Line: Why Corporations Make Good People Do Bad Things.* San Francisco: Berrett-Koehler Publishers, 1996.

FELTON, ROBERT F., ALEC HUDNUT, and JENNIFER VAN HEECKEREN. "Putting Value on Corporate Governance." *The McKinsey Quarterly,* no. 4 (1996): 170.

FIALKA, JOHN J. "EPA Pollution-Grading Plan Provokes Opposition of Companies, State Officials." *Wall Street Journal,* 17 February 1998, B8.

FIALKA, JOHN J. "EPA Puts Records About Polluters on the Internet." *Wall Street Journal,* 4 May 1998, B4.

FISHER, ANNE. "The 100 Best Companies to Work for in America." *Fortune,* 12 January 1998, 68–70.

FLEMING, PETER D. "What's Next for the Business Reporting Model." *Journal of Accountancy* 182, no. 6 (December 1996): 14(2).

FRANKEL, RICHARD, MAUREEN MCNICHOLS, and G. PETER WILSON. "Discretionary Disclosure and External Financing." *Accounting Review* 70, no. 1 (1995): 135(16).

FREEMAN, E. *Strategic Management: A Stakeholder Approach.* Boston: Pittman, 1984.

FRIEDMAN, MILTON. "The Social Responsibility of Business Is to Increase Its Profits." *New York Times Magazine,* 13 September 1970.

GALLHOFER, SONJA, and JIM HASLAM. "Approaching Corporate Accountability: Fragments of the Past." *Accounting and Business Research* 23 (1993): 320–330.

GARTEN, JEFFREY E. "Globalism Doesn't Have to Be Cruel." *Business Week,* 9 February 1998, 26.

GARVIN, D. A. "Building a Learning Organization." *Harvard Business Review* 71, no. 4 (July–August 1993): 79–91.

GENTRY, BRADFORD S., and LISA O. FERNANDEZ. "Valuing the Environment: How *Fortune 500* CFOs & Analysts Measure Corporate Performance." Geneva: United Nations Development Program, Office of Development Studies, 1997.

GILPIN, KENNETH N. "Shareholders Push for Tighter Rules Abroad." *New York Times,* 6 April 1998, D2.

GLASSER, JAMES J. "How EVA Works Against GATX." *Chief Executive (US),* January 1996, 42(2).

GOFF, JOHN. "Lawnmower Men." *EVAngelist* 1, no. 4 (1997): 9–18.

GORDON, LILLI A., JOHN POUND, and TODD PORTER. "High-Performance Workplaces: Implications for Investment Research and Active Investing Strategies." Waban, Mass.: Gordon Group, Inc., 1994.

GOUILLART, FRANCIS J., and JAMES N. KELLY. *Transforming the Organization.* New York: McGraw-Hill, 1995.

GOYDER, MARK, and NEIL HARTLEY. "Tomorrow's Company." London: The Royal Society for the Encouragement of Arts, Manufactures and Commerce, 1995.

GREEN, MARK D. "Executive Information Systems at Pitney Bowes Mailing Systems." In *New Management Accounting: How Leading-Edge Companies Use Management Accounting to Improve Performance,* edited by William F. Christopher. Menlo Park, Calif.: Crisp Publications, 1998, 71–84.

GREENBERG, HERB. "Shipping Bricks and Other Tricks." *Fortune,* 29 September 1997, 30, 34.

GRIFFIN, JENNIFER J., and JOHN F. MAHON. "The Corporate Social Performance and Corporate Financial Performance Debate: Twenty-Five Years of Incomparable Research." *Business and Society* 36, no. 1 (1997): 5 (27).

HAMMONDS, KEITH H., ROY FURCHGOTT, STEVE HAMM, and PAUL C. JUDGE. "Work and Family." *Business Week,* 15 September 1997, 96–99.

HANCHAK, NICHOLAS A. "From the Editor." *USQA Quality Monitor* 4, no. 1 (July 1997): i.

HANDY, CHARLES. *The Age of Paradox.* Boston: Harvard Business School Press, 1994.

HANFORD, DESIREE J. "States Face Pressure to Invest Morally: Pension Funds Unload Tobacco, Entertainment Stocks." *Wall Street Journal,* 9 June 1997, B7A.

HEALTHPARTNERS. "Prescriptions for Health Improvement (Report on the Partners for Better Health Program)." Minneapolis: HealthPartners, 1998.

HEALY, PAUL, AMY HUTTON, and KRISHNA PALEPU. "Stock Performance and Intermediation Changes Surrounding Sustained Increases in Disclosure." *Working Paper,* 1998, 49.

HEALY, PAUL, and KRISHNA PALEPU. "The Challenges of Investor Communication: The Case of CUC International, Inc." *Journal of Financial Economics* 38 (1995): 111–140.

HERMES INVESTMENT MANAGEMENT LIMITED. "Statement on Corporate Governance and Voting Policy." London: Hermes Investment Management Limited, 1998.

HERZLINGER, REGINA E. "Can Public Trust in Nonprofits and Governments Be Restored?" *Harvard Business Review* 74, no. 2 (March/April 1996): 97–107.

HESKETT, JAMES L., THOMAS O. JONES, GARY W. LOVEMAN, W. EARL SASSER, JR., and LEONARD A. SCHLESINGER. "Putting the Service-Profit Chain to Work." *Harvard Business Review* 72, no. 2 (March/April 1994): 164.

HESKETT, JAMES L., W. EARL SASSER, JR., and LEONARD A. SCHLESINGER. *The Service Profit Chain: How Leading Companies Link Profit and Growth to Loyalty, Satisfaction, and Value.* New York: The Free Press, 1997.

HOFFMAN, ANDREW J. "A Strategic Response to Investor Activism." *Sloan Management Review* 37, no. 2 (1996): 51(14).

HORNGREN, CHARLES T., GEORGE FOSTER, and SRIKANT M. DATAR. *Cost Accounting: A Managerial Emphasis.* 9th ed. New York: Prentice Hall International, Inc., 1997.

HOWELL, ROBERT A. *Developing Comprehensive Performance Indicators.* Vol. 31. Hamilton, Ontario: The Society of Management Accountants of Canada, 1994.

HOWELL, ROBERT A., JOHN K. SHANK, STEPHEN R. SOUCY, and JOSEPH FISHER. *Cost Management for Tomorrow: Seeking the Competitive Edge.* Morristown, N.J.: Financial Executives Research Foundation, 1992.

HRONEC, STEVEN M. *Vital Signs: Using Quality, Time, and Cost Performance Measurements to Chart Your Company's Future.* New York: American Management Association, 1993.

INTERFAITH CENTER ON CORPORATE RESPONSIBILITY. "Principles for Global Corporate Responsibility." *The Corporate Examiner,* 1 September 1995.

INTERFAITH CENTER ON CORPORATE RESPONSIBILITY. "The Proxy Resolutions Book." New York: Interfaith Center on Corporate Responsibility, 1998.

INTERFAITH CENTER ON CORPORATE RESPONSIBILITY. "The Proxy Resolutions Book." New York: Interfaith Center on Corporate Responsibility, 1997.

INTERNATIONAL BROTHERHOOD OF TEAMSTERS. "1996–1997 Proxy Season Overview." Washington, D.C.: International Brotherhood of Teamsters, Office of Corporate Affairs, 1997.

INTERNATIONAL BROTHERHOOD OF TEAMSTERS. "1997–1998 Proxy Season Overview." Washington, D.C.: International Brotherhood of Teamsters, 1998.

INTERNATIONAL BROTHERHOOD OF TEAMSTERS. "America's Least Valuable Directors: A Study of Corporate Board Directors." Washington, D.C.: International Brotherhood of Teamsters, 1998.

INTERNATIONAL BROTHERHOOD OF TEAMSTERS. "America's Least Valuable Directors: A Study of Corporate Directors." Washington, D.C.: International Brotherhood of Teamsters, Office of Corporate Affairs, 1997.

JENNINGS, KEN, KURT MILLER, and SHARYN MATERNA. *Changing Health Care.* Santa Monica: Knowledge Exchange, 1997.

JOHNSON, H. THOMAS, and ROBERT S. KAPLAN. *Relevance Lost: The Rise and Fall of Management Accounting.* Boston: Harvard Business School Press, 1987; paperback edition, 1991.

JOHNSON, ROY S. "The 50 Best Companies for Asians, Blacks & Hispanics." *Fortune*, 3 August 1998, 94–122.

JOINT COMMISSION ON ACCREDITATION OF HEALTHCARE ORGANIZATIONS. "ORYX: The Next Evolution in Accreditation—Questions and Answers about the Joint Commission's Planned Integration of Performance Measures into the Accreditation Process." Oakbrook Terrace, Ill.: Joint Commission on Accreditation of Healthcare Organizations, 1998.

KAPLAN, ROBERT, and DAVID P. NORTON. "Putting the Balanced Scorecard to Work." *Harvard Business Review* 71, no. 5 (September/October 1993): 134–147.

KAPLAN, ROBERT S. "Analog Devices: The Half-Life System (Case #190-161)." Boston: Harvard Business School, 1990.

KAPLAN, ROBERT S. "Mobil USM&R (A): Linking the Balanced Scorecard (Case #9-197-025)." Boston: Harvard Business School, 1996.

KAPLAN, ROBERT S. "Mobil USM&R (B): New England Sales and Distribution (Case #9-197-026)." Boston: Harvard Business School, 1996.

KAPLAN, ROBERT S., and ROBIN COOPER. *Cost & Effect: Using Integrated Cost Systems to Drive Profitability and Performance.* Boston: Harvard Business School Press, 1997.

KAPLAN, ROBERT S., and DAVID P. NORTON. *The Balanced Scorecard.* Boston: Harvard Business School Press, 1996.

KAPLAN, ROBERT S., and DAVID P. NORTON. "The Balanced Scorecard— Measures That Drive Performance." *Harvard Business Review* 70, no. 1 (January–February 1992): 71–79.

KAPLAN, ROBERT S., and DAVID P. NORTON. "Linking the Balanced Scorecard to Strategy." *California Management Review* 39, no. 1 (1996): 53(27).

KAPLAN, ROBERT S., and DAVID P. NORTON. "Using the Balanced Scorecard as a Strategic Management System." *Harvard Business Review* 74, no. 1 (1996): 75–85.

KARLGAARD, RICH. "SEC Loves IC; Commissioner Steven Wallman Sees a Future for IC Reporting." *Forbes ASAP* 159, no. 7 (1997): 38.

KERR, MARGARET. "Evolving the Business Ethics Function: From Compliance to Customer Value." Presentation to the Ethics Officer Association Annual Conference: Northern Telecom Ltd., 1995.

KERR, STEVEN. "On the Folly of Rewarding A, While Hoping for B." *Academy of Management Executive* 9, no. 1 (February 1995): 7–15.

KIRK, DONALD J., and ARTHUR SIEGAL. "How Directors and Auditors Can Improve Corporate Governance." *Journal of Accountancy* 181, no. 1 (1996): 53–57.

KORN/FERRY INTERNATIONAL. "25th Annual Board of Directors Study." New York: Korn/Ferry International, 1998.

KOTTER, JOHN P., and JAMES L. HESKETT. *Corporate Culture and Performance.* New York: The Free Press (Macmillan), 1992.

KPMG. "The KPMG Survey of Environmental Reporting." London: KPMG, 1997.

KURTZMAN, JOEL. "Is Your Company Off Course? Now You Can Find Out Why." *Fortune,* 17 February 1997, 128–130.

LALLY, ROSEMARY. "CEO Succession at Campbell Soup." *Corporate Governance Bulletin (Investor Responsibility Research Center),* July 1997, 3.

LANG, MARK H., and RUSSELL J. LUNDHOLM. "Corporate Disclosure Policy and Analyst Behavior." *Accounting Review* 71, no. 4 (1996): 467–492.

LANSKY, DAVID. "Foundation for Accountability (FACCT): A Consumer Voice on Health Care Quality." *JCOM* 3, no. 6 (1996): 54–58.

LEATHERMAN, SHEILA, and DEBORAH CHASE. "Using Report Cards to Grade Health Plan Quality." *Journal of American Health Policy,* January 1994, 32–40.

LEIPZIGER, DEBORAH. "Social Accountability 8000: CEP Accreditation Agency Launches Standard on Workplace Issues." New York: Council on Economic Priorities, 1998.

LEONARD-BARTON, DOROTHY. *Wellsprings of Knowledge: Building and Sustaining the Sources of Innovation.* Boston: Harvard Business School Press, 1995.

LEV, BARUCH. "The Boundaries of Financial Reporting and How to Extend Them." *Unpublished Paper,* New York University, 1996, 53.

LEV, BARUCH. "Information Disclosure Strategy." *California Management Review* 34, no. 4 (1992): 9–32.

LEV, BARUCH. "The Old Rules No Longer Apply." *Forbes ASAP,* 7 April 1997, 35–36.

LEV, BARUCH, and STEPHEN H. PENMAN. "Voluntary Forecast Disclosure, Nondisclosure, and Stock Prices." *Journal of Accounting Research* 28, no. 1 (1990): 49.

LEVITT, ARTHUR. "Investor Education: Disclosure for the 1990s." Speech given at McIntire School of Commerce, Charlottesville, Va.: Securities and Exchange Commission, 1995.

LEVITT, ARTHUR. "Shareholder Interests as the Director's Touchstone." Palo Alto, Calif.: Securities and Exchange Commission, 1996.

LEVITT, ARTHUR. "A Financial Partnership." Speech given at the Financial Executives Institute. New York: U.S. Securities and Exchange Commission, 1998.

LEVITT, ARTHUR. "The 'Numbers Game.'" Speech given at the New York University Center for Law and Business. New York: U.S. Securities and Exchange Commission, 1998.

LINDEN, DANA WECHSLER, and NANCY ROTENIER. "Good-bye to Berle & Means." *Forbes,* 3 January 1994, 100–103.

LINOWES, DAVID F. "Measuring Social Programs in Business: A Social Audit Proposal for Immediate Implementation." Paper presented at the American Accounting Association, Louisiana State University, Baton Rouge, Louisiana, 28 April 1972.

LORSCH, JAY W. "Empowering the Board." *Harvard Business Review* 73, no. 1 (January/February 1995): 107–117.

LORSCH, JAY W., and ELIZABETH MACIVER. *Pawns or Potentates.* Boston: Harvard Business School Press, 1989.

LOWENSTEIN, ROGER. "Coming Clean on Company Stock Options." *Wall Street Journal,* 27 June 1997, C1.

LOWENSTEIN, ROGER. "Earnings Not Always What They Seem." *Wall Street Journal,* 15 February 1996, C1.

LOWENSTEIN, ROGER. "Looking for Leaders in the Mahogany Jungle." *Wall Street Journal,* 14 November 1996, C1.

LOWENSTEIN, ROGER. "Microsoft and Its Two Constituencies." *Wall Street Journal,* 4 December 1997, C1.

LUBLIN, JOANN S. "CEOs Give Up More Clout to Boards." *Wall Street Journal,* 26 July 1996, A7A.

LUBLIN, JOANN S. "CEOs Have Less Say in Designating Successors." *Wall Street Journal,* 24 June 1997, B1, B8.

LUBLIN, JOANN S. "Minimal Disclosure Sparks Holder Suits." *Wall Street Journal,* 17 June 1998, B27.

LUBLIN, JOANN S. "Panel Suggests Independent Directors Take More Control of CEO Succession." *Wall Street Journal,* 13 July 1998, B6.

LUBLIN, JOANN S. "Pay for No Performance." *Wall Street Journal,* 9 April 1998, R1, R4.

LUBLIN, JOANN S. "Unions Brandish Stock to Force Change." *Wall Street Journal,* 17 May 1996, B1.

LYNN, BERNADETTE E. "Performance Evaluation in the New Economy: Bringing the Measurement and Evaluation of Intellectual Capital into the Management Planning and Control System." *Unpublished manuscript,* McMaster University, Hamilton, Ontario, 1996, 21.

MACDONALD, ELIZABETH. "Options' Effect on Earnings Sparks Debate." *Wall Street Journal,* 13 May 1998, C1, C2.

MACINTOSH, JOHN C. C. "The Issues, Effects, and Consequences of the Berle-Dodd Debate, 1931–1932." Paper presented at the 1994 Conference of the British Accounting Association, Winchester, Hants., England, March 1994.

MAHAR, MAGGIE. "How's Your HMO?" *Barron's,* 4 March 1996, 29–35.

MAKOWER, JOEL. *Beyond the Bottom Line.* New York: Simon & Schuster, 1994.

MALONE, MICHAEL S. "New Metrics for a New Age." *Forbes ASAP,* 7 April 1997, 40–41.

MATHIASEN, CAROLYN, MEG VOORHES, and HEIDI WELSH. "1998 Proxy Season Proves More Contentious." *Corporate Social Issues Reporter (Investor Responsibility Research Center),* July 1998, 1, 3–11.

MAVRINAC, SARAH C., NEIL R. JONES, and MARSHALL W. MEYER. "Competitive Renewal Through Workplace Innovation: The Financial and Non Financial Returns to Innovative Workplace Practices." Boston: Harvard Business School for the U.S. Department of Labor, 1995.

MAYER, MARTIN. "Why Secrecy Is Bad for Banking." *Wall Street Journal,* 30 December 1997, A10.

MAYNARD, HERMAN BRYANT, JR. *The Fourth Wave.* San Francisco: Berrett-Koehler, 1993.

MCCONNELL, PAT, and JANET PEGG. "Comprehending Comprehensive Income." In *Accounting Issues: Pat McConnell.* New York: Bear Stearns & Co. Inc., 1997.

MCCONNELL, PAT, JANET PEGG, and DAVID ZION. "Employee Stock Option Expense Pro Forma Impact on EPS and Operating Margins." New York: Bear Stearns & Co. Inc., 1998.

MCKINNON, SHARON M., and WILLIAM J. BRUNS, JR. *The Information Mosaic.* Boston: Harvard Business School Press, 1992.

MCKINNON, SHARON M., and WILLIAM J. BRUNS, JR. "Management Information and Accounting Information: What Do Managers Want." *Advances in Management Accounting* 1 (1992): 55–80.

MCTAGGART, JAMES M., PETER W. KONTES, and MICHAEL C. MANKINS. *The Value Imperative: Managing for Superior Shareholder Returns.* New York: The Free Press, 1994.

MEEK, GARY K., CLARE B. ROBERTS, and SIDNEY J. GRAY. "Factors Influencing Voluntary Annual Report Disclosures by U.S., U.K. and Continental European Multinational Corporations." *Journal of International Business Studies* 26, no. 3 (1995): 555(18).

MERCHANT, KENNETH A. *Modern Management Control Systems: Text and Cases.* Upper Saddle River, N.J.: Prentice-Hall, 1998.

MERCHANT, KENNETH A., and MICHAEL D. SHIELDS. "Commentary: When and Why to Measure Costs *Less* Accurately to Improve Decision Making." *Accounting Horizons* 7, no. 2 (June 1993): 76–81.

MEYER, CHRISTOPHER. "How the Right Measures Help Teams Excel." *Harvard Business Review* 72, no. 3 (May–June 1994): 95–103.

MEYER, MARSHALL W., and VIPIN GUPTA. "The Performance Paradox." *Research in Organizational Behavior* 16 (1994): 309–369.

MILLER, PAUL B. W. "Financial Reporting, Meet TQM." *CFO*, November 1997, 10.

MINTZ, S. L. "True Lies: How GAAP Conceals the Real Story at Stone & Webster." *CFO*, September 1994, 49–56.

MONKS, ROBERT. "Sears, Roebuck & Co. Annual Meeting of Shareholders: Robert A. G. Monks Remarks." Delivered in Atlanta, Georgia, 1992.

MONKS, ROBERT A. G. *The Emperor's Nightingale: Restoring the Integrity of the Corporation in the Age of Shareholder Activism.* Reading, Mass.: Addison-Wesley, 1998.

MONKS, ROBERT A. G., and NELL MINOW. *Power and Accountability.* New York: HarperBusiness, 1991.

MORGENSON, GRETCHEN. "Now You See It, Now You Don't." *Forbes*, 9 February 1998, 44–45.

MORGENSON, GRETCHEN. "Stock Options Are Not a Free Lunch." *Forbes*, 18 May 1998, 212–217.

MURRAY, DANIEL, ANDREW SMITHERS, and JOHN EMERSON. "USA: The Impact of Employee Stock Options." London: Smithers & Co. Ltd., 1998.

MYERS, RANDY. "Getting a Grip on Intangibles." *CFO*, September 1996, 49+.

MYERS, RANDY. "Indecent Disclosure." *CFO*, January 1997, 21–28.

MYERS, RANDY. "Measure for Measure." *CFO*, November 1997, 44–56.

NATIONAL ASSOCIATION OF CORPORATE DIRECTORS. "1997 Corporate Governance Survey." Washington, D.C.: National Association of Corporate Directors, 1997.

NESBITT, STEPHEN L. "The 'CalPERS Effect': A Corporate Governance Update." Santa Monica, Calif.: Wilshire Associates Incorporated, 1995.

NESBITT, STEPHEN L. "Long-Term Rewards from Shareholder Activism: A Study of the 'CalPERS Effect'." *Journal of Applied Corporate Finance* 6, no. 4 (Winter 1994): 75–80.

NOLAN, RICHARD L., and DONNA B. STODDARD. "CIGNA Property and Casualty Reengineering (A) (Case #9-196-059)." Boston: Harvard Business School, 1995.

NOLL, DANIEL J., and JERRY J. WEYGANDT. "Business Reporting: What Comes Next?" *Journal of Accountancy* 183, no. 2 (1997): 59(4).

O'HANLON, JOHN, and KEN PEASNELL. "Measure for Measure?" *Accountancy* 117, no. 1230 (1996): 44(3).

OPLER, TIM C., and JONATHAN SOKOBIN. "Does Coordinated Institutional Shareholder Activism Work? An Analysis of the Activities of the Council of Institutional Investors," 1997. See www.ciicentral.com

ORWALL, BRUCE. "Disney Holders Use Annual Meeting to Protest Lack of Independent Board." *Wall Street Journal,* 25 February 1998, B8.

ORWALL, BRUCE, and JOANN S. LUBLIN. "Investors Take Aim at Disney Board Again." *Wall Street Journal,* 20 February 1998, C1.

PALEPU, KRISHNA. "The Anatomy of an Accounting Change." In *Accounting & Management: Field Study Perspectives,* edited by William J. Bruns, Jr., and Robert S. Kaplan. Boston: Harvard Business School Press, 1987.

PALEPU, KRISHNA G., VICTOR L. BERNARD, and PAUL M. HEALY. *Business Analysis & Valuation: Using Financial Statements.* Cincinnati: South-Western Publishing, 1996.

PARKER, LEE D. "Broad Scope Accountability: The Reporting Priority." *Australian Accounting Review* 6, no. 1 (1996): 3–15.

PARKER, LEE D., KENNETH R. FERRIS, and DAVID T. OTLEY. *Accounting for the Human Factor.* New York: Prentice Hall, 1989.

PATTERSON, D. JEANNE. "The Link Between Corporate Governance and Performance." New York: The Conference Board, 1998.

PAVA, MOSES L., and MARC J. EPSTEIN. "How Good Is MD&A as an Investment Tool?" *Journal of Accountancy* 175, no. 3 (March 1993): 51–53.

PAVA, M. L., and J. KRAUSZ. "The Association Between Corporate Social Responsibility and Financial Performance: The Paradox of Social Cost." *Journal of Business Ethics* 15 (1996): 321–357.

PRICE WATERHOUSE CHANGE INTEGRATION TEAM. *Better Change: Best Practices for Transforming Your Organization.* Burr Ridge, Ill.: Irwin Professional Publishing, 1995.

RAPPAPORT, ALFRED. *Creating Shareholder Value: A Guide for Managers and Investors.* rev. ed. New York: The Free Press, 1997.

RAPPAPORT, ALFRED. "Three Ways Stock-Market Investors Can Stack the Odds in Their Favor." *Wall Street Journal,* 26 February 1998, R6.

REGAN, EDWARD V. "Non-Financial Measurements of Corporate Performance." In *Business Week's 1993 Forum of Chief Financial Officers.* Palm Beach, Fl., 1993.

REGAN, EDWARD V. "The Will to Act: Report of the Subcouncil on Corporate Governance and Financial Markets to the Competitiveness Policy Council." Washington, D.C.: Competitiveness Policy Council, 1993.

REIMAN, BERNARD C. *Managing for Value.* Oxford: Basil Blackwell Ltd., 1987.

RICHMAN, TOM. "Briefings from the Editors: Performance Measurement: Working Capital Productivity." *Harvard Business Review* 73, no. 4 (1995): 10–11.

ROSE, ROBERT R. "Call to Action: Labor Has Discovered the Perfect Issue for Galvanizing Workers: CEO Pay." *Wall Street Journal,* 9 April 1998, R6.

ROSENTHAL, GARY E., and DWAIN L. HARPER. "Cleveland Health Quality Choice: A Model for Collaborative Community-Based Outcomes Assessment." *Journal on Quality Improvement (Joint Commission on Accreditation of Healthcare Organizations)* 20, no. 8 (1994): 425–442.

ROSENZWEIG, KENNETH, and MARILYN FISCHER. "Is Managing Earnings Ethically Acceptable?" *Management Accounting* 75, no. 9 (March 1994): 31–34.

RUCCI, ANTHONY J., STEVEN P. KIRN, and RICHARD T. QUINN. "The Employee-Customer-Profit Chain." *Harvard Business Review* 76, no. 1 (January/February 1998): 81–97.

RUHL, JACK M., and SCOTT S. COWEN. "Breaking the Barriers to Value Creation." *Management Accounting* 73, no. 9 (March 1992): 44–47.

RUMMLER, GEARY A., and ALAN P. BRACHE. *Improving Performance: How to Manage the White Space on the Organization Chart.* San Francisco: Jossey-Bass Publishers, 1995.

SALMON, WALTER J. "Crisis Prevention: How to Gear Up Your Board." *Harvard Business Review* 71, no. 1 (January–February 1993): 68–75.

SANTIAGO, RAQUEL. "MetLife Scalpel to Lop HMO's Hospitals, Doctors." *Crain's Cleveland Business,* 18 July 1994, 1, 27.

SCHUETH, STEVE, and ALISA GRAVITZ. "1997 Report on Responsible Investing Trends in the United States." Washington, D.C.: Social Investment Forum, 1998.

SEBASTIAN, PAMELA. "Business Bulletin: Corporate Giving Would Face Scrutiny Under Two Proposed Bills." *Wall Street Journal,* 18 December 1997, A1.

SEBASTIAN, PAMELA. "Corporate Giving Needs Bigger Dose of Disclosure, Says a Professor." *Wall Street Journal,* 10 October 1996, A1.

SEBASTIAN, PAMELA. "A Workplace Code Gains Ground Among Multinational Companies." *Wall Street Journal,* 16 July 1998, A1.

SENGE, PETER M. *The Fifth Discipline: The Art and Practice of the Learning Organization.* New York: Currency Doubleday, 1990.

SESIT, MICHAEL R. "Firms' Reports Fail to Please Big Investors." *Wall Street Journal Europe,* 4 November 1996.

SHARPE, ANITA, and GREG JAFFE. "Cutting Edge: Columbia/HCA Plans for More Big Changes in Health-Care World." *Wall Street Journal,* 28 May 1997, A1, A8.

SHELLENBARGER, SUE. "Accounting Firms Battle to Be Known as Best Workplaces." *Wall Street Journal,* 21 January 1998, C1.

SHELLENBARGER, SUE. "Businesses Compete to Make the Grade as Good Workplaces." *Wall Street Journal,* 27 August 1997, B1.

SHELLENBARGER, SUE. "Companies Are Finding It Really Pays to Be Nice to Employees." *Wall Street Journal,* 22 July 1998, B1.

SHELLENBARGER, SUE. "If You Want a Firm That's Family Friendly, the List Is Very Short." *Wall Street Journal,* 6 September 1995, B1.

SHELLENBARGER, SUE. "Investors Seem Attracted to Firms with Happy Employees (Work & Family column)." *Wall Street Journal,* 19 March 1997, B1.

SHELLENBARGER, SUE. "Those Lists Ranking Best Places to Work Are Rising in Influence." *Wall Street Journal,* 26 August 1998, B1.

SHIELY, JOHN. "Managing for Value Creation at Briggs & Stratton." Wauwatosa, Wisc.: Briggs & Stratton, 1994.

SHIELY, JOHN S. "Is Value Management the Answer?" *Chief Executive,* December 1996, 55–57.

SIMON, WILLIAM L. *Beyond the Numbers.* New York: Van Nostrand Reinhold, 1997.

SIMONS, ROBERT. "Control in an Age of Empowerment." *Harvard Business Review* 73, no. 2 (1995): 81–88.

SIMONS, ROBERT. *Levers of Control: How Managers Use Innovative Control Systems to Drive Strategic Renewal.* Boston: Harvard Business School Press, 1995.

SIMONS, ROBERT, and ANTONIO DÁVILA. "How High Is Your Return on Management?" *Harvard Business Review* 76, no. 1 (January–February 1998): 71–80.

SOCIAL INVESTMENT FORUM. "After South Africa." Washington, D.C.: Social Investment Forum, 1995.

STEPHENS, VIRGIL. "Benchmarking CFO Effectiveness." Paper presented at the *Business Week* Conference, 20 March 1997.

STEWART, G. BENNETT, III. "EVA Works—But Not If You Make These Common Mistakes." *Fortune*, 1 May 1995, 117–118.

STEWART, G. BENNETT, III. *The Quest for Value.* New York: HarperBusiness, 1991.

STEWART, THOMAS A. *Intellectual Capital: The New Wealth of Organizations.* New York: Doubleday, 1997.

STEWART, THOMAS A. "Real Assets, Unreal Reporting." *Fortune*, 6 July 1998, 207–208.

STEWART, THOMAS A. "Will the Real Capitalist Please Stand Up." *Fortune*, 11 May 1998, 189–190.

STEWART, THOMAS A. "Your Company's Most Valuable Asset: Intellectual Capital." *Fortune*, 3 October 1994, 68–74.

STIVERS, BONNIE P., TERESA JOYCE COVIN, NANCY GREEN HALL, and STEVEN W. SMALT. "How Nonfinancial Performance Measures Are Used." *Management Accounting* 79, no. 8 (February 1998): 44–49.

SVEIBY, KARL ERIK. *The New Organizational Wealth.* San Francisco: Berrett-Koehler, 1997.

SWIERINGA, ROBERT J. "Challenges to the Current Accounting Model: Some Profound and Thoughtful Observations for the Next 100 Years." *The CPA Journal* 67, no. 1 (1997): 26 (6).

TAYLOR, SHELLEY. "Full Disclosure 1998." Palo Alto: Shelley Taylor & Associates, 1998.

TEACHERS INSURANCE AND ANNUITY ASSOCIATION–COLLEGE RETIREMENT EQUITIES FUND. "TIAA-CREF Policy Statement on Corporate Governance." Edited by Teachers Insurance and Annuity Association–College Retirement Equities Fund, 1997.

THE BUSINESS ROUNDTABLE. "Statement on Corporate Governance." Washington, D.C.: The Business Roundtable, 1997.

THOMAS, KENNETH H. *Community Reinvestment Performance: Making CRA Work for Banks, Communities, and Regulators.* Chicago: Probus Publishing Co., 1993.

TILT, CAROL ANN. "The Influence of External Pressure Groups on Corporate Social Disclosure: Some Empirical Evidence." *Accounting, Auditing and Accountability* 7, no. 4 (1994): 47–73.

UNITED STATES DEPARTMENT OF COMMERCE. "Results of Baldrige Winners' Common Stock Comparison: Third NIST Stock Investment Study, February 1997." Gaithersburg, Md.: Department of Commerce, 1997.

USEEM, MICHAEL. "Shareholders as a Strategic Asset." *California Management Review* 39, no. 1 (1996): 8–27.

VAN HEECKEREN, JENNIFER H. "Why Investors Push for Strong Corporate Boards." *Wall Street Journal*, 30 June 1997, A14.

VOORHES, MEG, MARK BATEMAN, and AMY WILSON. "Proxy Season Winds to Close with Autumn Meetings." *Corporate Social Issues Reporter (IRRC)*, August 1997, 1, 3–5.

WADDOCK, SANDRA A., and SAMUEL B. GRAVES. "The Corporate Social Performance-Financial Performance Link." *Strategic Management Journal* 18, no. 4 (1998): 303–320.

WALLMAN, STEVEN M. H. "Commentary: The Future of Accounting and Financial Reporting, Part IV: 'Access' Accounting." *Accounting Horizons* 11, no. 2 (1997): 103–116.

WALLMAN, STEVEN M. H. "The Future of Accounting and Financial Reporting Part II: The Colorized Approach." *Accounting Horizons* 10, no. 2 (July 1996): 138.

WETHERELL, VIRGINIA. "Counting Results." *The Environmental Forum*, January 1998, 21–26.

WHEELER, DAVID, and MARIA SILLANPAA. *The Stakeholder Corporation: The Body Shop Blueprint for Maximizing Stakeholder Value.* London: Pittman Publishing, 1997.

WHITE, ALLEN L., and DIANA M. ZINKL. "Raising Standardization." *The Environmental Forum* 15, no. 1 (January/February 1998): 28–37.

WIEGOLD, C. FREDERIC. "The Quest for Shareholder Value: Third Annual Guide to America's Best, Worst Companies." *Wall Street Journal*, 26 February 1998, R1-R20.

WILLIAMS, SUSAN. "Equal Employment and Disclosure: A Report on U.S. Corporate Practices." Washington, D.C.: Investor Responsibility Research Center, 1996.

WIRTHLIN WORLDWIDE. "Furthering the Global Dialogue on Corporate Governance: 1998 International Survey of Institutional Investors." New York: Russell Reynolds Associates, 1998.

WRIGHT, PHILIP D., and DANIEL P. KEEGAN. "Pursuing Value: The Emerging Art of Reporting on the Future." *PW Papers: Insights for Decision Makers* (1997).

WYNTER, LEON E. "Report Cards, Not Placards for NAACP (Business & Race Column)." *Wall Street Journal*, 3 September 1997, B1.

YAEKURA, TAKASHI. "The Interpretation of Accounting Information by Foreign Investors: Do We Really Need International Accounting Harmonization?" *Working Paper*, 1998.

YANKELOVICH PARTNERS INC. "A Study of Corporate Annual Reports." Cloquet, Minn.: Potlach Corporation, 1995.

ZADEK, SIMON. "Balancing Performance, Ethics, and Accountability." London: New Economics Foundation, 1997.

INDEX

Abt Associates, 241
Accountability
  aspects of, 8–12
  balancing interests of stakeholders,
    17–18
  benefits of, 14–16
  of corporation, 247–252
  culture of, 108–111
  decision making and, 17
  definitions of, 5
  developing, 4
  governance and, 53–60, 71–72
  information technology and,
    111–114
  management role in, 6–12
  management systems and, 101–108
  of manager, 245–253
  measurement and, 76–96
  misconceptions about, 4
  modern condition of, vii
  modern scope of, 143–144
  old attributes of, 143–144
  potential costs of, 15
  power of, 12–14
  reporting and, 115–140
Accountability cycle, 143–144
Accountants, 20
  and disclosure, 42–43

traditional role of, 164
updated role of, 164–167
Accounting
  financial, 20, 27–31
  management, 31–34, 145
  social, 139, 216–242
Activism, 48, 60–65
  rewards of, 70–71
  tools of, 65–69
Activity-based accounting (ABC), 32
ADT, acquisition by Tyco, 50–53
AES Corporation, 35
Aetna Health Plans of Ohio, 44
Aetna U.S. Healthcare, disclosure by,
  124
Affirmative action, 239
AFL-CIO, reform efforts by, 66, 69
Akers, John, 64
Albertson's, social pressures on, 236
All-above-board principle, 11
Allstate
  accountability of, 249–250
  case study of, 73–76
  corporate citizenship of, 131–132
  participatory decision making at,
    109
America's Least Valuable Directors
  (Teamsters), 65

American Institute of Certified Public Accountants (AICPA), 42
American Skandia Life Assurance, 191, 214
  case study of, 199–201
  Navigator of, 200
American Society for Quality Control, corporate ratings by, 49
Amoco, 47
Analog Devices, 124
  case studies of, 33–34, 82–84
  evolution of, 83
  measures at, 155–156
  quality management at, 84
Andersen, Arthur, 9
Annual report, 160–161
  revamping of, 161–164
Araskog, Rand, 64, 65
Argyris, Chris, 109
Auditing firms, positioning of, 166
Australia, financial reporting in, 184
Avon Products, social accountability by, 235

Balanced scorecard, 87, 90, 96
Baldrige Award, 99
Bank of Montreal
  case studies of, 91–92, 158–159
  measures at, 93, 147
  reporting at, 158–159
  stakeholders of, 148, 149
  strategy of, 92
BankAmerica, corporate citizenship of, 132–133
Banking industry, community reinvestment by, 132–133
Banks, Robert, 139
Barnes & Noble, 47
Barrett, Matthew, 91, 147, 149, 159
Bauer, Raymond, 241
Baxter International, environmental issues and, 227–229
Bay, Mogens, 78
Bednar, Ed, 182
Ben & Jerry's
  corporate citizenship of, 130, 231
  social audit by, 241–242
Benchmarking, 204
Bentham, Jeremy, 11–12

Berle, Adolph, 53
Blackburn, William, 227, 228, 229
Blakely, Robert, 29, 107
Boards of directors
  independence of, 56–57
  performance of, 58–59
  reform of, 59–60
  role of, 19–20
  traditional, 53–54
Body Shop, The
  corporate citizenship of, 130, 231
  social audit by, 241–242
Booth, MacAllister, 136
Boronow, Gordon, 191, 199–200, 206–207
Boswell, Ted, 140
Brache, Alan, 96
Brancato, Carolyn, 64, 72, 211
Brand value, 97
Brandeis, Louis D., 13
Briggs & Stratton, 186, 251
  case studies of, 174–176, 181–183
Bristol-Myers Squibb, corporate citizenship of, 138, 223–224
British Petroleum, corporate citizenship of, 246
British Telecom, corporate citizenship of, 229–230
Browne, John, 245, 246
Budgeting, operational measures and, 201–202
Burger, Warren, 165
Bush, Geoffrey, 227
Business Charter for Sustainable Development, 138
Business Week
  corporate ratings by, 48
  director ratings by, 66

California Public Employees' Retirement Systems (CALPERS), 62
  influence of, 65–66, 67, 68–69, 70, 71, 212
California Reinvestment Committee, 46
Calvert Group, 237
Cambrex Corporation, 185
  case study of, 121–122

Campbell Soup
  board of directors of, 57, 58
  case study of, 55–56
  performance of, 185–186
Carendi, Jan, 92, 94, 95
Cash flow return on investment
  (CFROI), 177–178
Caterpillar Tractor, case study of, 187
Chandler, Alfred D., Jr., 246
Chemical Manufacturers Association,
  137
Choate, Jerry, 5, 73, 74, 75, 131, 249,
  250
CIGNA Property & Casualty
  balanced scorecard of, 87
  case studies of, 35–36, 86–88, 199
  information technology at, 111–112
Cleveland Health Quality Choice
  Program, case study of, 44
Coalition for Environmentally
  Responsible Economies (CERES),
  46–47, 137–138
Coca-Cola, 15, 16
  case study of, 123
  stakeholders of, 149
Columbia/HCA
  lawsuits against, 68–69
  regulatory action against, 225
Communications strategies, 11
  for optimal reporting, 156–158
Community, as stakeholder, 147
Community Reinvestment Act, 132
Con Agra, 47
Confidentiality, drawbacks of, 12,
  34–35, 110
Consumerism, 149
Control systems, 99–101
  information technology and, 111–114
Cooper, Robin, 20
Copeland, Tom, 16
Corby, Francis, 17, 80, 81
Corporate family of measures, matrix
  of, 149–150
Corporate intelligence, access to, 149
Corporate Reference Guide (Families
  and Work Institute), 48
Corporations, ratings of, 48–49, 209
Cost measures, 153
Cost of quality, 29

Cost-of-quality measure, 153
Council of Institutional Investors, 69,
  71
Council on Economic Priorities, 235
  corporate ratings by, 49
Creating Shareholder Value
  (Rappaport), 76
Crystal, Graef, 66
Customers
  advantages derived from, 146
  disclosure to, 43–46

Deavenport, Earnest, 99, 103, 252
Decentralization, 206–207
Decision making
  financial measures and, 172–176
  operational measures and, 195–199
  social measures and, 223–224
Denham, Michael, 6
Denmark
  financial reporting in, 184
  social accounting in, 235
Diageo, 133
  corporate citizenship of, 226–227
Director Professionalism (National
  Association of Corporate Directors),
  58–59
Disaggregated data, 113–114
Disclosure
  of forward-looking information, 39
  legal aspects of, 13–14
  mandatory, 186–189
  of nonfinancial information, 39
  operational measures and, 209–210
  regulation of, 39, 41–42, 186–187,
    210–211
  required by marketplace, 188–189
  of social responsibility figures,
    130–140
  to stakeholders on the outside,
    36–40, 41, 49
  See also Reporting
Disney, 66, 67
  reform at, 68
Domini Social Index, 237
Dow Chemical
  case study of, 195–199
  intellectual asset measures of, 197,
    210

Drucker, Peter, 9, 246
Dunlap, Al, 148
DuPont, environmental commitment
    of, 3–4, 16, 135–136
DuPont Dow Elastomers, 198

E.B. Eddy Group, corporate
    citizenship of, 138, 140
Eagleburger, Lawrence, 65
Eastman Chemicals, 99, 124
    case study of, 103–105
    customer orientation of, 104–105
    measurement at, 155, 180–181
    mission of, 253
    planning and control at, 104, 105
    quality management at, 104, 109
    stakeholders of, 148, 149, 151–152
Eastman Kodak, 99
Eco-Management and Audit Scheme
    (EMAS), 137
Economic profit, 77–79
    case study of, 123
    creation of, 79–80
Economic value added (EVA), 80, 181
    case study of, 174–175
Education, future of, 216–218
Edvinsson, Leif, 94, 95, 192, 205, 215
Eisner, Michael, 67, 68
Elliott, Robert, 42
Emergency Planning and Community
    Right to Know Act (SARA Title III),
    135
Employees
    advantages derived from, 146
    and ethics, 240
Environment, reporting on, 134–140
Environmental Protection Agency, 234
Epstein, Marc, 241
Equal Employment Opportunity
    Commission, 130–131, 234
Equal opportunity, documentation of,
    130–131, 234
Estes, Ralph, 241
Ethics
    and employee satisfaction, 240
    importance of, 225–226
Evans, Lane, 235
Executive compensation, 64
Exxon, corporate citizenship of, 231

Families and Work Institute, 48
Feedback
    financial measures and, 176–179
    operational measures and,
        202–206
    social measures and, 227–230
Feigenbaum, Val, 106
Fenn, Daniel, 241
Figure of merit, at Bank of Montreal,
    147
Financial accounting, 20
    drawbacks of, 27–31
    flexibility in, 29–31
    purpose of, 27
    See also Financial measurements
Financial Accounting Standards Board
    (FASB), 187–188
Financial measurements
    adapting to individual situations,
        170–172
    modern, 76–81
    power of, 172–186
    relation to nonfinancials, 214–215
    stakeholders and, 171–172
    traditional, 27–31
    See also Financial accounting;
        Measures
Financial officers, role of, 21
Financial statements, ambiguities in,
    37–38
Fishman, Jerry, 34, 84
Fortune
    corporate ratings by, 49
    generosity index of, 239
Foundation for Accountability
    (FACCT), 127–128
France, social accounting in, 235
Friedman, Milton, 219

GAAP (generally accepted accounting
    practices), 5
GATX, 171
General Electric, performance of,
    184
General Motors, governance of, 8–9
Gillmor, Paul, 13
Glass Ceiling Commission, 234
Global Reporting Initiative, 137
Goizueta, Roberto, 5

Governance, 8–9
    reform of, 71–72
    restructuring of, 54–60
    shortcomings of traditional, 53–54
Grade, Jeffery, 80
Grand Metropolitan, corporate
    citizenship of, 133–134, 227
Griffin, Jennifer, 239
Group Health Cooperative of Puget
    Sound, 128
Guinness, 133
Gupta, Vipin, 155

Hake, Ralph, 84, 85, 86
Hall, Loren, 109
Halvorson, George, 129
Hampton, Philip, 52, 56, 57
Hanchak, Nicholas, 209
Handy, Charles, 5
Hansen, Kent, 61
Harnischfeger Industries, 17
    case study of, 80–81
Harrah's Entertainment, 67
Harris Bank, 91, 147
Health care industry
    case study of, 44–45
    operational measures in, 202–204
    reporting in, 115–119, 124–130
Health Plan Employer Data and
    Information Set (HEDIS), 126, 128,
    129
HealthPartners, 128–129
Heimbold, Charles, 224
Heinz, H.J., disclosure by, 238
Hellman, Thomas, 138, 233
Hendrickson, Gene, 32
Hermes Lens fund, 61, 62,
Hero Motor, 176
Heskett, James, 16, 146
Hillman, Philip, 47
Hoffman, Robert, 169, 177, 178, 179
Hoffmeister, Jan, 192
Hoshin, 84
Howell, Robert, 153
Hronec, Steven, 102, 154

IBIT (income before interest and
    taxes), 28
IC index, 192

In Search of Excess (Crystal), 66
Information technology
    and accountability, 111–113
    and disclosure, 113–114
    drawbacks of, 114
Input measures, 153
Institutional investors
    importance of, 48, 60–65, 188
    and social responsibility, 237–238
    tools of, 65–69
Intellectual capital, 94, 192
Interest groups, clout of, 46–47
Interfaith Center for Corporate
    Responsibility (ICCR), 47, 235–237
International Paper, 185
    case study of, 119–120
International Standards Organization
    (ISO), 137
Investment decisions, criteria for, viii
Investor Responsibility Research
    Center, 66, 221
ISO 14000 standard, 137
Isom, Gerry, 35, 36, 86, 88, 111, 112,
    199, 201

Japanese competition, 174–175
Jenkins, Edmund, 42, 117, 118
Jenkins Report, 42–43, 161
John Deere, 174
Johnson, David W., 55, 57, 185–186
Johnson, Samuel, 41
Johnson, Thomas, 20, 31
Joint Commission on Accreditation of
    Healthcare Organizations (JCAHO),
    45, 128
Juran, Joseph, 194

Kaiser Permanente, disclosure by,
    124
Kaplan, Robert, 10, 20, 31, 82, 86, 89,
    165, 180
Kawasaki, 174
Kennedy, Joseph P., 41
Kerr, Margaret, 225, 238–239
Kerr, Steven, 251
Kinder, Lydenberg, Domini, 237, 239
Klinger, Scott, 222
Kotter, John, 16, 17, 146
Kozlowski, Dennis, 50–52, 56

Lagging indicators, 152
Larcombe, Frederick, 121–122
Leading indicators, 152
　vs. lagging indicators, 152
　See also Measures
Learning
　financial measures and, 176–179
　fostering, 109–110
　operational measures and,
　　202–206
　social measures and, 227–230
Lee, Thomas A., 157
Lego, Paul, 64
LENS fund, 60
Lev, Baruch, 77, 120, 124, 158
Levitt, Arthur, 30–31, 41, 166, 187,
　234
Liddy, Edward, 75
Linkage
　of financials and nonfinancials,
　　212–214
　of social with financial and
　　operational measures, 238–241
Linowes, David, 241
Lippincott, Philip, 57
Loeppke, Ronald, 203, 208
Loyalty
　performance measures and,
　　183–186
　social measures and, 230–233

MacAvoy, Paul W., 55
Macleod, Donald, 183
Maffei, Gregory, 122
Mahon, John, 239
Mahoney, Richard, 177
Management
　and accountability, 6–7, 245–253
　control systems in, 101, 102–108
　governance by, 8–9
　hoshin, 84
　information technology and,
　　111–114
　measurement by, 9
　planning in, 100, 102–108
　reliance on financial accounting by,
　　27
　reporting by, 11–12
　role of, 19, 246–247

Management accounting, 145
　problems with, 31–33
　revamping of, 33–34
Management cockpit software,
　113
Management planning and control
　(MPC), 106
Management systems, 10, 100–101
　information technology and,
　　111–114
McCall, Carl, 68
McClain, Terry, 78, 79, 171
McCool, Bob, 89, 109
McGuire, William, 115, 116, 118,
　125
Mead, Dana, 5, 25, 26, 28, 29, 98, 106,
　107, 110, 201, 249, 251, 252
Means, Gardiner, 53
Measures
　of brand value, 97
　constituency of, 154
　corporate family of, 149–154
　through corporate hierarchy,
　　154–156
　devising, 152–154
　financial vs. operational and social,
　　152
　formulation of, 146
　ideal number of, 153–154
　importance of, 73–76, 145, 247
　input, 153
　insufficiency of modern, 168
　new forms of financial, 76–81
　new forms of nonfinancial,
　　81–96
　output, 153
　process, 153
　stakeholders and, 147, 248
　types of, 9
　See also Financial measurements
Media, 149
Merrill Lynch Principled Values
　Portfolio, 237
MetLife, 44
Meyer, Chris, 110
Meyer, Marshall, 155
Microsoft, case study of, 122–123
Millstein, Ira, 8, 59
Minow, Nell, 61, 62

Mobil Corporation
  balanced scorecard of, 90, 109
  case study of, 89, 91
Modern Corporation and Private Property (Berle and Means), 53
Monks, Robert, 60–62
Monsanto, case studies of, 168–169, 177–179
Morrison, Dale F., 57

N.E.T. Research of Belgium, 113
Nash, John, 58
National Association for the Advancement of Colored People (NAACP), corporate ratings by, 49
National Association of Corporate Directors, 58
National Association of Regulatory Utility Commissioners, 21
National Committee for Quality Assurance, 126–128
National Semiconductor, 183
NationsBank, 132, 133
Nesbitt-Burns, 147
Net operating profit after tax (NOPAT), 79
Newcomer, Lee, 125
Nonfinancial information
  importance of, 39–40
  measurement of, 6, 9, 20, 81–98
Nonfinancial measures, 81–82
  case studies of, 82–96
  new, 96–98
  relations with financial measures, 214–215
Northern Telecom (Nortel Networks), 251
  quality issues at, 250–251
  social accountability of, 216–220, 225–226, 240
Norton, David, 10, 82, 86, 89, 111, 180, 206
Novo Nordisk, corporate citizenship of, 138

Objectives, importance of, 38–39
Occupational Safety and Health Administration (OSHA), 234

OECD (Organization for Economic Cooperation and Development), reform of, 70
Open management principle, 11
Operational measures, 152, 190–192
  power of, 195–210
  stakeholders and, 192–195
Opler, Tim, 71
Options, cost of, 38
ORYX PLUS, 45–46
Output measures, 153
Ovitz, Michael, 67

Palepu, Krishna, 189
Patterson, Bill, 69–70
Pension funds
  clout of, 48, 62–69, 188
  importance of, 62
  and social responsibility, 237–238
Performance
  financial measures and, 183–186
  organizational measures and, 207–209
Performance measures, ix
  case studies of, 92–96
  financial, 170–189
  new, 96–98
  operational, 190–215
  social, 216–243
Performance paradox, 155
Petersson, Lars-Eric, 5, 205
Petrash, Gordon, 196, 198, 210
PhyCor, priority setting at, 202–204
Pitney Bowes, case study of, 194
Planning, 100
  annual, 102
  information technology and, 111–114
  operational measures and, 201–202
Polaroid, environmental commitment of, 136
Porter, Michael, 5–6
Portfolio$creener software, 221
Power and Accountability (Monks and Minow), 62
Process efficiency, 214–215
Process measures, 153
Product life cycle (PLC) reviews, 224
Profit, as preeminent measure, 152

Proxy fights, 66–67
Proxy rights, 63–64
Public Environmental Reporting
   Initiative, 47
Public relations, 37
Publicity, importance of, 41

Quality management, 82–86
Quality measures, 153

R & D (research and development),
   accounting of costs of, 29–30
Rappaport, Alfred, 76, 174
Reebok International, 67
Relevance Lost (Johnson and Kaplan),
   20
Reporting, 115–119
   annual report, 160–164
   communications strategy for,
      156–158
   environmental, 134–140
   of financials, 119–124
   importance of, 247
   by management, 11–12
   myths about, 159–160
   of nonfinancials, 124–130
   rationale for, 124–126
Resource allocation, operational
   measures and, 201–202
Return on capital (ROC), 180
Return on capital employed (ROCE),
   78
Return on equity (ROE), 78
Return on investment (ROI), 78
Return on net assets (RONA), 78
Robertson Stephens, 133
Robinson, James, 64
Roosevelt, Teddy, 234
Roth, John, 216, 217–218, 225, 250
Rouse Company, case study of,
   120–121
Royal Bank of Canada, corporate
   citizenship of, 232
Royal Dutch/Shell, corporate
   citizenship of, 130, 134, 140, 230
Rummler, Geary, 96

SA 8000 standard, 235
SARA Title III, 135

Schneiderman, Art, 33
Scott, Richard, 225
Scott Paper, restructuring of, 148
Sears, Roebuck
   accountability at, 60–61
   commitment to nonfinancial
      performance, 213–214
SEC, 41
   disclosure orders of, 187
Securities Act of 1933, 13
Shapiro, Robert, 169
Shareholders
   advantages derived from, 146
   importance of, 148
   influence of, 67
   vs. other stakeholders, 16–18
   value of other stakeholders to, 149
Shiely, John, 175, 186, 189, 253
Simons, Robert, 201
Skandia Group
   American operations of, 191–192
   case studies of, 92, 93–95, 205–206
   Navigator of, 94–95, 124, 195, 205
Social audit, 241–242
Social dividend, 252–253
Social measures, 139, 152
   linkage with other measures,
      238–241
   maturing of, 220
   outside pressures and, 233–238
   power of, 223–233
   regulators and, 234–236
   stakeholders and, 220–222
Sokobin, Jonathan, 71
Solutia, 178, 179
Stakeholder scorecard, 93, 96
Stakeholders, 248
   accountability to, 148–149
   competing interests of, 16–19
   dealing with, 151
   disclosure to, 36–40, 41, 49,
      211–212
   discontent of, 40–41
   financial measures and, 171–172
   importance of, 146–147
   loyalty of, 230–233
   operational measures and, 192–195
   types of, 146, 148
Stasey, Robert, 84

Stempel, Robert, 64
Stone & Webster, 61
Strategy, 10
    financial measures and, 179–183
    operational measures and, 199–201
    social measures and, 224–227
Stratton, Frederick, 175
Sun Company, corporate citizenship
    of, 139
Suzuki, 174
Swedbank, performance measurement
    at, 9
Swiss Bank Corporation, social
    responsiveness of, 237

Taco Bell, case study of, 97
Tektronix, case study of, 32–33
Tenneco
    accountability at, 98, 107–108,
        251–252
    case studies of, 25–26, 27–29,
        106–108, 201–202
    information flow at, 110
    measures used by, 153
    planning and control at, 106–108
Teslik, Sarah, 69
Texaco, case study of, 222
TIAA-CREF, 62
    influence of, 65, 68
    screening activities by, 69
Time measures, 153
Toro, 174
Total value impact (TVI), 78–79
Toxics Release Inventory, 239
Transparency, 11, 156
Transparent management principle, 11
Tyco
    acquisition of ADT by, 50–53
    board of directors of, 56, 57

U.S. Quality Algorithms, 208–209
United HealthCare
    case study of, 115, 116–117
    customer satisfaction with, 118
    report card of, 127
    stakeholder satisfaction with,
        124–125
United States Trust Company of
    Boston, social responsiveness of,
    236
United States v. Arthur Young, 165
University of Michigan Business
    School, corporate ratings by, 49
University of Nebraska-Omaha,
    corporate ratings by, 48
Utilitarianism, 12

Valerio, Tom, 112
Valmont Industries, 171
    case study of, 78–79
Value, creation of, 78
van Heeckeren, Jennifer H., 55
Vancouver City Savings Credit Union,
    corporate citizenship of, 231–233

Wallman, Steven, 41, 161–162
Walsh, Michael, 25, 26, 28, 248–249
Wambold, Richard, 106, 201–202
Wells, Robert, 91, 147, 159
Whirlpool
    quality management at, 84–86
    top sheet of, 85
Whitwam, David, 84
Wichita State University, corporate
    ratings by, 48
Wolrath, Björn, 92, 95
Woolard, Ed, 3, 12, 135, 253
Working capital productivity, 214
World Wide Web, 113